STAR TREK LIVES!

Somewhere in the world (allowing for time differences) at all times, STAR TREK is being avidly watched—four years after it went off the big U.S. national hookup.

The STAR TREK phenomenon has puzzled the TV experts, accustomed as they are to the over-rated rating methods, the good or bad time-slots, that normally spell death or life for a show. Everyone knew that putting the third year of STAR TREK into a 10:00 p.m. Friday slot was only a prelude to dropping the show altogether. Naturally, STAR TREK was stopped in mid-flight—its five-year mission incomplete.

But TV experts did not know about science fiction fans—and most particularly, the "Trekkies." Local stations found that running the episodes through each season had a powerful pull. Even though many were chopped and cut to accomodate new sponsors, the faithful fans watched, and *new* fans joined them. The strength of STAR TREK grew and grew. The fans themselves took the world that Gene Roddenberry and a talented group of actors had made into the first intelligent SF TV series and made a whole new wonder of it.

This is the story of how the first world was conceived, how the second was developed, and how the third grew. Like Kirk and his crew, it is the story of victory in the face of certain defeat.

LIVE LONG AND PROSPER

THE WORLD
OF
STAR TREK

David Gerrold

BALLANTINE BOOKS • NEW YORK

ISBN 0-345-24938-0-195

Manufactured in the United States of America

First Edition: May 1973
Eighth Printing: May 1976

For Henry and Gail Morrison

The opinions expressed in this book are the author's and do not necessarily reflect those of the Universe.

The World of STAR TREK—
Or should that be the Universe of STAR TREK?

No. World is correct. *World* in the sense of a self-contained reality, an alternate to *this* reality. A universe to match is implied.

Actually, there are three worlds of STAR TREK. First, there's the STAR TREK that Gene Roddenberry conceived—the original dream of a television series about an interstellar starship. Then there's the STAR TREK behind the scenes, how the cast and crew made Gene Roddenberry's ideas come true, how they were realized and sometimes altered in the realization. And finally, there's the STAR TREK Phenomenon, the world that the fans of the show created, the reality that they built in response.

All three of these worlds are fascinating, and all three of them are dealt with in this book. Each of the worlds of STAR TREK created the next; and like interlocking rings, each had its effects on the others. The show created the stars, the stars engendered a fandom, and the fans kept the show on the air.

I've already written one STAR TREK book—it's called *The Trouble with Tribbles*, and it's the story of how I made my first sale to television, and how "The Trouble with Tribbles" episode of STAR TREK was written. This is the second part of that story, *this is the book to place it in context.*

This book is about the STAR TREK myth, what it was and how it happened—the truth behind it. The fascinating part about the myth is that even after you strip away the flackery, the studio puffery and ballyhoo—

1

STAR TREK is *still* a piece of magic. It lives and breathes by itself. The *Enterprise* and her crew have become a new set of gods in the science fiction pantheon.

So the reason for this book (as well as the first one) is to try to preserve some of that magic so that years from now some yet unborn "Trekkie" may open it up and be able to recapture at least a hint of STAR TREK's magic seasons.

PART ONE

The First World of Star Trek—Gene Roddenberry's Dream

First, there was Gene Roddenberry's dream, a television show called "STAR TREK."

The idea was described as "Wagon Train to the Stars," or "Hornblower in Space"—the adventures of a far-traveling starship and her crew.

Perhaps the best description of the show is in the lines spoken at the beginning of every episode:

"Space, the final frontier. These are the voyages of the starship *Enterprise,* her five year mission to explore strange new worlds, to seek out new life and new civilization, to boldly go where no man has gone before."

Or, more exactly, from *The Star Trek Guide*:*

(Excerpted from orders to Captain James T. Kirk)

III. You are therefore posted, effective immediately, to command the following: The U.S.S. ENTERPRISE.

> Cruiser Class—Gross 190,000 tons
> Crew Complement—430 persons
> Drive—space-warp
> Range—18 years at light-year velocity
> Registry—Earth, United Space Ship

* The *Star Trek Guide* (in its earliest form) was a 20-page mimeographed book, distributed to all writers and prospective writers for the series. It contained descriptions of all the characters and sets as well as notes on the capabilities of the *Enterprise* and what kind of stories the series could use.

It was revised twice as the show progressed. New material was added and old material was updated. In the third edition, for instance, the *Enterprise* was upgraded from Cruiser Class to Starship Class—the feeling being that a "starship" was a special kind of vessel with greater range, speed, power and other capabilities than other vessels in space. Much of this material was reprinted in Stephen Whitfield and Gene Roddenberry's *The Making of Star Trek.* (Available from Ballantine Books.)

IV.   Nature and duration of mission:

   Galaxy exploration and investigation:
          5 years

  V.   Where possible, you will confine your landings
       and contacts to Class "M" planets approximating
       Earth-Mars conditions.

 VI.   You will conduct this patrol to accomplish pri-
       marily:
       (a) Earth security, via explorations of intelli-
            gence and social systems capable of a gal-
            axial threat, and
       (b) Scientific investigation to add to the Earth's
            body of knowledge of alien life forms and
            social systems, and
       (c) Any required assistance to the several Earth
            colonies in your quadrant, and the enforce-
            ment of appropriate statutes affecting such
            Federated commerce vessels and traders as
            you may contact in the course of your mis-
            sion.

In sum, "Hornblower in Space." Just as Captain
Horatio Hornblower was the highest representative of
English law in the far waters in which he sailed, so
would Captain James T. Kirk of the *Enterprise* be the
highest legal representative of Starfleet Command in the
far reaches of the galaxy.

He would be explorer, ambassador, soldier, and
peacekeeper. He would be the sole arbiter of Federation law wherever he traveled—he would be a law
unto himself.

The implication here is that *there are no other channels of interstellar communication.* At least, none as
fast as the *Enterprise.*

Let's examine this for a moment, because it's essential to understanding the STAR TREK format. Captain
Kirk is an autonomous power. Purely from a television
point of view, he *must* be an autonomous power—oth-

erwise the series lacks drama and he lacks interest. If Kirk could check back with Starfleet Command every time he was in trouble, he would never have any conflicts at all. He would simply be a crewman following orders. He wouldn't be an explorer or an ambassador at all—just the Captain of the local gunboat on the scene.

For Kirk to be a dramatic and interesting human being, he must be wholly responsible for his own actions as a representative of the Federation. As such, every decision he has to make becomes an important one.

Fortunately, the exigencies of space travel—especially faster-than-light travel—support this kind of dramatic concept.

We must make one assumption, though—that faster-than-light travel is possible. This is the basic asumption of STAR TREK: that man *can* reach the stars. It is the only assumption we need to make, but it is the hook on which the whole series (and much of science fiction, in general) hangs. Without faster-than-light travel, we are stuck in our own solar system—and that's too much of a limitation for our storytellers. Why should we deny ourselves a background as broad and irresistible as a whole galaxy—or a universe?

Science fiction is the contemporary fairy tale, it's the twentieth century morality play. At its worst, it's merely romantic escapism; but at its best, it is the postulation of an alternate reality with which to comment on this one. Strictly from a dramatic point of view, we *need* the assumption of faster-than-light velocities. It is as necessary to the genre as the assumption that miracles can happen is necessary to the artistic success of a medieval religious pageant. (In either case, the implication is optimism about the workings of the universe.)

Despite the fact that almost everything we know about the workings of the universe suggest that it is impossible to achieve the speed of light or velocities faster than that, we can still make the assumption. We are violating Einstein's Theory of Relativity, as well as the vast body of scientific knowledge that backs it up, but we *can* make the assumption. Not just for dramatic reasons, but for scientific ones as well.

You see, if it *is* possible to travel faster than light, the method will not be discovered by anyone who has already decided that it is impossible. Rather, the discovery will require a man who assumes that it *is* possible, and who will speculate at length on the conditions necessary to achieve such. In fact, this is how the hypothesis of the tachyon was arrived at—a tachyon, *if it exists,* is a particle that cannot travel at less than the speed of light, only faster. If tachyons can now be proven to exist, then we will know that faster-than-light travel *is* possible. So, the assumption is not so outrageous as some science purists might insist.

STAR TREK postulates an alternate reality where faster-than-light travel is an established fact. Granted this one assumption, we can then proceed to establish the nature of an interstellar society. One of the things we must know is the nature and quality of that society's communications.

Given the STAR TREK format, given the workings of the universe derived from the one basic assumption that we have to make, we can establish that there are only four possible channels of communication between the planets of different stars.

Three of them are impractical.

If we examine them all, we'll see why they're impractical. And also, we'll see why Captain James T. Kirk can't help but be an autonomous power.

The first method of communication, of course, is radio. Or television. Or modulated laser beams. Or any kind of wave modulation that travels exactly at the speed of light. Obviously, if the speed of light limits our spaceships, it also limits our radios.

The nearest star to our own sun, Sol, is Alpha Centauri. It's 4.3 light-years away—that means that light, traveling at slightly more than 186,000 miles *per second,* will still take four and one third years to get there. *Any* quantity traveling at the speed of light will take that long. And that's assuming that the signal was still strong enough to be detected when it arrived. (Even a pencil-thin laser beam will spread, when projected from the Earth to the moon, to cover an area more than a half-mile in diameter. And that's only to the moon. How far is it to Alpha Centauri?)

No, the reason why we can't use radio or light waves is that they're self-limiting. The key word is *limit*. Hang on a minute and you'll see.

STAR TREK *almost* got around this. The TV series postulated a "subspace radio." While this was never explained in detail, the implication was that this was a method of communication much faster than light, *but still not instantaneous.*

A message to Starfleet Command sent by subspace radio might take several hours or days. Beyond that, either the time lag was too great or the *Enterprise* was out of range. The answer was too slow in coming.

This is the same limitation as with radio waves —only the scale is different.

When you are thinking in terms of interstellar distances, there is no such thing as a small number. Even the small numbers are big ones. If your subspace radio is not instantaneous, if it functions at a measurable speed *then that speed is its limit*. And no matter how fast it is, the distances of the galaxy are still vast enough to make that speed seem insignificant. The point can be reached where, even if your ship is not yet out of range, a dialogue still becomes impossible. Given enough distance, even the smallest time-lag will magnify eventually.

Let's try another.

The third method of interstellar communication involves the use of robot-torpedoes; that is, unmanned faster-than-light ships, guided by inboard computers. They would be launched from one planet to deliver a message to another, light-years away. The torpedoes would not be spaceships per se; rather, they would be propulsion units, guidance system and payload only. There would be no life-support capabilities at all.

As couriers, these torpedoes would be as fast as their propulsion systems would allow; at least as fast, probably faster, then comparable manned ships.

This particular channel of communication was never used or shown on STAR TREK—but given the technology that could design and build a starship *Enterprise,* the capability to build robot-torpedoes as well also had to be there.

The use of such torpedoes would be highly practical for planet-to-planet communication. A robot can deliver mail just as easily as a manned ship.

On the other hand, the torpedo would be almost completely *im*practical for ship-to-planet or planet-to-ship communications. (How does a preprogrammed torpedo find an unprogrammed ship?) From the dramatic standpoint alone, the faster-than-light torpedo is as impractical as the radio and the subspace radio. There is a time lag.

The torpedo is the equivalent of an interstellar carrier pigeon. Like the other two methods, it can deliver a message or it can send one—but it cannot serve as the vehicle for a dialogue. And a dialogue is *precisely* the kind of interstellar communication that we are looking for. A *dramatic* story requires it.

If there were such a communication channel available, then a ship like the *Enterprise* would be unnecessary and her mission redundant. Obviously, there is no such instantaneous channel—at least, not in the STAR TREK universe. The existence of the *Enterprise* proves it.

You see, the *Enterprise* is the fourth method of interstellar communication. It is the only practical vehicle of interstellar *dialogue* between two far removed existences—and as such, it is the one we are primarily interested in as a basis for stories about divergent planetary cultures clashing with one another.

The situation of this interstellar society is almost exactly analogous to the Earth of the eighteenth century. Then too, communications over vast distances were slow and uncertain. The arrival of a ship or courier was always an event. Even if the news he was carrying was several weeks, months, or years old, it was still the most recent news available.

When one government had to deal with another, they used diplomatic notes and couriers—and in matters of highest policy, they depended upon their ambassadors. Because communications were so slow, an ambassador could be a particularly important individual. He was the arm and authority of his government. He was its voice. He was the man who determined and enacted the policies of his nation with regard to his specific area of authority.

Likewise, the Captain of the *Enterprise* must be just such an ambassador. He will be a minister with a portfolio of his own making. Carefully briefed as to Starfleet's goals and policies, it will be his responsibility to interpret them and act in the wide variety of situations he will confront. He is a piece of Starfleet itself. He is the piece entrusted with the mission of conducting the "interstellar dialogue."

Now, let's translate that into television.

A successful dramatic television series needs (a) a broad-based format about (b) an interesting individual or group of individuals whose responsibilities force them into (c) unusual situations and confrontations, requiring (d) decisive and positive action on the part of the protagonist and his cohorts.

Any successful dramatic series will fulfil these requirements. The *better* it fulfils them, the more likely it is to be a success.

Let's define our terms here:

Dramatic: synonymous with conflict. A confrontation is implied. The story is man against _____. Man against man, man against nature, man against himself. The protagonist, or hero, is prevented from reaching his goal by an obstacle or series of obstacles. The more difficult these obstacles are, the more heroic he has to be in order to overcome them. How he overcomes them tells us what kind of a person he is.

The story is told as a series of climaxes rising in intensity, each more exciting than the one before. Every climax involves a confrontation with an obstacle, until the final climax when either the obstacle or the hero is defeated.

In drama *other* than series television—say, a play or a movie—the event that is being told is the most important event in the hero's life. It is the whole reason for the existence of a story about this person. We are not interested in Gary Cooper's actions after *High Noon;* we don't care about Fletcher Christian after the *Mutiny on the Bounty;* we are through with Robert Armstrong after *King Kong* topples from the Empire State Building. Only the final confrontation is important—and what the hero learns from it.

What the hero learns from the event is what makes it the most important event in his life. The hero *must learn something.* (Or *fail* to learn something, but in that case, the audience has to recognize that he has failed.) Scarlett O'Hara learns that she really does love Rhett Butler. Dorothy learns that you need brains, a heart, and courage, and that it's inside you all the time or you never had it at all. Ryan O'Neal learns that Being In Love Means Never Having To Say You're Sorry.

The story is about the lesson that this person has to learn—and these are the events that will teach it to him. Hamlet learns how to make a decision. Oedipus learns humility.

This is the point of *all* drama. It is the sole justification for any play—

—except on series television.

Or for that matter, in any kind of a series. Whether it be Doc Savage, Tarzan, Sherlock Holmes, or James Bond.

In a series the form has to be turned upside down —the events depicted must *not* be the most important events in the hero's life. Otherwise, there's no point in going on with the series. Everything after that would be anticlimactic.

This is the dilemma of series television. On the one hand, the producer must present dramatic stories week after week—on the other, he must not be *too* dramatic. Otherwise, he damages the series as a whole, ending up with a cumulative body of work that is essentially *melodramatic*. And then the ho hum reaction sets in.

Thus, the television producer's problem becomes one of how to tell exciting stories week after week without descending into melodrama. As there is only one *real* kind of dramatic excitement, the problem is intensified—how many changes can you ring on one theme?

The single dramatic element which provokes excitement in a play is this: *your identity is in danger*. All others are merely variations: your life is in danger, your country is in danger, your girl friend might leave you, your wife might find out, your brother might die, the police might catch you. Something threatens to prevent you from being the person you already are or want to be. This is the hero's problem and we identify with him. He copes with it and learns something about his identity and why it's so precious to him. The audience identifies with him and his problem and learns something too.

But if you endanger the hero's identity week after week, not only do you run the risk of melodrama—you also run the risk of falling into a formula kind of storytelling. This week Kirk is menaced by the jello monster, he kills it by freezing it to death; next week Kirk is menaced by the slime monster and kills it by drying it out; the week after that he is threatened by the mud monster and defeats if by watering it down; the following week Kirk meets the mucous monster . . . Again, the ho hum reaction. Or even the ha ha reaction.

Fortunately for the dramatic arts, the number of possible identities and the number of ways of endangering them is unlimited. And therein lies part of the answer to the TV producer's problem.

You don't have to endanger *the hero* every week. You can endanger someone else, someone around him—and it is his responsibility to come to that person's aid. If he incidentally has to endanger himself in the process, so much the better. The result is a semi-anthology format, and it is the only way possible in which to avoid falling into the trap of doing formula stories.

Thus, a good series format should be one which allows its hero to be primarily a decision-maker, especially as concerns other people's lives. The requirements of television also necessitate a certain amount of excitement and danger—so that if there is not true drama (i.e. identity-danger) there is at least a passable imitation of same.

This is the reason why there are so many doctors, cops, cowboys and private eyes on television. Also spies and lawyers. (And variations thereof.) These are the professions that fill the needs of series television exactly. Each of them revolves around a human identity that provides services to other human identities, thus the hero *has* to be involved with other people—and due to the nature of the services he is providing, the people are generally caught in tense and dramatic situations. The hero will have to make decisions that will affect their lives. And sometimes his own life will be endangered in the process.*

The number of professions that lend themselves to excitement and danger is not all that limited—but the number of *genres* that provide a broad background to play a multitude of stories against *is* limited. How many *different* stories can you tell about a fellow who puts out oil well fires for a living?

The number of genres suitable or practical for television is small. Despite twenty years of experimentation (and fifty years of film history before that) the field remains remarkably limited: cowboys, cops and doctors.

Science fiction, as a genre, has had a singularly unhappy representation on American video. The few *true* science fiction TV series that have managed to have any impact at all have been primarily anthology-type series, like Rod Serling's *Twilight Zone*. A series about a set of continuing characters had never quite made it on American network television—until STAR TREK.

But STAR TREK was a genre unto itself. And it opened a whole new range of possibilities for the television series.

* One of the things that modern audiences have come to respect in a hero is his ability to keep his cool—his ability to stay objective in a trying situation. I suspect that part of this is a cumulative subconscious cultural identification with too many *slick* TV heroes. To me, the slick TV hero is the result of *bad* writing. He isn't allowed to get too involved emotionally with the people he is dealing with—to do so would increase the importance of each event to him, turning the story from melodrama into drama. (Think of *Dragnet*. Or *Adam-12*. Joe Friday must never care about the people he arrests or what happens to their lives. They are merely objects in a game he is playing: good guys vs. bad guys.)

Apparently, emotional involvement would destroy a hero's ability to do his job. But I think a much more basic answer is that it takes time and artistry to create true drama—neither of which television has any great abundance of. Thus, our cheap heroes remain aloof and seem super-cool, when in fact, they are merely unreal. A pity, because we should learn to admire the people who can reach out to each other, not those who have learned how to make catatonia a viable life-style.

Examining it as a genre, it is a near-perfect genre: a galaxy is an unlimited background. In it a writer can postulate any kind of individual and any number of ways of endangering his identity. Captain Kirk, as representative-at-large for Starfleet Command, is the perfect hero. The viewer identifies with Kirk and his attempts to fulfil the duties of a Starfleet Captain. The viewer also identifies with those whose identities are endangered. If in helping them, Kirk is *occasionally* endangered himself, the viewer's excitement is increased. (The viewer's excitement can be increased by this trick only so many times. If Kirk *persists* in placing himself in danger, we begin to question his credibility as a Starfleet Captain.*)

Kirk is the Captain of a mighty starship. He commands a crew of 430 persons. He is the highest Starfleet authority in the quadrant. And his responsibilities are manifold—to himself, to his ship, to his crew, to his mission, and to the government that commissioned him.

He is interesting because he is a decider. A Captain's job is *to make decisions*.

A Captain is not a scientist, not an explorer, not a soldier, not a policeman. He can easily add a specialist to his crew to handle any of those jobs—and handle them better than he could. These things are only a small part of his responsibility. His real job is to be the executive decision-maker, to decide what research is of primary importance for the scientists to consider, to decide what planets should be explored for their resources and civilizations, to decide when and where a military

---

* It is by a character's actions that we discover what kind of a person he is. If a person hedges in a clinch, we will think him unsure and uncertain. If he does a foolhardy action, we might consider him a decisive risk-taker; but if he makes a habit of it, we will know him for a crazy fool. If his actions are all reflexes without thought, he becomes a stereotype, a cardboard puppet that the writer is arbitrarily moving around. It is only by variation that a character comes alive; the more varied his actions, the more depth he has dramatically.

operation is necessary, to determine which laws should be enforced and how. And once those decisions are made, it is for his crew to implement them; their jobs are to execute the orders that are given them.

Thus, the true function of a Captain is to *lead* a team; he must know how to delegate authority to those best able to handle the specific tasks at hand. Considering Captain Kirk in particular, we must refer again to the *Star Trek Guide:*

> "With the starship out of communication with Starfleet bases for long periods of time, a starship captain has unusually broad powers over both the lives and welfare of his crew, as well as over Earth people and activities encountered during these voyages. Kirk feels this responsibility strongly *and is fully capable of letting the worry and frustration lead him into error.*"

That last sentence (the italics are *not* mine) is especially important. Obviously it was realized quite early in the conception of the series that Captain Kirk would have to be aware of himself and his duties—and that he would be very much affected by the decisions he would have to make.

Otherwise, he simply would not be a very interesting human being.

And it's human beings that we're primarily interested in. Captain Kirk *should* worry—that's what distinguishes him from an android. The viewers will identify with his concern for others.

It is Captain Kirk's concern that makes the story important. If a decision is less than crucial, it can be made by a subordinate officer. Only the crucial decisions will be passed up to the Captain. And if it isn't important enough to make him sweat, then it's not worth telling a story about.

Thus STAR TREK neatly fulfils all of the requirements

for a good TV series: a broad-based format allowing a wide variety of stories, an interesting hero, an unusual set of situations and confrontations, and the requirement of decisive and positive action from a protagonist whose job and training is to do just that.

Plus, STAR TREK has that one added virtue mentioned before—it is a genre unto itself. And that makes it unique.

Let's consider some specifics now. We'll start with the crew of the *Enterprise*.

To make good decisions, a Captain needs good advisors. Good decisions can be made only when *all* the facts can be considered. A Captain needs advisors who are experts in the many fields he will have to deal with.

Aboard a ship like the *Enterprise,* one of the most important officers would be the Science Officer. If the *Enterprise* had been purely a military vessel, this would not be so. In that case, military advisors would have outweighed science officers.

But because the *Enterprise*'s mission is the exploration of new worlds, the Science Officer is second in importance only to the Captain.

"His bridge position is at the library-computer station which links the bridge to the vessel's intricate brain, a highly sophisticated and advanced computer which connects all stations of the ship, collects information, makes computations, and provides information. While personnel at other posts can feed in or extract information relating to their specific duties, the Science Officer from his central panel can tap the resources of the entire system—including a vast micro-library on man's history, arts, sciences, philosophy, including all known information on other solar systems, Earth colonies, alien civilizations, a registry of all space vessels in existence, personnel information on any member of the *U.S.S.*

Enterprise, or almost anything else needed in any of our stories."

Those are the requirements of the job—now who is the best man to fill it?

From a dramatic consideration alone, he must be an interesting person. Just as the captain must be the man who will be most affected by his responsibilities, so must every other character in the story be an individual who is aware of the conflicts in which his job places him. (This is a series we're talking about—we don't have just one hero, we must have a set of heroes.)

The Science Officer must be able to correlate vast amounts of information presented very rapidly and synthesize accurate summaries for his captain. This demands a being of superior mental prowess, either human or otherwise.

STAR TREK postulated an alien race called Vulcans—originally from the planet Vulcanis, but this was later shortened to Vulcan.

Physically, Vulcans resembled human beings—except that they had pointed ears and arched eyebrows. Their skin had a distinct yellowish tinge*—but that's because their blood was green, it was copper-based. (Instead of iron-based as in human beings.) They were capable of great feats of physical and mental prowess, and they had unique powers of telepathy: the Vulcan mind-meld allowed a Vulcan to enter into another being's thoughts. The Vulcan nerve-pinch could be used to momentarily stun a human being (and probably a Vulcan as well. After all, how would a culture

---

* Actually Spock started out with reddish skin, but the makeup tests on almost all colors, while okay for color broadcast, made him look as if he was wearing phony makeup on black & white TV. Therefore it was decided to use the yellowish hue. It was the local station mixers who made Spock look green on some sets. In another color freakout, the green command level shirts never looked green on the TV set, but rather a kind of gold.

develop such a weapon if it didn't work on its own kind?) †

Last of all, the Vulcan culture placed a great premium on rationality. Open displays of emotion were worse than gauche—they were savage. Barbaric. An unpleasant reminder of the basic animal origins of every Vulcan. The bestiality of the Vulcan heart had to be stifled.

Vulcans were consciously trying to forget their past—or at least, live it down. According to STAR TREK episode "All Our Yesterdays" written by Jean Lisette Aroeste, Vulcan had had a long and savage history, with wars much more vicious and destructive than anything that has ever been experienced on Earth.

The Vulcan culture finally rejected its savage heritage—rejected it so thoroughly that they rejected anything that smacked of it as well. Wars are emotional experiences, they stem from individuals and groups of individuals and nations acting irrationally, reacting with their adrenals instead of their brains. In rejecting war and savagery, Vulcans were forced to also reject emotions.

Just as Freedom and Opportunity are the spoken goals of most Earth cultures, so did Rationality and Logic become the keystones of the Vulcan culture. Vulcans carefully bred emotionality out of themselves. They conditioned themselves and their children to be logical. They consciously altered the direction of their evolution.

The result is the supra-rational Vulcan society that produced the First Officer of the starship *Enterprise*, Mr. Spock.

Spock's father was a Vulcan who married an Earth-

† The Vulcan mind-meld required the Vulcan to be in physical contact, or at most, only a short distance away from the being with whom they were in telepathic touch. The farther away, the less clear and distinct the impressions received.

woman, because "it seemed the logical thing to do." It was never stated whether there were any other offspring to this union, but if so, they would also be half-human, half-Vulcan, like Spock, and prey to the same internal conflicts.*

The half-and-half nature of Spock's persona is part of what makes him such an interesting character. There is too much Earthman in him for him to be completely Vulcan, and there is much too much Vulcan in him for him to even try to be Human.

Spock was raised on Vulcan, consequently he thinks like a Vulcan. More importantly, he thinks of himself *as* a Vulcan. Not a human being, not even a half-breed, but a *Vulcan.* He shows pride only in his Vulcan heritage, he almost flaunts his Vulcan rationality and inherent superiority to emotional human beings. He is ashamed of his human inheritance. He tries to hide it as a weakness, as one would be ashamed of the great-uncle who was hung as a horse thief. Thus, Spock is ashamed of the fact that he has feelings. He tries to pretend he doesn't, or that he has them strictly under control, but occasionally we see that this just isn't so.

From a dramatic point of view, Spock is a beautiful character—he is the perfect character to be the ship's Science Officer. His superior brain powers give him the ability to accurately handle the large amounts of information that are his responsibility. But the fact that he is the only Vulcan on an all-human ship sets up a host of internal pressures and conflicts. All around him are individuals flaunting their emotions—a disgusting display of fears, prejudices, loyalties and friendships.

---

* Dorothy Fontana, story editor for STAR TREK's first two seasons, as well as author of the script "Journey to Babel" in which Spock's parents were introduced, comments thusly: "To stamp out all the obvious stories in which half a horde of Spockian brothers, sisters, half-brothers and half-sisters showed up, I arbitrarily decreed he had no other siblings. And, in my own mind, this vastly strengthened the drama in the conflict between Spock and his father in 'Journey to Babel.' "

While the human part of him wants to react to this and yearns to express itself too, the Vulcan half must keep a continual tight control.

His job as Science Officer aboard the *Enterprise* is probably one of the most difficult tasks he could be assigned. As such, it forces him to continually reexamine his own identity; but it also provides him with an unparalleled opportunity to exercise his intellectual capacities. So if Mr. Spock suffered the need to feel at home anywhere, the *Enterprise* would probably be it.

Captain Kirk's second advisor—one who is every bit as important as Mr. Spock—is Dr. McCoy, the ship's Medical Officer.

In many respects, Dr. McCoy is diametrically the opposite of Spock. Just as Spock is responsible for the ship's "mind," McCoy is responsible for its "body."

McCoy cares about the people he treats—he cares about them as individuals and he treats them as such. He is very much an emotional being—not simply that he expresses his emotions, but that he recognizes that there are fundamental biological, physical and mental reasons for the existence of emotions. Probably he feels that Spock is somehow incomplete because the Vulcan deliberately suppresses even those feelings he does experience.

To McCoy, Spock is a bit of a neurotic—the annoying kind, the one who brags about his neurosis as a strength. To Spock, McCoy is also an annoyance because of his unscientific demeanor. McCoy not only is not logical, he doesn't even *care* about logic.

The doctor realizes that people *aren't* logical, never were meant to be, so why worry about logic at all? Because of this, he is the most outspoken officer aboard the *Enterprise*.

And, just as Captain Kirk and Mr. Spock would seem to be the perfect dramatic entities for their responsibilities, so is Dr. McCoy. Because one of the worst failings a doctor can have *is to have feelings*.

A doctor has to be callous. Really. Given the amount of suffering that he will have to deal with, he can't allow himself to care about his patients as individuals—that would mean taking on their pain and sickness as his own. Even the best of doctors will not be able to save all of his patients; many of them will die. A doctor, in order to preserve his own sanity, has to think of them as anything but human beings. How many friends can you lose—especially when it is your responsibility to save them—and still continue to function rationally?

Granted that future science and technology will provide fantastic advances in medicine. Granted that doctors will be better trained and better equipped. But planetary exploration will still be a dangerous business and men will be encountering threats and menaces that will be totally unfamiliar. A ship's doctor is going to be continually reminded that all of the people around him are mortal. For his own sake, he had better not get too close to them.

And yet, McCoy is a man with emotions—he wants to feel for other human beings. He wants to, but he must not.

Understand the contrast here: Spock prefers logic over emotions. McCoy prefers emotions over logic. But each is in a position where they must stifle part of who they are in order to fulfill their duties aboard the ship. Spock is continually reminded of his own emotionality and McCoy is continually forced to reject his.

Perhaps each of these characters recognizes the dilemma that the other is in, and more than anything else, this could be the reason for the unspoken affinity between them—the mutual shock of recognition in a topsy-turvy mirror.

They are united also by a deep-seated regard for the Captain. And make no mistake, Spock does indeed have strong feelings of loyalty and respect for Kirk. The Vulcan betrays himself in this respect time and time again. For McCoy, of course, his relationship with the Captain is one of deep affection and warmth—an old, tried friendship.

In another respect, McCoy and Spock are symbolic opposites.

Remember that Captain Kirk's job is to be a decider. These two are his chief advisors. As such, they will represent the two aspects of every decision he will have to make—especially the difficult ones that will affect other people's lives.

As advisors, each of them will express his opinions; but their opinions will not only be derived from the nature of their jobs, they will be colored by who they are as individuals. Spock represents Rationality, McCoy represents Compassion. Thus, the two of them are more than just characters aboard the *Enterprise;* they symbolize Captain Kirk's internal dilemmas. The two of them serve to verbalize the arguments that the Captain must consider. Because we cannot get into the Captain's head to hear what he is thinking, Spock and McCoy are doubly important to the series' ability to tell its stories well—*it is primarily through them that Kirk's internal conflicts can be dramatized.*

The symbolism can be extended into the other crew members of the *Enterprise*:

Lieutenant Uhura represents the ship's ability to communicate. Mr. Scott represents the ability to take action once a decision has been made. Mr. Sulu, as helmsman, is the tool of that action. Ensign Chekov, as a Kirk-in-training, represents the next generation of command that must be raised to understand its responsibilities.

Actually, it is not the characters themselves that represent these elements, it is their jobs as crew members.

Think of the starship as a living being itself, a single entity of which her human complement is merely the equivalent of individual cells within a body. These are the pieces of the *Enterprise*'s *soma*.

Like any living creature, she needs judgment centers —a Captain; centers of rationale and emotion; organs of communication and action. It is not the personalities of the individuals that establish these symbolisms; rather these are the basic conditions of intelligent life. The people who execute these functions for the living *Enterprise* become symbols of these conditions not because of any inherent personal distinguishment, but because it is the nature of the jobs that they have assumed.

It doesn't have to be Captain Kirk at the helm, or Mr. Spock at the library-computer station. It could just as easily be Captian McGillicuddy and Mr. McGuffin. Or Captain Klutz and Mr. Cool. Anyone. It doesn't matter.

The situations they will find themselves in will remain very much the same, will call for specific patterns of response from each position, and will be precisely tailored *to test each individual the most*.

The responsibilities of Captainhood are such that whoever were to be commissioned to the helm would feel the same self-doubts in the equivalent situations. If not, then he'd be neither *human* nor interesting. And if he's not interesting, then the writers—the good ones, anyway—will tell their stories about someone else. Any writer who hacks out an adventure in which the hero *isn't emotionally involved* is not only a bad writer, he's cheating his audience.

This analysis of STAR TREK is based on the (unlikely) assumption that the full measure of creative ability can be brought to every aspect of the series' production. (We *will* deal with this later.) Purely in terms of story, the key word is *human*.

We are all human beings.

At the moment, we are *only* human beings. There are no other intelligences or entities with which we can establish dialogues.

As human beings, we are self-centered. It is a natural human trait, common to all of us. We like nothing more than to see ourselves in mirrors—especially the kind of mirrors that distort us, or show us the backs of our heads, or make us look prettier than we really are. And this is reflected in our arts.

Our drama is oriented to the study of man and the human experience—what it means to *be* a human being. Human beings don't come with instruction books, and we have to learn who we are every step of the way. We gaze into the mirror of drama not just because we want to be entertained, but because we want to get closer to other people by sharing a piece of their lives—and by learning about others, we hope to learn more about ourselves. We are delighted when we can gain a piece of new insight. We treasure it and cherish it as a piece of wisdom—and polish it so frequently that we reduce it to cliche. Given enough time, all of the world's great wisdom will be expressed in cliches. But this is the highest mark of success that an idea can achieve—to become so familiar to all men that it becomes a shorthand statement for a whole experience.

Whether a story is true drama or merely hackwork melodrama, our reasons for being interested in it remain the same—we are interested in ourselves and how *we* would react in a similar situation. Hence, we look for interesting and unusual situations in our drama, puzzles and exercises with which to test ourselves, problems against which we can measure the strength of our own identities.

We want to be as brave as our Captain Kirks, as cool as our Mr. Spocks, and as outspoken as our Dr. McCoys. We long to be as colorful and as larger-than-life as they are. But failing that—being trapped into a nine-to-five, consume or be consumed existence—we have to let our actors and writers provide these dreams for us vicariously. We will content ourselves with just *identifying* with Captain Kirk and Mr. Spock and Dr. McCoy. If we can't *be* them, well, we can still *dream* about being them.

The other characters in the series, Mr. Scott, Mr. Sulu, Mr. Chekov, Nurse Chapel and Lieutenant Uhura were not as fully developed as the three major leads.

This is not to say that they were not important to the series—they were very important—but they were never treated with the same depth of feeling. We rarely, if ever, were allowed to see if any of these individuals had any *inner* conflicts.

It was as if Kirk, Spock and McCoy were consciously designed to be the most dramatic possible individuals for their responsibilities, while the others were merely individuals assigned to their specific jobs without much regard for any inherent dramatic conflicts. Scotty was known to love his engines, Uhura liked to sing in her off-hours, Sulu was a hobbyist, a botanist as well as a swordsman, Chekov showed great pride in being Russian, and Nurse Chapel had a crush on Spock. Period.

In the *Star Trek Guide,* each is treated with only a paragraph or two of personal description—but the descriptions are all of surface characteristics. We are not told what *drives* any of these people. We don't know what they think about, or what they fear. We might as well be told Scotty is a Scotsman, Sulu is an Oriental, and Uhura loves watermelon. There simply hasn't been enough presented to let us picture these individuals as fully rounded people.

Of course, things were developed for each of these characters in the course of the series, but too often this was only the result of specific story needs. Attempts to redefine (or maybe just define in the first place) the subordinate characters *as human beings* were minimal. There were too many other things to be worried about in a hectic production schedule.

A great deal of this stems from the exigencies of television production and the basic series format. Subordinate characters are meant to be just that—*subordinate*. They are supposed to do their jobs, support the main characters, and be otherwise unnoticeable. They are not to detract from the story. They are never to be treated as if they were a main focus of an episode—there are usually only two focuses: the regular star and the guest star.

If a subordinate character starts becoming too important, the impact of the series is changed. And this is dangerous, because it's equivalent to changing the series itself into a whole new concept. A series is designed to appeal to a specific audience; if you change too much, you might lose part of that audience. If a producer does decide to make changes in his format, he has to be very careful that they are the right ones, that he is emphasizing what the audience will react well to.

An example of this is the character of Mr. Spock. As STAR TREK progressed, the role grew in importance until finally STAR TREK was no longer the adventures of Captain Kirk and the crew of the *Enterprise,* but Captain Kirk and Mr. Spock of the U.S.S. *Enterprise.* The relationships of the rest of the crew, and even the starship itself were downplayed in favor of the relationship between Kirk and Spock. It was only because the relationship between the two was so interesting that the change was justified.

None of the other subordinate characters ever commanded that kind of interest, however, and so, they remained subordinate. They remained functions of the starship rather than becoming *dramatis personae.* Lt. Uhura continued to open hailing frequencies—any robot could have done that; Mr. Scott found some trou-

ble with the doubletalk generators—but fortunately he
fixed it in time; Mr. Chekov had trouble with the helm
because some superior force had overpowered the
ship—he didn't know what to do about it.

As such, none of these aspects of the various STAR
TREK plots required these characters to be individuals
concerned about themselves and their responsibilities.
They were simply there to dramatize the external conflicts of the leading characters. They were functions of
the starship, not of the story.

Among the subordinate characters, the only exception to this rule was Nurse Chapel. She was the only
regular character who was not a function of the starship as such. A Doctor's Nurse simply is not important
to the overall hierarchy of command. She has no purpose except to be someone for the doctor to talk to—
and anybody in a nurse's uniform could fulfil that role.

Nurse Chapel was the only subordinate character
whose internal motivation was seriously developed. We
were never told the trifling facts of her ancestry or her
preference in music. Instead we were shown quite
bluntly that Nurse Chapel loves Mr. Spock—and make
no mistake, it is a tragic love because it is doomed to
be unrequited. Mr. Spock could never allow himself to
respond to her interest. It might be the best thing in the
world for him—but he would never do it.

This is probably the primary reason for Nurse
Chapel's existence aboard the *Enterprise*—to love Mr.
Spock. She fulfils no other dramatic function, and no
other symbolic function either. The most important
continuing event in her life is her love for the ship's
First Officer. She was obviously created specifically for
this. The need to dramatize Spock's Vulcan aloofness
requires that a woman fall in love with him and be continually rebuffed. Hence, Nurse Chapel.

This is why Nurse Chapel sometimes seems slightly
out of key with all of the other subordinate roles. Hers
is a basically human motivation, while the other char-

acters are basically symbolic with human aspects super-imposed upon them.*

The characters of Uhura, Chekov, Sulu and Scott might seem a little uncomfortable with Nurse Chapel, unable to deal with her except strictly on the most professional level. The bridge crew have minimized their inner drives, Nurse Chapel has not. Perhaps there is a mutual recognition of this, perhaps not. In any case, although there may have been trust between them, there did not seem to be a great deal of affection.

What this means to the format of the show, however, is that the characters of Uhura, Chekov, Scott and Sulu have a great deal more dramatic versatility than Chapel. She has been too thoroughly limited by her creation to a single dramatic function, while the others, having been created for no specific dramatic function at all, can be assigned various dramatic responsibilities throughout the course of a season.

The roles of the others have been left open for development, they are blank books for the series' writers to fill as they choose. We haven't been told what drives Uhura or who Sulu loves—this can be developed later. The only flaw is that there is no guarantee than any of it *will* be developed later. We might end up with just as many questions about these people as we started with. Or maybe not. It depends on the man who sits in the producer's chair.

---

* This was probably the reason why Nurse Chapel was the least popular member of the STAR TREK family. It was because of her love for Spock and his occasional moments of gentleness toward her that Christine Chapel was largely a hated character among the Trekkies who adored Spock. Female fans saw her as a threat to their own fantasies and male fans saw her as a threat to Spock's Vulcan stoicism.

But those fans who have been lucky enough to meet Majel Barrett in person (now Majel Roddenberry) at science fiction or STAR TREK conventions have been surprised and delighted. The most frequently heard comment is, "But, she's beautiful!" And she is. They just couldn't see it in her as Chapel because of the relationship between her and Spock.

Fortunately, STAR TREK struck a reasonably safe middle ground with these characters. They were developed enough to be personalities, but never so much as to damage their ability to reappear the following week in the same role. If a story required a particularly violent upheaval in a character's life, generally, a character was created specifically for that upheaval. (Part of it, of course, involved keeping the lesser roles from becoming too complex to be handled by individual writers. No writer is going to know all the scripts that went before, or all the other scripts in development, hence the subordinate roles must be kept fairly simple and unchanging from episode to episode.)

The real strength of these roles is shown by their cumulative effect on the viewer. Although very little is presented about these characters in any specific episode, the sum total feeling after viewing five or six episodes is that these *are* real people.

The involvement that results is quite deep. In a sense, the involvement is very much akin to real-life relationships. One does not meet a person and immediately find out who they are—we do not very often meet people when they are at the height of an emotional crisis. We rarely meet them even in situations which would distinctively delineate an overall set of reactions for them. Rather, we meet people as they are "maintaining"—moving from one situation to another. Or just existing between situations.

Generally, if there is a situation, it is one of "I am on my guard while I am meeting you, and you are on your guard while you are meeting me." It takes time and several exposures to an individual before the guard is relaxed. During that period, data is gathered and correlated. Little things, like whether one prefers peanut butter or mildew, big things, like attitudes and angers. A total picture is built up, but only gradually.

Such is the way the lesser STAR TREK characters developed in the viewer's mind. He wasn't shown much in any given week—but over a period of time, he was shown quite a bit, developing a feeling of recognition and familiarity. Enough data was eventually presented to bring the characters completely to life, and the result was that despite the hasty treatment given them in any specific script, they still seemed as real and as fully developed as the three major leads.

STAR TREK's "bad guys" however, were never fully realized as characters. As villains they were more symbolic than individual, and consisted primarily of two distinct groups—

The Klingons and the Romulans.

Klingons first:

Klingons are professional villains. They are nasty, vicious, brutal and merciless. They don't bathe regularly, they don't use deodorants or brush their teeth. They don't even visit their dentists twice a year. They sharpen their fangs by hand because they think pain is fun. They eat Blue Meanies for breakfast.

Think of the Mongol Hordes with spaceships and ray guns. To the Klingons, Genghis Khan was a phony and Attila the Hun was a fairy. And Hitler was only a beginner. Remember Ming of Mongo from all those old Flash Gordon serials? Well, these are his descendants, selectively inbred for sheer awfulness.

A Klingon is a good person to invite to a rape—or even a murder, providing it's your own. Klingons build their battlecruisers without toilets; it makes them nastier. Klingons pick on old ladies. Klingons fart in air locks. Klingons drop litter in the streets. Klingons pick their teeth in public. And those are their good points.

Klingons do all the things that men pretend they don't—only Klingons are proud of it.

The Klingons are perfect villains.

They were introduced in an episode entitled "Errand of Mercy," by Gene Coon. In that episode, the neutral planet, Organia, is threatened by a Klingon takeover. Kirk tries to persuade the Organians to accept a Federation base on their planet for their own protection. but the Organians refuse. Although they are seemingly unprotected, they insist that they are able to cope with the Klingon threat unaided. Kirk doesn't see how, the planet is totally unarmed, and the Organians are confirmed pacifists. The Klingons are murderous butchers and Kirk fears a massacre.

When the Klingons arrive, Kirk naturally ends up getting into a fight with the Klingon captain. Excuse me, a confrontation. At which point, the Organians reveal themselves to be superior energy beings with the power to nullify all weapons of both sides. "Thou shalt not fight!" insist the Organians. At this, Kirk gets mad, "How dare you forbid us to fight with each other! It's our right!!" And then he realizes that the whole purpose of his mission was to *prevent* a war. The Organians are right! The Organians have the power to enforce a peace treaty between the two empires. Grudgingly, Kirk and his Klingon counterpart, Kor, agree to a *détente*. They have no choice.

The Klingons were such delicious villains, however, that they began to crop up in other episodes: the author's own "The Trouble with Tribbles," Gene Roddenberry's "Private Little War," Jerome Bixby's "Day of the Dove," Dorothy Fontana's "Friday's Child," and so on.

—But all of the Klingon episodes were, in one way or another, restatements of the original: Klingons and Earthmen must *not* fight.

The Organian peace treaty is a convenient limit. Otherwise any confrontation with the Klingons would immediately result in an all-out war.

From a series point of view, if the Klingons are going to appear regularly as villains in stories, then they need to be "controlled" villains. That is, the situation should be equivalent to the American-Russian cold war of the fifties. (Remember that?) Not only does this provide a good background for a wide variety of stories, both humorous and dramatic, but it is a lot more optimistic and (hopefully) believable than a space war.

After all, a race that can achieve space travel is going to have done so only through large scale programs of social cooperation, and hopefully, in the process will have learned that there are better ways than aggression to accomplish one's goals. Perhaps they would have even forsaken goals that require aggression (in any of its forms) for their accomplishment.

Besides, if STAR TREK needs to tell a *real* war story, that's what the Romulans are for . . .

Speaking of Romulans, there's another situation. Romulans were precursors to the Klingons, they were developed first. They weren't quite as nasty, but they were a lot more intelligent and that made up for the missing nastiness.

Romulans first showed up in "Balance of Terror" by Paul Schneider. They also figured in "The *Enterprise* Incident" along with some Klingons.

In both of these stories, the *Enterprise* was shown in direct battle with Romulan ships, thus implying that a state of war existed between the Earth Federation and the Romulan Empire. As long as each government's ships kept to their own side of the line, however, the war was limited to minor skirmishes. If at any time it had been shown that a state of *all-out* war existed, then STAR TREK would have had to either become a space war TV series, or the two groups would have had to run into some more Organians . . .

Turning to the *Enterprise* itself, the ship was designed more for its visual impact than out of any particular sense of "this is what it will be like."

Matt Jefferies, designer for the show and the man responsible for the overall STAR TREK "look," submitted several designs to Gene Roddenberry. Roddenberry winnowed, suggested and corrected, and Matt tried again. Eventually, the familiar disc and pylons began to take shape and proportion.

One of the early forms of the *Enterprise* had the disc *below* rather than above the central Engineering pod.

The capabilities and design of the *Enterprise* as presented in the *Star Trek Guide,* as well as seen on the show, were an incredible mixture of the clumsy and the brilliant.

For instance, the bridge set was one of the best designed science fiction sets in motion picture history. There are few that can equal, let alone surpass, the bridge of the *U.S.S. Enterprise.* (Offhand, I can only think of two: the interiors of the spaceships used in *Forbidden Planet* and *2001: A Space Odyssey.* And maybe the one from *Silent Running.* Maybe.)

As a design for the control of a giant starship, the bridge is a model of logic and efficiency. The Captain's eyes are before him in the form of a giant viewscreen. So is the pilot console, which is the equivalent of his hands. The Science Officer is to his right, ready to present whatever information is needed. Communications and Engineering are to the rear, right and left respectively, where they are out of the way, but convenient.

The upper walls are lined with information screens and the Captain's chair swivels so he can survey the whole bridge easily. The lights and controls on each panel are set in curved banks—curved to match the reach of the human arm. Whatever operator is seated at a console, he will find all of his controls in the most convenient possible position.

So workable is this design that the United States Navy sent a delegation to the studio to examine the bridge set in detail. They were considering a similar layout for a new aircraft-carrier bridge. (The new *Enterprise* maybe. . .?)

That's the brilliant part.

The clumsy part is that so many writers and directors continually *misused* this beautiful set.

Example: (A familiar scene.) The *Enterprise* is under attack. She's hit by a photon torpedo—*kaboom!* —everything tilts and everybody falls out of their chairs! They climb back into them and another torpedo comes zooming in—*kaboom!*—again, they're knocked to the floor! A third time—*kaboom!*—the camera tilts and they all fall down again!

And Scotty reports, "All defenses out, Captain. The next one will get us for sure."

Several years ago, Bob Justman, associate producer of the show, was asked by a fan about this: "Why don't you put seat belts on the chairs?"

"Because," he replied, "if we did, then the actors couldn't fall out of them."

—But the above scene—and Bob Justman's easy answer—are *wrong*. Both scientifically and dramatically. There has been little thought put into either.

From a scientific standpoint, the scene is fallacious. Each of those torpedoes would have had to have been a direct hit in order to shake the *Enterprise*. If they had been misses—even *near misses*—the ship wouldn't have been shaken at all. Shock waves don't travel through the vacuum of space. Hence, in order to shake the ship, they must have been direct hits. If they were direct hits, the ship should have been destroyed three times over.

Or try it another way. Let's assume that a near miss *does* have the power to jolt the *Enterprise*. But the *Enterprise* has an artificial gravity—no, not just an artificial gravity, a whole force field to neutralize the effects of momentum, acceleration and inertia. Assuming the speed and maneuverability already postulated for the vessel, a protective force field is a necessity to keep the ship's crew from being smeared into jelly every time she made a rapid change of direction or speed. If this is so, a near miss with a photon torpedo would no more be able to rattle the crew of the *Enterprise* than it would be able to dislodge a fly trapped in amber.

(And assuming that such an artificial gravity/force field did exist, isn't it amazing that it was never knocked to hell and gone by one of those missiles?)

Actually, I could just as easily argue the other side of the question:

Well, you see, the *Enterprise* had her shields up. The torpedoes exploded against the ship's force screens and the shock of the explosion was transmitted to the ship via the shields. Or: the shields didn't stop all of the explosion, part of it leaked through. Just enough to shake everyone, but not kill anybody.

Sure.

It doesn't really matter. Whichever side of the question you argue, it's only doubletalk. But when doubletalk is designed to justify a piece of *bad* writing, that's a reprehensible cheating of the viewer. "Let's make it look exciting. We'll have all the actors fall out of their chairs. Three times."

The same scene could have been a lot more tense—and a lot more believable as science fiction—if it had been written with even the simplest awareness of the postulated capabilities of the *Enterprise*.

The purpose of the scene is to dramatize the menace of the attacking ship. Fine. Very simple. Instead of three missiles, just one. The *Enterprise* tracks it all the way in—and can't stop it. The officer at the weapon control console (let's put him at the upper left side of the bridge) reports all of his attempts to intercept the torpedo—phasers, anti-missile missiles, force screens, tractor beams, and various other doubletalk devices—and also reports the failure of each device to stop the approaching torpedo. The torpedo strikes the *Enterprise*'s *last* set of screens and detonates, and in the process knocks out that line of defense. This is all reported on the bridge—at the moment of detonation, nobody falls out of their chairs and no sparks fly from any panels (somebody has invented fuses). The lights simply dim momentarily, then come back up again as (implied) the emergency power supply cuts in.

Kirk calls for a status report and Scotty replies: "All defenses out, Captain. The next one will get us for sure."

And that brings us to the exact same place that the first scene did.

The major difference is one of credibility. The scene with the people falling out of their chairs is visually exciting, but it is not dramatically valid. We are abruptly and arbitrarily *told* that the *Enterprise*'s defenses have been knocked out.

The latter scene—admittedly a harder one to write—*shows* how those defenses are taken out, and in the process, it builds to a tense climax. The scene involves the viewer in the destruction of each line of defense and makes him more a participant in the action. The real point of the scene is to leave Kirk with no defenses at all—that's when he has to open his hailing frequencies and start talking. Fast. But it feels a lot better if the writer has brought us to this point *honestly*.

Science fiction is not a western with ray guns and spaceships. It is a genre so demanding that few of its practitioners are more than moderately competent at it. The responsibility to be logical and scientifically accurate, while at the same time telling a good dramatic story, will continually defeat any writer who approaches the field with less than total respect for its requirements.

Because so few screen writers are well versed in science fiction, STAR TREK should have had not just its technical advisors, but also a full time science fiction writer on its staff. A multi-faceted scientist like Dr. Isaac Asimov would have been an ideal choice, someone with a good background in science as well as science fiction. Such a staff advisor would have worked closely with the writers, the directors, the producers and the actors, as well as the designers and the decorators, to make everything as logical, believable and accurate as possible.

There were too many instances of clumsiness in STAR TREK's production that a science fiction advisor could have corrected. Doubletalk cannot disguise bad writing—and it will only hurt good writing. It's a little harder, yes, to be accurate, but the results are worth it.

Consider:

The *Enterprise*'s corridors seemed awfully roomy, they were about twice as wide as they should have been. In fact, the whole ship was too roomy. Space is at a premium in any kind of enclosed environment. Anyone who's ever been aboard a submarine—or even an aircraft carrier, for that matter—knows that they are designed for the maximum utilization of their volume. Efficiency is a necessity, and a spaceship is going to have to be designed the same way.

In fact, the requirements of a spaceship are much more stringent—for instance, the interior atmosphere must be maintained with the correct combination of gases, at the right temperature, pressure, humidity and ionization, to maintain not just the lives, but the comfort as well, of the crew. The margins for deviation are narrow; therefore, *every* cubic inch of interior volume means airspace that must be maintained—and maintenance requires the expenditure of energy. When you have to conserve your ship's power, you don't waste airspace.

The reason for such broad corridors? They had to be wide enough for a camera dolly, cables and a film crew.

To attempt to show that the ship was cramped would have required the construction of cramped sets—which are harder to work with and would have meant much more in the way of production time.

(So, instead, we're told that the ship has power to

waste—it's implied, not specifically said. But if that's so, then we should never see a story in which maintenance of life support functions becomes a critical factor for building suspense. A ship can't be both wasteful *and* limited.)

Another example: the turbo-elevators. These were the machines that took the various crew members from one part of the ship to another. Good idea; especially as we are told that the thickest part of the *Enterprise*'s disc is twelve stories thick.

But—the elevators seemed to be the *only* way to get from one deck to another. If the ship's power supply were cut off, every deck would be separated from every other. Oh, well, not really—somebody could always crawl through the air vents, or through the Jefferies Tube, or down one of the ladders which we saw very infrequently. *All except for the bridge.* Cut off the turbo-elevators and you isolate the bridge. Tsk. That's *bad* designing. Illogical.

Another one: the Captain's cabin. Or anybody's cabin for that matter. They were all redresses of the same set. If any of those cabins had a bathroom, it was never shown. There weren't even any doors to *imply* a bathroom. We were never shown any cleanup facilities on the whole ship—not even in the sick bay. And the *Enterprise* was on a five year mission—isn't that a long time to hold it? Isn't that carrying it a bit too far?

Also, about those cabins—all of the major officers aboard the ship had their own cabins, and roomy places they were too. No complaint here, but what about the crew's quarters? Those were never even shown or suggested. Did each member of the crew have a cabin too? That would have made the *Enterprise* more of a hotel than a starship. Or did they have bunkrooms?

If they did have bunkrooms, how come they were never mentioned or shown? How come we never got into the crew's lives?

Or was the crew just a collection of some 400-odd

androids to walk up and down the halls—scenery behind the main characters, to be moved around as necessary, but not really important to the story except as another part of the background to support the overall illusion?*

These examples are not just casual errors in the STAR TREK format. They are part of a general pattern. The glossy surface and flickering lights of the show's gaudy technicolor production could not make up for what was *not* there. In its execution, STAR TREK tended to lack the kind of *deep* extrapolation that characterizes good science fiction.

Consider the ship's galleys, for instance—they were never clearly defined. In "Charlie X" there are references to the ship's cooks, yet when I worked on "The Trouble with Tribbles" I was told that there was only a Mess Officer, and everything else was done by machines. But what machines?!! A slot in the wall? Whatever a character ordered appeared almost immediately behind it. While this may have been admittedly convenient, the processing machinery necessary to perform this miracle—just the myriad moving parts necessary to bring the food from storage to the wall slot—seems prohibitively wasteful of *space.*

And those damned wall slots were *everywhere.* In

---

* About this, Gene Roddenberry says, "Well, yes, we did make mistakes. There were things that worked and things that didn't work, and if we were ever to do STAR TREK again, we would make improvements in those areas. The one elevator to the bridge *was* a mistake, and no emergency exit in sight. Yes, we would correct that. And we should have had a head in Captain Kirk's stateroom, certainly.

"We had hoped to build on the basic format as the show progressed. Each year we would have a little more money to spend on new sets and we had intended to add more and more sets gradually to answer some of these questions. My feeling about the crew was that indeed they did have their own staterooms. The services today have always annoyed me, putting up enlisted men like cattle. I think all men deserve dignity and it was my feeling that by that century, we would have come to understand that."

"Tomorrow Is Yesterday" we were even shown that the transporter room had a food slot. Good Grief!* It makes you wonder what's going on behind the walls of the *Enterprise*.

A justification can be made for any of these elements of the show's conception. The wide corridors are necessary to prevent claustrophobia in the crew. Separate cabins for everyone are necessary because the culture of the future places a high premium on privacy. Food slots must be plentiful for the same reason—the crew needs to be reassured as to the security of their basic requirements. (And a dumbwaiter system isn't all *that* complex.) Okay—but if you accept this, then what does that imply about the culture that built it?

What kind of a culture would place such a high premium on privacy and security? It does not seem likely that it would be a totally healthy one, or even likely that it would be a spacegoing culture. Space travel implies hardships—insecurity as well as being thrown together with the same group of people for a very long time. The amount of energy needed to establish security and privacy for 430 people is enough to make a starship prohibitively expensive, especially if it is designed in a wasteful manner. The first commandment of the Universe is very simple: Thou Shalt Not Waste. (There are no other commandments, there are only variations.)

These flaws are all part of a pattern—but not a pattern of commission, rather one of omission. And the omission is a serious one. At no point was the *Enterprise* given a background culture.

* Quoting Dorothy Fontana: "There was a food slot in the Transporter Room in 'Tomorrow Was Yesterday' because production people wouldn't let me take the Air Force Sergeant out of the Transporter Room or send an extra for some chow for him. It was, of course, never used again. Same reason, essentially, for never seeing bunk rooms and other variations of crew quarters. Have to build a set which might be used once—for one scene—costly, etc. You had to fight with Bob Justman (Associate Producer) on this. And mostly, writers lost."

Oh, we know that Kirk is an Irishman, Spock is a Vulcan, Scotty is a Scot, Sulu's an Oriental, Uhura is African, and McCoy is from the deep South. But these aren't cultural attributes, they're matters of inheritance and have nothing at all to do with the environment that produced this ship and this crew.

In general, the viewers were given so few clues about the social background of the starship that the result was occasionally grotesque. The walls of the recreation rooms were barren even of the simplest decoration. There were no paintings, no screens, nothing to look at, not even patterns of tile or enamel, just a simple stark gray. The basic bulkheads of the ship seemed as grim as a prison, as utilitarian as a hospital.

If these were real people, vitally alive, as intelligent and able as postulated in the *Star Trek Guide,* they would make the impact of their individuality obvious on their "home away from home." They would make the ship their own. They would decorate their galleys and rec rooms, they would make the sick bay a cheerful place with bright walls and colorful artwork. These people are not automatons—and they would not live in an environment seemingly designed for such.

A starship is not an independent entity—no more than a jet plane is independent just because it can leave the ground.

Imagine for a moment, a fully loaded 747 jet airliner flying from Los Angeles to New York. That's several hundred thousand pounds of airplane and three hundred people. First of all, there's the technology to build that airplane. (Not just one factory in the city of Seattle—but aerospace contractors all over the United States supplying components for every part of the plane, from blades for its jet engines to light bulbs over the seats.) Then there's the technology to maintain it; the schools to train the mechanics, the teachers to teach the stewards; the simulators and mockups on which they'll learn; the equipment with which the plane will be serviced, the specialized trucks and tools and devices; and the men and the training to support *all* of these levels.

There's more than the airplane alone. There are airports. Lots of them. That means the equipment and technology to lay down a perfectly flat runway two miles long. There are ground controllers—that means radar and scopes and computers. And reservation desks and communication systems to service those desk. Luggage handling systems, porters, allowances for taxis, parking lots, restaurants, rest rooms—and the people to clean, maintain and work in them.

Then you have to be ready for emergencies—so there will be rescue planes and fire trucks and medical equipment on hand. And detectives to protect the passengers and Federal Marshals to look for hijackers with metal detectors and psychological profile charts.

An airplane burns fuel—a lot of it. A 747 gulps enough petroleum in a single flight to drive an automobile for a year. That requires refineries to crack that oil (men to build and operate those refineries) and trucks to deliver it, tanks to store it. Passengers need meals, that demands another whole service industry. And entertainment—and specialized insurance—and airsickness bags in the back of each seat.

None of these things just *happen* by chance; they are designed into the system as it grows. The 747 could not exist until most of the support technology had already developed. What did not exist had to be built. All of it was oriented to fit the needs of the passenger as our culture has determined them. The very existence of the 747 as the kind of plane it is, is a direct result of what our culture considers important to the traveler. Imagine an airplane with 14 bathrooms!

That airplane is a piece of living America. It is an active vital symbol of our national technology, but it is no more independent of that technology than is a bird independent of the air in which it flies. The air holds up the bird. Our technology holds up that airplane.

Now. Apply that to a starship.

Extrapolate the needs of the *Enterprise*. Her fuel requirements, her crew requirements, her maintenance and training needs, her supply needs, her communication and control structures, her relation to the culture that produced her—and *why* that culture produced her.

Think about it.

Do you think the *Enterprise* is really an independent entity?

It isn't. It never could be. Her independence is an illusion, just as the independence of the 747 is an illusion. Sooner or later that ship is going to have to return home to have her exhausted energies recharged. Or, if not home, then to a base with an equivalent technology.

And if all of this is true technologically, then it must follow sociologically too. The men and women who crew the starship are no more independent of their cultures than is the starship independent of her technology. They're going to take their culture with them to the stars—and even if they were stripped of every physical aspect of their home cities, they would still reflect their social conditioning in their attitudes.

Yet, the *Enterprise* that we saw on NBC television was a strangely stripped *Enterprise*. Too often, she seemed to be independent of the rest of the galaxy, only occasionally taking orders from Starfleet. She seemed also to be sociologically independent. Indeed, there seemed to be nothing at all which could really be pinpointed as distinctive to the Starfleet culture.

Not in the people. Not in the ship.

Part of the answer is in the *Star Trek Guide*:

What is the Earth like in STAR TREK's *century?*
For one thing, we'll never take a story back there and therefore don't expect to get into subjects which would create great problems, technical and otherwise. The

"U.S.S." on our ship designation stands for "United Space Ship"—indicating (without troublesome specifics) that Mankind has found some unity on Earth, perhaps at long last even peace. References by our characters to Earth will be simply a logical projection of current scientific and social advances in food production, transportation, communications, and so on. If you want to assume that Earth cities of that future are so splendidly planned with fifty-mile parkland strips around them, fine. But for obvious reasons, let's not get into any detail of Earth's politics of STAR TREK's century; for example, which socio-economic systems ultimately worked out best.

Right there, in one paragraph, we are told that we cannot *really* postulate where these people or this starship came from. We may find out what drives various individuals aboard the ship, but we do not know, nor do we have any way of finding out, what drives them culturally—what motivates their government in sending them out on this mission and equipping them for what eventualities? We can only surmise from what is implied. Nothing has been told to us to let us guess what is culturally important, what is approved and what is taboo.

We can only imply the basic cultural overview by the cumulative actions of the crew of the *Enterprise* and the people they meet. On our first meeting with them, because we want to identify with them, we might surmise them to be like ourselves—but after observing them for several weeks or months, we begin to see that they have a much nobler outlook than most of us seem to have. At least, they appear to be more able to live up to those goals which too many of us only pay lip service to in our own lives.

Of course, it's easy to be noble in any situation, when it's only for an hour and you'll be leaving it for a new situation next week. But that's neither here nor there. We also saw that our crew of the *Enterprise* could sometimes be less than noble—quite often we discovered charming human weaknesses. Scotty's drinking, McCoy's sarcasm, Kirk's impetuousness.

But to really understand *who* these people are, we have to look to another section of the *Star Trek Guide*:

> *But projecting the advanced capabilities of your starship, wouldn't Man by that time have drastically altered such needs as food, physical love, sleep, etc.?*

> Probably. But if we did it, it would be at the cost of so dehumanizing the STAR TREK characters and surroundings that only a small fraction of the television audience would be interested, and the great percentage of viewers might even be repulsed. Remember, the only Westerns which failed miserably were those which *authentically* portrayed the men, values, and morals of 1870. The audience applauds John Wayne playing what is essentially a 1966 man. It laughed when Gregory Peck, not a bad actor in his own right, came in wearing an authentic moustache of the period.

The giveaway words here are: "1966 man."

Or, what they really mean: "Contemporary man."

The crew of the *Enterprise* is in no way meant to be representative of future humanity—not at all. They are representative of the American Sphere of Influence *today*. Their attitudes, their manner of speaking, their ways of reacting, even their ways of making love, are all *contemporary*.

We have met the *Enterprise*—and they are *us*.

The crew of the *Enterprise* is twentieth century America in space.

And—although it takes a bit of justification—that's the way it *has* to be.

Remember, this is drama we are talking about, as well as *American television*. It *has* to make money.

That means it has to have appeal and that its characters must be attractive and interesting—an audience has to be able to relate to them. Even if the show is alien to the audience's experience, the characters have to be recognizable.

Neither *Gunsmoke* nor *Bonanza* are really about 1880. They are about 1972 men in an 1880 world. The *Untouchables,* when it was still on, was about 1966 men in a 1929 world. And STAR TREK also is about 1966–69 men in a 2??? world.

This is the essential appeal of drama. As mentioned earlier, we watch a story because we are really testing ourselves. We are curious as to how we would react in an equivalent situation. In science fiction, we are also testing our culture. Thus, both the characters and the culture have to be recognizable parts of ourselves. They have to reflect contemporary values—not totally, but enough so that the viewer can follow.

STAR TREK is *not* pure science fiction. It is not predictive science fiction, and it is not accurate science fiction.

It was never meant to be.

Anyone who tries to shoehorn the series into that kind of arbitrary definition will be making the same mistake that every hardcore aficionado who grumbles in his beer about SF and the dramatic arts (grumble grumble) has been making since the very first episode of STAR TREK began.

What STAR TREK is, is a set of fables—morality plays, entertainments, and diversions about contemporary man, but set against a science fiction background. *The background is subordinate to the fable*.

I'm going to quote my earlier definition of SF:

Science fiction is the contemporary fairy tale, it's the twentieth century morality play. At its worst, it's merely romantic escapism; but at its best, it is the postulation of an alternate reality with which to comment on this one.

That definition could almost be applied to STAR TREK, but the difference between STAR TREK and science fiction is that *true* science fiction requires that the background be logical, consistent, and the overall shaper of the story. The world in which the character moves determines the kind of actions he can make, and hence the plot of the tale. In true science fiction, the background is never subordinate to the plot.

As we have already seen, the *Enterprise* and her crew were able to function almost independent of their backgrounds. The only thing about them that remained consistent was their contemporary attitudes.

STAR TREK's backgrounds were always subordinate to the story—and because of that, it never quite achieved the convincing reality of true science fiction. Its use of a science fiction background gave it the appearance of science fiction; but in reality, STAR TREK was a science fiction-*based* format for the telling of entertainments for and about the attitudes of contemporary America. And that's called science fantasy.

The format is a flexible one—in other hands, it could be about other people. It doesn't have to be Americans. The STAR TREK idea could easily be translated into Russian or Chinese or Swahili or Polish. The basic format is that of reflections of the viewer confronting a wide variety of alternate realities.

These realities are so varied as to provide opportunities for high comedy ("The Trouble with Tribbles"), satire ("Bread and Circuses"), farce ("I, Mudd"), tragedy ("City on the Edge of Forever"), psycho-case studies ("Space Seed"), morality fables ("Errand of Mercy"), soap opera ("Is There in Truth no Beauty"), theology ("Who Mourns for Adonais?"), melodrama ("The Lights of Zetar"), and even high camp ("Spock's Brain").

As such, STAR TREK is the most flexible format for a television series ever to have been postulated for commercial network broadcasting. And as such, STAR TREK had the potential to be the finest dramatic series in TV history:

The reflection of American man—no, make that just Man—freed from the context of the American culture (or any specific culture) and placed in a series of alternate realities, would be a powerful dramatic vehicle for educating, enlightening—and especially for entertaining the American public. *If* the dramatists scripting the series were allowed to do so with no holds barred.

Just as Archie Bunker is forced to confront his own attitudes week after week, so would such a STAR TREK allow its heroes to examine their attitudes in a multitude of situations—and the viewer with them. Captain Kirk would become a symbol not for American ingenuity—but more important, for the American dilemma: how best can we use our strength? Each week, he would be making crucial decisions about problems that we would see relating to our own lives and environments.

This writer submits that STAR TREK *was—and still is—the finest format ever designed for* American *series television.*

There are few shows that can match it for potential.

But, potential must be realized. An unfulfilled potential is a very special kind of failure.

We'll consider that aspect of STAR TREK later.

PART TWO

The *Star Trek* Family—The People Who Made The *Enterprise* Fly

The reality that was STAR TREK was only an illusion. A very skilled and carefully contrived illusion. Even when American television has little or nothing to say, it still can say it beautifully. And when American television does have something to say—as with STAR TREK—the illusion is convincing enough to alter the shape of reality. As witness the fans' response.

The people who made that illusion work were the STAR TREK family. The cast and crew of the show. The creative talents that worked together to make a totality that was more than the sum of its individual parts.

In writing this book, I spoke with and interviewed all of the cast members of the show, as well as producer Gene Roddenberry, line producer Gene L. Coon, and story editor Dorothy Fontana. I also spoke with other actors and crew members whenever possible.

One theme kept repeating itself over and over. "STAR TREK was a family. It was a special show and we had a special feeling about it. Gene Roddenberry knew what he was doing in the casting and in the production of the show. He was what made it great." Without exception, every person interviewed recalled STAR TREK as one of the high points of their careers.

A couple of notes about the following interviews: The reminiscences of the cast members are reported all as transcribed off the tapes I made of each session. Their comments on what they liked—and disliked— are included with only the minimum of editing. Editing was for grammatical purposes only.

The only member of the STAR TREK cast whose comments are not included in this book is Majel Barrett

Roddenberry. As she puts it, "I let 'Pussycat' do all my talking for me. He's the expert on STAR TREK."

The comments of Gene L. Coon and Dorothy Fontana are scattered throughout the book in the text or as footnotes. In addition, much of the background material that they presented became the foundation for whole sections of analysis of the show.

William Campbell's remarks are included as representative of the guest star's attitudes toward STAR TREK—also, because his interview was too good to omit. I believe it presents valuable insight into some of the workings of television relationships as well as the difference between series acting and guest star spots.

Time and space considerations prevented as detailed a report on the sound stage crew as I would have preferred. However, the individuals involved were so thoroughly presented in Stephen Whitfield and Gene Roddenberry's *The Making of* STAR TREK that the reader is referred to that work for further information. Much of the material available to me for this book only duplicated what was previously published in the above.

Gene Roddenberry's remarks about STAR TREK and also about his future plans are included in a special chapter later on, entitled, "The Return of STAR TREK. . . ?"

Undeniably, the most popular character on STAR TREK was Mr. Spock, the alien First Officer. His mother had been an Earthwoman, his father, a Vulcan. Spock was a half-breed, torn between two worlds.

And because of that, he was the show's most *interesting* character.

But when STAR TREK was conceived—and even in

the first two pilot episodes—very little thought had been given to Mr. Spock as a character. The details hadn't been worked out yet, just the basic conception, a half-breed alien without emotions. He was simply *there*.

Gene Roddenberry had thought it would be nice to have an alien on board the *Enterprise,* but the real development of Spock as a character did not come until later—and much of the credit belongs to Dorothy C. Fontana, a thoughtful and sensitive woman who started out as Gene Roddenberry's secretary and ended up as the show's story editor. She wrote several of STAR TREK's best scripts, including the excellent "Journey to Babel." That was the story that introduced Spock's parents and also presented quite a bit of his background.

The impact of Mr. Spock on the show is almost too vast to be clearly defined. More than any other character, he is the one closest identified with the show—unfairly and unfortunately perhaps, because it is at the expense of so much else that is worthy of attention. When you mention STAR TREK to a non-STAR TREK fan, the reaction is generally, "Oh, yeah—that's the show about the guy with the pointed ears."

The fans took to Mr. Spock—and everything related to him. To many of them he was the sole *raison d'être* for STAR TREK. No less an authority than the *Saturday Review* voiced the opinion that Captain Kirk should be booted off the ship and Mr. Spock put in command. (To which a number of people disagreed vehemently, not the least of whom was the good Captain. Too many of the Spock-fans who expressed this kind of thinking simply hadn't realized that Spock was generally at his best when he had Captain Kirk to play off of. And vice versa.)

Neither could the writers resist Mr. Spock. He was too interesting a character to leave alone. There was too much to do with him. And they did—they used him at every opportunity. Because he was the most interesting crew member for Kirk to take with him on a mission, he was written into more scripts than anyone else. Pretty soon he was on screen as much as the Captain. Within one season, Mr. Spock grew incredibly in his importance to the show—almost, it seemed, until he had taken over the series, if not the ship. When I met William Shatner for the first time in 1967, on the set of STAR TREK, he even touched on this himself. "When you write your script," he said, "remember that Kirk is the Captain of the ship. The story has to center around him and his decisions."

I don't know if he told that to every writer he met—but if he had, there were obviously quite a few who hadn't listened.

A good part of Mr. Spock's appeal, of course, was Leonard Nimoy himself. Before STAR TREK, he'd appeared in shows like *Thriller, The Lieutenant,* and *Outer Limits.* (And even an incredibly bad B-picture called *The Brain Eaters.* Fortunately, it was a very small part and he was heavily made up. If you didn't know it was Leonard, you'd never recognize him.) As an actor, he was not known to the general public—not by his name, perhaps only occasionally by his face. But the casting directors and the producers knew of him, and he was working regularly. He was also training to be a director.

And then STAR TREK happened.

"For me," says Leonard Nimoy, "it started in 1964 or '65. I did an episode of *The Lieutenant,* a TV series that starred Gary Lockwood.* Gene Roddenberry was the Executive Producer, and he was away when we

---

* Gary Lockwood played Lt. Commander Gary Mitchell in STAR TREK's second pilot episode, "Where No Man Has Gone Before." In that episode, the *Enterprise* tried to go out beyond the edge of the galaxy and Lockwood got zapped into a funny-eyed superman. Lockwood may be better known though for his role as Astronaut Frank Poole in *2001: A Space Odyssey.* He was the spaceman murdered by the computer, Hal 9000.

shot it, so I never did meet him. A month or so later, my agent said he had talked to Gene—he said he had liked me in that show and that he had a part in mind for me in a science fiction pilot he was writing.

"I didn't take it very seriously or think much of it, because the man was only *writing* the pilot—that's an awfully long trip before he gets it done. It has to be examined and reviewed by the studio and the network—and then getting it into production and all that that involves is another whole story. Who knows where I'll be at that time, or whether he might find somebody else? I had learned not to get very excited about that kind of conversation, although it was always nice to hear that somebody was interested.

"But about six months later, he called and said he wanted to meet me. So I went to see him and he was well into it by then. He took me around and showed me the various designs for the sets and the props that were being built. the phasers, the communicators, and wardrobe sketches that were being done. And we talked about this character—the original idea was, from the onset, that this character would be half human, half alien. The pointed ears were specifically established, but the rest of it was somewhat vague. It was in the process of being developed, what color the character's skin would be, the nature of the rest of his makeup—the eyebrows, the haircut, the color of his skin, all came later.

"And so we started serious negotiations. Serious negotiations—in that case, I had no leverage. they made me an offer, we quibbled over a couple of dollars, you know, and made a deal. I liked the idea of the character. At first, when Gene started talking about it, I was a little concerned—it sounded like Mickey Mouse time with the pointed ears. Of course, that was everybody's reaction at first, including the press; but as we discussed it, and as he began to tell me what the character was going to be about and what he hoped for the character in terms of dimension, I thought, 'this is a valid thing—within the genre, this is a valid character. We might be able to make it work.'

"The biggest problem we had developing the character was the ears. It was very difficult—we were with the wrong makeup people. The studio had made a deal with a special effects house that makes monster heads and things like that, and they were going to do the work—they had made a flat deal for X number of dollars to do something like three monster heads and a pair of pointed ears.

"Now, I don't know if you know how those things are made. You have to have a plaster cast made of the area of the face or body where the appliance is going to fit, and then they make a positive piece from the plaster negative—a head, or in this case, the ears. Then, in putty, they work up the shape of the appliance, and then they cast that and make the piece. I went there and they cast my ears, and a few weeks later they came up with the first pair of ears.

"They were gruesome. They were very rough and crude. They were very very porous, almost like alligator skin. The shape wasn't right. Aesthetically, they just didn't work at all. They were awful.

"By this time, they had a makeup man assigned to the show, Fred Phillips, and he started working with me, putting them on, and working with skin colors and eyebrows and so forth. And we both agreed that the ears were pretty bad. He went to the production department and said, 'These ears are being made by the wrong people.' Fred had done an awful lot of appliance work and he *knew* good appliances. He'd started at Universal—he went all the way back to Lon Chaney and Boris Karloff. He told them that there are people who are specialists in the appliance field. These people we were with were very good for shock heads, but for a delicate appliance that we have to really believe is part of the body—like puffy eyes, or a broken nose or scar tissue—it's very delicate work and it has to blend in very evenly with the rest of the face.

"But the studio said no, keep working with these people, because we paid them, we want them to do the job. And about four or five days before shooting, they came up with another pair—which weren't much better. So Fred decided to do it on his own—we were working one afternoon at the studio makeup department—he made a phone call to MGM and said, 'Come with me.' There was a man he knew at MGM who was a specialist in pieces like this. We went over there and told him what we had in mind. He drew us a sketch— which I could see immediately had the right feeling and we did a cast, I was out of there in about twenty-five minutes. And about forty-eight hours later, he delivered the ears that I finally wore. And they came just in time—they came just a day or two before we started shooting the show.

"A pair of ears might last anywhere from three days to five or six shooting days—each appliance had its own little idiosyncrasies, they were all different, some lasted longer than others. Only once in a great while did we get a pair that hadn't baked properly, or something that meant that we couldn't use them.

"You know the ears were painful. They irritated, particularly inside the ear where they had to be glued down. And of course, what we don't realize is that when we talk or move, we do have facial skin movement—and there is a little bit of movement of the ears—so there's a little rub from the appliance. Every once in a while, I'd get a sensitive raw area. But, you know, you can get used to hanging by your thumbs, as they say.

"Meanwhile, Gene Roddenberry and I were having lengthy conversations to develop the character, ideas about how the character would walk, talk and function. And so we went to work, and I was in that first pilot with Jeff Hunter. I didn't have a heck of a lot to do in it, it was a nice job, I was on it for three weeks—which I think was the longest job I'd ever had in this business in fifteen years. Prior to that, I'd always been in and out in a couple days. I'd had maybe half a dozen jobs that ran two weeks, most of them were one week television jobs.

"So this one was a giant project—very esoteric show, very cerebral. It scared everybody half to death because it cost a fortune and most of the network people didn't understand it.

"And then I forgot about it. I thought, well, that settles that. It's done.

"My contract ran out—but about seven months later, they called me and said, 'We're going to do another STAR TREK pilot and we want you back.' So, we did that, and you know the rest. The rest has all been documented.

"Actually, I felt very comfortable playing the character. I felt, particularly in the first season of scripts, even before we went on the air, that the character was good—that I could stand behind the role. I didn't have to be ashamed or self-conscious in any way. I felt I was finding things in the character, that there was room for exploration. Gene Roddenberry was open to exploration. I felt very good about it—I hoped that the show would work. But I had no idea that the character would become as popular as he did.

"When the fans began to respond, it was exciting—very exciting. There were times when it was even scary. It happened so fast and with such intensity, it changed our whole way of life in a matter of a few weeks.

"The very first thing that gave us a real physical indication of what was happening was a trip I made to Medford, Oregon, for NBC. The show had been on the air a few weeks and my mail was coming in pretty strong . . . —Uh, let me give you an idea of how limited my expectations were. When the first mail started coming in, I answered it myself, responding to each piece personally, writing handwritten notes and handsigning each photograph. And I would do that during lunch hour. Once a week they would give me my mail, so the first week there was about thirty-five pieces, and I thought, 'Well, if that's the mail for the week, I can handle that.' Then the second week there was, I don't know, fifty or sixty pieces. The third week there was a couple of hundred—and after that, it was all over. From that point on it just kept multiplying geometrically until there were thousands of pieces of mail coming in every week.

"Then I went on my first promotion trip—this public appearance I mentioned. NBC called me and said there's this nice little town called Medford, Oregon, that has a Pear Blossom Festival every year and they have a little parade through the town and they'd like you to come and be the Grand Marshal of the parade. John F. Kennedy had done it one year. So, I said, yeah, okay, I'll be the Grand Marshal.

"I went up there and rode in the parade, and what happened was that several thousand people turned out, a very large turnout for this parade. The problem was that they had announced that I would sign autographs in a park at the end of the parade. And as we rode down the street, all of the kids started coming off the sidewalks—the police couldn't control them; there were too few police and too many people—and they surrounded the car, and stayed with the car all the way to the end of the parade. So we were gathering this entire crowd through the city and down to the park. And at the park —there was one man there, he was the park supervisor, who was trying to control the situation—it was physically impossible to get in or out.

"Finally, the police had to come in and get me by force. When I got back to Hollywood, I talked to the NBC promotion department about it, and they said,

'That's the way it's going to be from now on.' They'd been through it all before with people like David McCallum—it had happened to him too, with *The Man From U.N.C.L.E.* And they said, 'Any time that we send you out in the future, we'll see to it that there's proper security measures for getting into places, getting out of places, privacy, secrecy about where you're going to be and so on. Because it becomes impossible for you otherwise.' And they were right.

"In some cases people *refused* to let me appear because they were concerned about what the results might be. In fact, Macy's department store in New York said, 'We don't want the crowds that you'll bring.' I was offered to them in connection with a promotional tour I was doing for a new record album. And Macy's said, 'We can't handle it.'

"We did a show early in the first season, called 'Naked Time.'* which was the show in which, at least for me, and I think the audience too, there was the first very definitive—miniscule, but very definitive—study of the kind of schizophrenia that moved Spock, the nature of the dynamic of the split being, the human versus the alien. This was an episode that took place on board the ship. There was a virus that was passed hand to hand, and it very quickly brought about a change in the character of the people it infected. The person's subconscious levels became expressed. And in Spock's case, he started to have feelings. The feelings in him started to overwhelm the control, and there was this fight for control of the being. Would he be an emotional being or a Vulcan? He had to fight it out with himself. And that, I think, very clearly and specifically defined, for a long time to come, the nature of the character.

"There were other shows that were important to Spock for various other reasons. When Gene Rodden-

* Written by John D. F. Black.

berry first came up with the Vulcan mind-meld—you know, he had a great talent for that kind of thing—what happened was, we had a scene where a disturbed man had been brought aboard the ship and was in sick bay and Spock had to question him to get certain information out of him. Well, as the scene was originally written, it was simply an expository scene where Spock asked a lot of questions and through his garbled conversation the man came up with a lot of information. But Roddenberry rewrote the scene so that we went into the man's mind and *past* his problem—we got past the fact that he was in a psychotic state. That was the first time that we used the mind-meld and it was very successful.*

"When we went to Vulcan the first time and did the show about Spock's impending marriage, it was a very rich and lush show.† We were seeing something about the Vulcan society for the first time—and I came up with the Vulcan greeting, the salute.* I felt that there should be *something*. There was a moment that seemed to call for some signal between Spock and the Matriarch of the planet. Fortunately, Celia Lovsky, who played T'Pau, could do it too. You know, not everybody can do that. If she hadn't been able to do it, we probably would have lost that bit.

"You know, that reminds me of a funny incident. I

---

* "Dagger of the Mind," by Shimon Wincelberg (pen name for S. Bar David.)

† "Amok Time," by Theodore Sturgeon.

* The salute is given with the right hand, palm facing the person you are greeting—like an Indian about to say "How"—but the fingers are spread in the middle. The first and second fingers are together, the third and fourth fingers are together; the gap is between the second and third fingers. The gesture is very reminiscent of the V-For-Victory Peace Sign. When done with two hands close together, it is an old and esoteric Rabbinical gesture, used in certain types of Jewish blessings. The congregation is supposed to cover their eyes, but Leonard used to peek. (Theological humility prevents me from speculating here that Vulcan was colonized by the ten lost tribes of Israel.)

was in Cleveland one day—it was later in the year—
and I was being driven in a car and we stopped at a
traffic light. I was sitting in the back seat and a girl
pulled up next to us at the traffic light. She looked over
and recognized me and she gave the salute. So I rolled
down the window and I said, (saluting so) 'Can you do
it with your left hand?' She tried—she got about that
far (a claw-like gesture)—and said, 'I speak it with an
accent.'

"I remember very vividly the day we came up with
the Vulcan nerve-pinch. We had a script* in which
Captain Kirk had been fragmented into two characters.
It was a Jekyll-and-Hyde type of story where there was
the good Kirk and the evil Kirk. And in the scene
where they confronted each other and the good Kirk is
about to shoot the evil Kirk, it was written that Spock
slips up behind the evil Kirk and knocks him out with
the butt of his phaser. And I rebelled against that—I
said that's a hangover from westerns. In the 22nd century, you don't have to slip up behind people—*Vulcans*
don't have to slip up behind people and hit them over
the head with butts of guns. We should find some other
way of doing this. And the director, Leo Penn, said,
'What would you suggest?' And I said, 'Well, I happen
to know that Vulcans have this power to render people
unconscious through their knowledge of the human
anatomy plus a particular Vulcan vibration. And this is
the way it's done.' I told Bill (Shatner) what I planned
to do, and Bill understood immediately, and I reached
up behind him and did that—and Bill just kind of
froze up and went unconscious. And that's the way that
was born. Roddenberry saw it the next day in the
dailies, and loved it. He started including it in future
scripts.

"So that's the way that things were developing. Each

* "The Enemy Within," by Richard Matheson.

day was a very creative day for that reason. Bill was finding his things, De Kelley was finding his things, I was finding mine, and it was a very fertile time. There were a lot of good things happening."

Because of Mr. Spock's popularity, and because of Leonard's many other responsibilities, he decided to hire his own secretary—oops, excuse me. Not secretary. Girl Friday. There's a difference. The responsibilities are a great deal heavier.

He hired Teresa Victor in 1967 (she's been with him ever since), and her job is to make his easier. Sometimes she has to be a buffer between Leonard and some of his more overenthusiastic fans.

It's not that the actor doesn't appreciate the fans' attentions—he *does,* they're the ones who have put him where he is—but if he spent as much time with the fans as they wanted, he'd never have any time for acting or directing. And it's the acting that's the *raison d'être* for the whole thing.

Teresa began working for Leonard shortly after STAR TREK went on the air. She had never had any previous experience with the fan phenomenon, so when the head of the mail department phoned her one day and asked, "What should we do with Leonard's mail?" she said, "Well, bring it up here to his office, of course."

And they did. Two huge sacks of it.

And that was just one week's worth of mail. Fortunately, she had the presence of mind to have it delivered somewhere else after that. Within a couple of weeks, it would have filled the office. Shortly thereafter the show's mail was turned over to a service anyway.

When Teresa started working for Leonard, she

wasn't too sure if the job would work out, so she and Leonard both agreed to give it a few weeks to see if they could work well together. If she liked the job and they were getting along, then she would stay on.

After three weeks it was pretty obvious that they meshed well, but Teresa wanted to do something to *show* Leonard how she felt, something that would say to him, "Yes, I am happy working for you."

So she decided to get herself a pair of Vulcan ears and on the day when the trial period was up, she planned to wear them—it would be a pretty obvious gesture.

The first problem lay in getting the ears. She didn't know who to talk to or where to go. The demand for these, the most precious of all STAR TREK souvenirs, was already phenomenal. After all, if Leonard Nimoy's own employee couldn't get a pair . . . Finally, one of the casting directors located a pair and presented them to her just the night before she needed them.

Then she had to figure out how to put them on—and remember, these ears had *not* been cast to fit her, but Leonard Nimoy—she had to use a very strong adhesive. She spent almost an hour the next morning getting them on just right and then combing her hair over them so they wouldn't show until she wanted them to. Unfortunately the tips kept poking through.

All day long she wore those ears, up and down the lot, delivering messages, running errands, taking care of all the big and little things that were her responsibilities. And nobody noticed. No one said a word. Not one person realized that she was wearing a pair of pointed ears.

She was crushed. The few who did notice just looked at her a little strangely and apparently thought that those two odd shaped projections were part of her *own* ears. Teresa felt so hurt because no one realized—not even Leonard—that she began to wonder if she really was going to stay on.

If the ears were uncomfortable for Leonard Nimoy, who they had been molded for, they were even more uncomfortable for Teresa Victor. By the end of the day she was in real pain and close to tears. Finally, she said, "Leonard, I have something to show you." And she pulled her hair back to reveal her pointed ears. "I am dying from the pain!" He cracked up laughing— but he realized by that gesture how important it was to her that she show him how she felt.

That evening, however, Teresa and a girl friend were supposed to attend one of those parties where they sell cookware or clothes or things like that. Teresa didn't know any of the people there, it was the girl friend's invitation, but she realized she was going to be in a very embarrassing situation—*she couldn't get the ears off*.

All of the people there were strangers to Teresa, and as it was still fairly early in STAR TREK's first season, not one of them had seen the show yet, or knew about Vulcans and pointed ears. For half the evening they thought she had some kind of unusual birth defect, and for the other half they thought she was wearing hearing aids. She could not convince them that she was Mr. Spock's "girl Friday." "Mr. Spock? Who's that?"

For a while, Teresa was having trouble getting pencils and other supplies. So she got into the habit of "borrowing" what she needed from other offices. Finally, Bob Justman wrote a memo—he was famous for that sort of thing—to the studio heads:

I should like to report to you that pens and pencils have been disappearing from my office at a phenomenal rate. I don't have proof, so I don't think that I can logically accuse anyone of these thefts. However, I staked out my office the other night in an attempt to identify the guilty party.

Unhappily, some unknown assailant sneaked up behind me and clamped a fiercely vise-like grip upon me somewhere between my neck and shoulder. I lost consciousness within a split second and did not awaken until several minutes later. To my dismay, I noticed that there were more supplies missing from my office.

Whoever attacked me and my supplies must have been endowed with quite superior sense of hearing as I am certain that I made no noise and in fact, was quite careful to breathe as lightly as possible.

There is one very strange fact which has emerged from this incident. I had rather cleverly concealed a naked razor blade within my pencil box so that whoever would be stealing my pencils would have an opportunity to slice open his or her finger. Upon investigating my now empty pencil box, I discovered a slight amount of the oddest green liquid present on the razor blade and around the bottom of the pencil box. I can't imagine what it can be. It certainly isn't blood as we all know that human blood is red.

Incidentally, on the subject of fan letters, I have received three fan letters this season. I answered them post-haste. Please send me fifteen cents to cover postage.

Sincerely,
Bob Justman

Of course, that wasn't the end of it. Leonard wrote a memo too, also to the studio heads:

I should like to file a complaint about the first aid facilities here at the studio. It seems that late one night last week, while doing some very important work in my office, I had a minor accident and cut a finger. I went to the first aid office only to discover that they are closed after shooting hours. I think it highly illogical to assume that accidents only take place during shooting hours. What can be done?

Spock

Finally, the studio heads replied to all these little notes:

Come on, you guys! Is that the only thing you have to do all day—write memos?

But Teresa did get her pencils.

Much of STAR TREK's business was conducted by memo. This was by necessity. A memo is an effective way for each member of a team to make the best use of his time. It lets each person record his opinions while they are still important in his mind, and it preserves them until the intended recipient has the opportunity to read them. The advantage is that neither has to have congruent office hours. When Executive Producers, Line Producers and Associate Producers all have dovetailed responsibilities and a limited amount of available time, the memo makes it possible for each of them to handle all their responsibilities more efficiently.

For instance:

Dear Encino Fats:

Reference your comment the other day I should give you a memo on Bob Bloch's script "Wolf in the Fold," I gave you a memo on it! In fact, a splendid memo, one which I would not have thought would be so easily forgotten by one who professes to admire incisive writing and clear thought.

Yours very truly,

THE BIRD

There. You see how that works? Now isn't that a lot more efficient than a phone call where you might waste ten or fifteen minutes just going over things already discussed?

Memos were also written for more mundane matters. Like getting the show produced.

One of the problems that persisted for all three years of the show's production was that of William Shatner's weight. Shatner is a very athletic actor, and takes great pride in his ability to do strenuous scenes such as fights; he exercised regularly, but as the strain of each season's production began to tell on him, he would begin slacking off on the exercises, and well . . .

As Gene Roddenberry put it, "We found ourselves having to stay away from longer shots wherever possible, as the simple plain lines of our basic costume render most unflattering any extra poundage around the waist. I did get concerned about this since we were playing to an audience that was most weight conscious —and also very *youth* conscious, and poundage adds years photographically."

At one point, near the end of the second season, a couple of very concerned memos were written about "William Shatner's Equator."

The memos discussed the possibility of selecting some particularly unflattering film clips, a face view, a full belly body view and sending them to Shatner without comment.

But the pictures were never sent. It wasn't necessary. William Shatner is too much of a professional, he took too much pride in his own appearance to allow the show to be damaged. The *Enterprise* was not going to be commanded by "Captain Fatty."

William Shatner has appeared on such television shows as *Twilight Zone, Thriller, Outer Limits,* and in such TV-movies as *Vanished* and *The Andersonville Trial*. He was also in the motion picture, *The Brothers Karamazov*. He has worked in television, movies and stage for far too many years to be unaware of the importance of keeping himself fit. There are too many good parts that require an athletic hero, and those are the parts that William Shatner likes to play.

When the part of Captain Kirk was offered to him, Shatner grabbed it because he believed in the dramatic possibilities of the show. And in the course of the production, he not only made himself synonymous with the role of the starship commander, he brought his wide-ranging expertise in all areas of the art to the STAR TREK set.

Because STAR TREK had many different directors, this meant an increased burden of responsibility on the cast and the rest of the crew to keep the STAR TREK "look" consistent. Specifically, there were times when, for one reason or another, a director could *not* handle the show—those were the times when William Shatner (as well as the rest of the cast and crew) had to cope with the situation on their own. Shatner's long experience with stage and television proved itself time and time again on the set. Even with experienced directors, like Marc Daniels and Joe Pevney, he did not hesitate to offer his own suggestions.

On the matter of his weight, William Shatner is quite candid and willing to talk. And it is a good example of just how much discipline is required of an actor in a weekly television series.

To quote Shatner, "On the time off between seasons, or prior to starting, for that matter, I'd be involved in my usual regimen of whatever, running hysterically around from place to place, and also doing a lot of exercise. So when I'd start the season I'd be at my optimum weight and everything would be fine, but then as the season progressed and as I got more and more tired, I couldn't get up early enough to work out, and gradually the fatigue began to defeat my ambition to keep in shape. And so I'd gradually—well, deteriorate, to the point where the first shows came on, the first thirteen, and I would see how much weight I had gained. Then I'd go on a crash diet—and I'd lose weight by the end of the season.

"I'd start off slim, and get to my fat period, and then taper off again. And the knowledgeable people who watched the show have written me or told me in person that they've made bets as to what time of the season a particular show was shot, based on the fact of how much weight I had gained.

"They used to leave these lead weights lying around—they were used for counterweighting the camera crane—and the crew would leave them all over the set. So I used to pick them up and heft them a few times between takes, trying to keep in shape that way. —Oh, they played a joke on me with them. That was another practical joke. The weights came in twenty-five and thirty-six pound sizes. And the special effects department went to great time and expense to make a wooden one up and leave it lying where I usually left the ones I worked out with. So I lifted this thing up, I expected it to weigh thirty-six pounds—and it went flying into the air. Luckily it didn't hit anybody, but there was a lot of clowning around with that false weight for a while."

Perhaps the only episode where William Shatner's weight was unimportant was one called "The Deadly Years," written by David P. Harmon. In that script Captain Kirk, Dr. McCoy and Mr. Scott were all victims of a virus that aged them rapidly. They were *supposed* to look old.

In the course of the production each was made up in varying degrees of old-age makeup to indicate the rapid progression of the disease. To some extent, William Shatner objected to this—he didn't want to look old. And if you'll look at stills from the show, you can see that he is wearing considerable less makeup than the other two actors. (I refer you also to the photo section in *The Making of Star Trek,* by Stephen Whitfield and Gene Roddenberry.)

Putting on this makeup was a very lengthy process as it involved facial appliances to give the appearance of baggy eyes, heavy jowls, wrinkles, crow's feet and sagging skin. Appliance work—like Mr. Spock's ears —is always complicated. Each appliance has to be specially molded and then blended into the actor's skin so that no dividing line shows. Old-age makeup requires an appliance for almost every part of the face. Says William Shatner, "I spent three hours in the makeup chair one afternoon, just getting made up, and finally, I was ready about five-thirty or six o'clock. I came out on the set after having spent three hours with this painful—and boring—process of application, and they said, 'Okay, you're ready? Well, we have to quit. We have to cut at six-twelve.' And I said, 'You can't. I just spent three hours getting made up.' And they brought the producer down, Gene Coon, and he tried to go longer, but it was the policy of the studio to quite at six-twelve.

So with great reluctance, they quit for the day—and I ripped off three hours worth of work without ever once having stepped before the cameras."

Because he was the star of the show, William Shatner was the focus of its attention. Everything *had* to revolve around him. Neither STAR TREK nor the *Enterprise* could function without Captain Kirk. And if some of the incidents that happened to him were funny or annoying, there were others that were just as moving.

"My father died during one of the shows and I had to leave to pick up the body and fly to Montreal for the funeral. And I did that all on a weekend. I left on a Friday and I came back on a Monday, and we picked up the scene where we had left off.

"I'd heard about his death on my lunch hour, my mother had called me, and the company was willing to shut down immediately. But for some reason I insisted on going on for the rest of the afternoon to complete this particular scene. And I remember vividly, Leonard standing very close to me—almost like a herd instinct, it was a very touching moment—just being there, and trying to comfort me.

"And Jerry Finnerman, the Director of Photography, was standing behind the camera and crying for the whole afternoon. Not only for me, but because *his* father had died on a set some years before. His father had been a cinematographer too, and Jerry had been his father's crane operator. He had collapsed on the set and Jerry had held him in his arms while he died. So now, he was identifying with the death of my father and he was very broken up by it.

"Bob Justman kept running in and out—but he was unable to take it, unable to stand being on the same set, so he'd run out again. Then he'd come back a half hour later to see if he could help. He was torn as a man and as a production manager.

"That was the show with the Horta, you know, the

rock monster.* And I know exactly where the scene was that I stopped, and the scene where we picked up again on Monday. But the shots were all usable and nobody ever spotted any noticeable difference."

In a lighter vein:

"I used to keep my dog on the set the last year because I had no place else to leave him—my marriage was breaking up at the time—so everybody got accustomed to seeing this giant black doberman hovering around me, going to my dressing room with me and back and forth to the set. And nobody could get in my dressing room—which reminds me of another story, although it's not about STAR TREK.

"The same dog, his name was Morgan, used to come with me everywhere I went. After STAR TREK ended, I went on summer stock tour. It was the first of four that I did, and the dog came with me and stayed in my dressing room—but he wouldn't allow anybody else in, which was fine with me, because usually in the plays that I did I was on stage the whole time. In this particular play, there was a bit of business where I dropped my pants and the underwear that I was wearing would get a laugh. It was a special kind of underwear because it was commented on in the play. So I had to wear a particular type of boxer underwear.

"Well, one evening I was onstage and we were getting close to the moment where I would drop my pants and I suddenly realized I'd forgotten to put the shorts on. And I couldn't drop my pants—it was essential to the plot that I get this underwear shown. So while I was talking onstage to the character, whoever was on, I edged over to the side of the stage and I said to the

* "The Devil in the Dark," written by Gene L. Coon. The script was written in four days. Monster-maker, Janos Prohaska had crawled into Gene Coon's office wearing a rubber costume. Coon had said, "That's great! What is it?" Prohaska said, "I don't know. It can be whatever you want." Coon replied, "I'll write a script around it." And he did. It proved to be one of the most popular episodes of the first season.

stage manager, '*Get my underwear!*' Of course, he realized the problem immediately. So I kept on talking and acting in this scene, and I could hear backstage, I could hear him running to my dressing room, I heard the door open, I heard this ferocious barking—and now I realized, I'm still talking and carrying on, but I'm totally aware of what must be going on backstage. This giant doberman would not allow the guy who could save my life into the dressing room. I had about ten seconds in which I came offstage for something or other and I was planning—my mind was leaping ahead to possible solutions—I was planning to change into my underwear at that moment, if I could indeed get the underwear. Well, I didn't know what was happening backstage, but when I came offstage for that ten second bit, there was my underwear waiting for me. And I slipped it on and got back onstage and everything worked out well. It was only when the curtain went down that I had a chance to ask what happened. Another actor in the company also had dobermans, he was very accustomed to dealing with them, and when he realized what the problem was, the stage manager had apparently told him, he went running into my dressing room and told my dog in no uncertain terms, '*Lie down!*' The dog laid down. The guy ran in, grabbed the underwear and ran out. So, I was lucky there that there was another dog fancier in the cast."

"Getting back to STAR TREK, I remember that the fan reaction was tremendous. I would go out on personal appearances and the fans would just come running. Sometimes there was a danger of them being crushed. It happened at Macy's in New York once, it was very scary; and another time in South Carolina. I had just flown in from New York—it was late at night, about midnight—and I got off this commuter airplane, this smallish airplane and I couldn't see because there were so many lights on it. I didn't know what they were, and suddenly I realized there was a crowd of hundreds and hundreds of people and that all those searchlights were for me. It was absolutely astonishing. They had signs saying 'Up STAR TREK!" And 'Go, Captain Kirk, Go!' It was a tremendous turnout for a small town at this airport, giving it the aura of a grand opening. Well, I had come to appear in a parade—those people followed me all the next day.

"I know that the show is more popular now in its syndicated run than it ever was on network. I know it from the personal appearances I've made across the country that it's the result of it being at an earlier time slot in the independent stations. The network had it on at 8:30 and finally 10:00, but now that it's in the 6:30–7:30 time slots, somewhere around that area, it has outpulled any show at that time, network or independent station. In other words, when an independent station buys STAR TREK, at least up to the point that I was following it, they could be sure that they would have the highest market of any station in their area. I was crisscrossing the country for a while. I was in Seattle, then I flew to Miami, then I went up to New York and then Los Angeles, and in every one of those cities, plus the cities in between, without exception, every station manager told me STAR TREK was more popular than any other show at the same time . . . it's a phenomenon in television history in terms of syndication.

"I think that taken as a whole STAR TREK is one of the best television series ever on the air. I was approached after the first pilot was made. They showed me the first pilot and asked if I were interested in playing the part that Jeffrey Hunter was playing. I was intrigued by it and Gene Roddenberry and I had many talks about what the character would be like, what kind of a person he was, and that sort of thing.

"For instance, there was a question of how to play a commander of a ship every week with the responsibilities he has to bear without getting too heavy and pompous. That was a problem. I didn't solve it until about halfway through the first season. I had to learn not to take myself so seriously. I was being told to do certain things, but there was no precedent to follow. We were establishing our own precedent, and I found out as soon as I began to see it on the air. I realized what I had done wrong and began to change. In a play, you get immediate reaction from an audience and can start to change immediately, but until you're on the air in TV, you just don't know. There were things I had to create, like Captain Kirk's sense of humor, that was one of the things I began to develop.

"I've been an actor for many years and a director too. I feel I know a great deal about the way to make a film. I know what I would do in given instances. I don't like to impinge my feelings about a scene or a moment on a director who knows what he is doing because he may have a point of view himself. Certainly Marc Daniels is a first rate director, but there are times when I can say to somebody who I respect—why don't you try it this way . . . and because they respect me, they'll accept an idea from me where they might throw it away out of hand from some other actor. Besides which, as the star of a series, you have more influence than you would under normal circumstances.

"I felt very strongly about every area of the show. If I could see a point in the story line that could be improved, I would not hesitate, but leap eagerly into the fray and say, 'Here's what I think.' There were many times when the point was taken and used, and there were other times when they said, 'We can't do that.' And I accepted that. There were times when I suggested dialogue or script changes or ways to play a scene. There were times when directors finked out for one reason or another, either personal problems or lack of talent. Jerry Finnerman and I would complete the show.

"There was one show, I've forgotten the name of it, which somebody said to the director, if you bring the show in in five days, you'll get $500 extra. And it was a show I was mostly alone in. I did fourteen pages of dialogue in one day. The average was nine or ten pages a day, but I did fourteen. The show came in on time, the director got the 500 bucks and I didn't even get a thank-you."

There were occasionally problems on the STAR TREK set. Not all of them were *easily* solved. But all of them were eventually solved. For instance, Gene Roddenberry recalls: "One little incident that happened was one of the assistant directors asked me to go to the stage and talk to Bill Shatner about not being available when the camera was ready to roll, he was either on the phone or in the bathroom, or whatever. I went up to talk to him and Bill Shatner said, 'All right, Gene. It's reasonable for you to say this, but may I suggest something to you? I am in practically every scene in this show. Now there's a certain amount of personal business I have to conduct, there are times when I have to use the john, there are times when a friend will drop in on the set to say hello, and so on. The reason that it looks that I am late more often than other people is that I am in more scenes. Another person who has a smaller part can do these necessary things and it will never be noticed.'

"I said, 'My God, Bill, you're quite right. There is a certain amount of personal life and professional life an actor has to keep up and you're absolutely right. You're bound to appear more often late than others because you are in every scene. Forgive me for not seeing that first.' And we shook hands and that's how most of our problems were really resolved.

"We had an exceptional relationship. Not just Bill

and I, everybody on the show. We hardly ever had a problem that in the end we couldn't sit down and resolve."

One of the problems, however, was "The Great Shatner and Nimoy Feud."

There wasn't one. Not really.

—There were rumors, but they were unfounded. They were born out of the show's popularity. But, as rumors, they caused trouble.

When so much attention is focused on anything or any*one*, even the smallest incident will be magnified out of all proportion. A discussion becomes a disagreement. A disagreement becomes an argument. An argument becomes a fight. A fight becomes a feud.

Look, a movie set is a lot of things. It's a tourist attraction, it's a sweat-shop, it's an altar for idol-worshippers, it's a political convention, it's an encounter group, it's a hostility session—but to the people who have to work on it, day in and day out, it's a *family*.

And STAR TREK was one of the happiest families. Probably it was one of the most congenial sets in Hollywood—most of the cast and crew members seemed to think so. Even the casual visitor was likely to notice that this particular set was a fun place to be. In fact, there were times when the studio had to restrict the number of people allowed to visit—they were starting to interfere with the shooting.

Like all families, however—even the happiest—the STAR TREK family was not without its little bumps and crises. And it was these that gave rise to the persistent and annoying rumors of a feud.

In the STAR TREK family, Gene Roddenberry was the father-image—affectionately known as "The Great Bird of the Galaxy" or sometimes just "The Bird." As a producer, he is one of the most skilled. The hardest problem for any producer is keeping his regular people happy and functioning at their best—and this is one of the things that Gene Roddenberry is very very good at.

Nothing but *nothing* is every allowed to get in the way of production. The producer's goal is to get a good show on film and into the can. And that means that the cast and crew *have* to be kept happy. Gene Rodden-berry should have been called "The Man with the Silver Tongue." He could charm the venom out of a cobra—and make the cobra enjoy every moment of it.

He gave frequent parties for the cast and crew, he was called "the Pearl Mesta of Paramount." He encouraged a good practical joke, and he set up some of the best himself. ("Steve Carabatsos was our story editor for a while. Matt Jefferies got hold of a weather balloon and we got some helium. We poured about a pint of cheap perfume in it and then we put the balloon in his office and blew it up so it completely filled his office and pushed the door closed against it and waited for Steve to come to work. He opened the door and walked right into this thing and we knew the only way he could get into his office was to break it, and breaking all the helium and air mixed with perfume would make his office smell like a Turkish whorehouse for a month, and indeed, that's what happened.") And he saw that there was a STAR TREK "blooper reel" for every season, an expense that most producers won't go to.

Gene Roddenberry always did what he believed to be best. His basic goal was to see that STAR TREK was the best TV show that he could make it.

Along about the middle of the second season, the little grumbles and gripes began to get annoying, almost out of hand. In this case, the hassle was not limited to Shatner and Nimoy—there were complaints from all of the actors.

You see, by this time, the show was beginning to settle into shape. Most of the development of the *Enterprise*'s capabilities and her characters' personalities had already been done. We had seen the Vulcan nerve pinch and the salute and the mind-meld. We had seen two or three super-computers driven crazy with illogic, we'd met the Klingons and the Romulans, and we'd determined the relationships of the various principal characters. Nearly every other episode had some girl tumbling into Captain Kirk's arms. Some of these things, once determined, began to turn into *shticks* and formulas and overworked devices.

The cast began to chafe. For a variety of reasons, each of them was unhappy with many of the scripts that were being sent down. For one thing, the show was a hit; it was established by now that STAR TREK had the most devoted fans of any TV show on the tube. Every member of the cast was concerned with making his character interesting and important. *And* keeping true to the original concept that these are warm, intelligent *human beings,* who have dedicated their lives to the stars.

For instance, Nichelle Nichols was very unhappy with the fact that so few of the writers were giving Lieutenant Uhura anything of importance to do—she felt that she was being used as a token Negro, opening and closing the hailing frequencies and staying safely in the background in most of the episodes. James Doohan felt that Scotty had not been treated as importantly as the Chief Engineer of a vast starship should be. After all, he was third in command after Kirk and Spock. And he really hadn't been allowed to be much of a human being either. James Doohan is an accomplished actor of considerable experience—he wanted to use his abilities to the fullest.

De Forest Kelley was generally unhappy that Dr. McCoy was not being used as a real doctor; too often, he felt, McCoy was being slighted. In the original conception, the Medical Officer was as important as the First Officer; but lately, it seemed that a lot of scenes were being written for Spock and Kirk, when the nature of the information being presented demanded that it be the Medical Officer who deduces and explains what is going on. De felt that he wasn't being given enough to do.

Shatner and Nimoy were unhappy too.

Now, this was not a major crisis—but there was a deterioration of morale. And Gene Roddenberry felt that much of the grumbling was unwarranted. He was aware of the problems and was working to solve some of them.

So he wrote THE letter.

It was a very confidential piece, sent only to the cast, only the regulars. No one, not even Gene Coon, saw copies of it. There were five pages directed to William Shatner, four or five pages to Leonard Nimoy, half a page to De Forest Kelley, half a page to James Doohan, and so on.

In this letter, Gene Roddenberry—the silver-tongued bird of the galaxy himself—took his actors to task and gave them all a proper bawling out. What was said to each is unimportant—what is important is that it *worked*.

Afterwards, things settled down. Somewhat. With only an occasional bruised ego, the cast went back to work.

But shortly after that, Gene Coon and Gene Roddenberry walked onto the set and De Kelley came up to them with murder in his eye and a copy of the letter in his hand. "Now, *this* is exactly what I'm talking about. Shatner gets five pages. Nimoy gets five pages. And I get only half a page!"

About this incident, Gene Roddenberry said: "A time did come during one of the years when I felt some criticism of the major performances were in order, which is the producer's job, of course. But I decided to keep it soft. I think it's safe to say that it is impossible to make any show with a group of actors who are proud of themselves and their performances—and have reason to be—and have them work together ten hours a day, under the pressures of television production, day after day after day without their feuds coming and going. They have it on every show, it happened on STAR TREK. I think it's to the credit of all the performers on STAR TREK that the fights rarely interfered with performances and most of them were over just as soon as they started."

Both Leonard Nimoy and William Shatner can confirm the truth of this. For instance, Leonard Nimoy says, "Bill and I are both very committed to and concerned with the work that we do, and we both tend to have strong personalities—we're both Aries—and we both have strong feelings about what's right and what's wrong. So, yes, there were times when we had differences of opinion about how a thing should be done or whether it should be done at all. But, we are very good friends, we're very close. We have a very very close relationship, even though we don't see each other a lot. But that's not by choice—Bill has done a lot of traveling in the last couple of years and so have I. It's just the nature of the business. But when we do meet, it's babble time. The stuff just pours out of us and we turn each other in a way that's really unique. I don't really know of anybody else in my life that does that—that I have that kind of thing with. I went to Chicago just to surprise him on a television show. They called me and asked me if I would do it and I said I would be glad to. And not only was he genuinely surprised, but he was obviously terribly moved. It was really a terrific thing. And we sat on that TV show for about an hour and we just *babbled* about old times.

"The whole feud thing, I think was amplified out of proportion by the fan magazines* who needed something exciting to write about. And it's much more excit-

---

* Not to be confused with *fanzines*. Leonard Nimoy was referring to the professional magazines, the kind that alternate pictures of David Cassidy and Donny Osmond on their covers.

ing to write about arguments on a set than to simply report that all is peace and quiet and that the show is being done professionally.

"The one problem that I did run into is the time that Bill and I spent together was that we'd be together in the makeup department in the morning and we'd start talking about something that happened the previous day. And we'd get so animated and so involved—we'd get so hilarious and hysterical just laughing that we literally couldn't even sit in the chairs. We'd have to get up out of the chairs to laugh it out. And by the time 8:00 came around—you know, I'd be there at 6:30 in the morning, Bill would arrive at 7:00 and it would start—and by 8:00, many days, I was just wiped out, exhausted emotionally, from having talked and laughed so much. Sometimes it was pure craziness in there. And then I had to go out and start a twelve hour day of shooting, and I would walk out *limp*."

William Shatner's reply to the same question was almost identical:

"There was never any feud. There were, on occasions, mostly between Leonard and I, a difference of opinion and sometimes, in a moment of pique, one or the other of us would get angry. You've got to realize that for three years, all of us—but particularly, Leonard and I—were thrown into each other's company for twelve hours or more a day. And here were two people who had never met before, we never asked to be married to each other—but we were, in effect, *married*. We were more constant companions than each other's wives. And, if you use that as a basis for judging the relationship, we had a far happier marriage than most marriages are. We got along famously.

"And, I think, any analysis of our relationship with each other has to be based also on the feelings we have for each other now, which is very interesting. I hadn't seen Leonard for three years, not since the cancellation of the show. The first time I saw him was only for a brief second in the commissary at Universal Studios. We just kind of clutched each other, pounded each other on the back and said 'Hi, how are you?' But then, a couple of months after that, I was playing in the Chicago area and I was doing a live television show, a talk show, and while we were on the air, the host asked, 'What do you think of Leonard Nimoy?' And I began to praise Leonard. And the host said, 'Well, I'm glad you said that, because—' And in walked Leonard. They had flown him from Los Angeles to Chicago, to appear on this hour show. Well, we just laughed and giggled our way through the whole program—and I think that demonstrates more than anything the basic good fellowship between us."

And that's about that. End of paragraph, chapter and feud.

DeForest Kelley, who played sarcastic Dr. McCoy, used to love clowning around on the set. Like all the actors, he couldn't resist a good joke.

For instance:

"We'd had these tribbles everywhere. They had them in the prop room and they kept showing up here and there for weeks after we filmed the episode. A tribble might show up as an extra breast on Nichelle or something like that. I guess everybody was still kind of tribble happy and every time we got a chance to work a tribble in somewhere, we were working them in. Instead of pulling out a communicator, somebody would pull out a tribble. They'd continually pop up somewhere. Pull out a drawer and somebody would reach for something and there'd be a tribble there. So I delivered one. I don't remember what show it was, but I was performing surgery on someone—probably Mark Lenard in 'Journey to Babel'—and after a supposed incision, I took a tribble out of him. I remember doing it and having the whole crew crack up completely. It took weeks to get all the tribbles off the set.

"Another time, we did a show with Shatner where he was playing a man and a woman both. I think it might have been 'Turnabout Intruder.' Anyway, he had this very dramatic scene and I was checking him over and he had his moments of becoming quite feminine every so often. And he had a line something like, 'What do you think it is?' And I looked at him very sincerely and said, 'Captain, you're pregnant!' He almost fell off the table. Shatner loved that stuff.

"Of course, Shatner loved to do it to people too. He was an artist at it, certainly with me. You know, we all had our differences here and there, but we had this thing going, and no matter what we thought of the other one, he could look at me in a certain way or do something and crack me up completely. But he's a very in-control actor under very adverse circumstances.

"There were some things that weren't so funny at the time, but they're funny to think back upon. The first year of the show, I was driving an old '57 Ford that I had, and Leonard was driving an old Studebaker or something like that. By the time we were into the second year, we found ourselves in the position of being able to afford new cars. So I bought a new Thunderbird, and Leonard bought a new Buick Riviera. We were both very proud of them. You know, they had stereo radios and were just lush. We'd back in every morning in our same spots, side by side, all three of us, parked on the lot there. The third space was Shatner's, of course. He went from a Corvette—that's what he had when we started—to something like a Pontiac sports car. A GTO, something like that. He was always the hot-rodder of the group, the motorcycle king, the athletic one.

"But anyhow, I got off early one day and I went out and got in the car, and I had left the wheels turned when I had parked in the morning. Leonard was just coming around the corner of the soundstage, I didn't really see him until a moment later; I started the car and the wheels were turned and I went right into his new Buick.

"So here comes Leonard on his bicycle, and I'm out looking at the cars. And I said, 'Leonard, I wrecked our cars!' And he said, 'You're kidding.' And then he looked over and saw it and he almost fell off his bicycle. It would have been a great shot—there we were standing there and exchanging insurance information, me in street clothes and him in his costume and ears. It was very funny—and at the same time, it wasn't.

"You know, I remember how I came on to STAR TREK. Paul Fix was the doctor in the first couple episodes, and then I came on. It's a strange thing with casting. Roddenberry is a very talented man and he has a great knack for casting—I've done other things with him. I've seen how he works and it's not easy to get principals together where a certain chemistry works. If you don't have that chemistry that's flowing between three people or four, it doesn't work and you can't force it. It's one of the things that was a major factor with the three of us, me and Leonard and Bill. A lot of people thought there was a great deal of luck involved in it, but I think a great deal of it was shrewd casting.

"When Gene first called me in for this show, and to meet with the director, he said he wanted me for the doctor. At the time I thought it was Roddenberry's decision to say yes or no. So I thought I had the part, but apparently somebody didn't want me, I don't know who, because I didn't get it. Gene was doing another show, called '*Police Story*' with Rafer Johnson and myself and the late Steve Ihnat. It was a threesome thing going again, and it was a hell of a show, a very good show. It should have sold, but it didn't. In the meantime, NBC had made the first pilot of STAR TREK, but they couldn't get together with the late Jeffrey Hunter. That's when Shatner came into the picture, so they went ahead and made the second pilot with him.

"Now, *Police Story* was shown on one of these audience reaction things and evidently I got lucky and I received a good response. So I called Gene Roddenberry after I found out *Police Story* didn't sell. He had already made the second pilot on STAR TREK and I called him to thank him, to tell him I was sorry that the show hadn't gone, and he said, 'Well, don't hang up, De. Something has just happened.' And he said that the network was impressed by the response on that other show and that he wanted me for the doctor on STAR TREK. So that's how the whole thing started.

"Now, to be perfectly honest, I had never been much of a science fiction fan. I read very little of it. But I saw the pilot that Jeffrey Hunter made, and I was absolutely fascinated by it. I had never seen anything like it. I walked out of the projection room—I felt *stoned*! You know, really! It was the first time that I had ever seen any science fiction that had impressed me so much. And I thought, well, it's either going to be the biggest hit on television, or the biggest flop. I didn't think there would be any middle road at all. So when I was finally called upon to be in STAR TREK, that's when I began reading science fiction.

"It was a fascinating time—particularly the first year. The first year was very hard work. It almost killed us all. We were working terribly long hours. We were pushing to get these things done and done right. We all felt we needed so much more time than we were getting. I was pleased with it, but I felt that McCoy wasn't being used to his fullest extent. I began to see and feel the possibilities for him, and I think they did too. In the second year they began to expand him somewhat, and in the third year, they really began to get to him.

"Our first year was the kind of a year, even though it was experimental because we were really trying to find our way, we were trying to set the characters and give each character definition, Bill and Leonard and myself, we were all looking for ourselves that first year—but we did some material that I think people enjoyed most, which was more science fictional than some of the stuff we did later.

"We did a lot of crazy things on the set. In the beginning, when everything was rosy, everyone was having a lot of fun working with the show. And after working long hard hours, you do certain things to break some of the tension that builds up. You need a good laugh, and then you go back and work some more.

"I remember when we were doing the Halloween show—'Catspaw'—and Nichelle and Bill and Leonard and Walter and myself were behind huge double doors in this big castle, and we were supposed to burst through these doors and come running into this place. We were all standing around in the back and we were laughing about whether we were going to go in according to billing, Shatner, Leonard and me, then Nichelle and finally Walter. Well, Bill said, 'The hell with it, let's just bust through the door all at once like we're supposed to.' And Nichelle was standing there, and I said, 'Okay, the last one out's a nigger-baby.' And Nichelle, she got the biggest kick out of it, she cracked up completely. And then we all came out of this door, just roaring with laughter, falling down. Of course, it ruined the take. The director yelled 'Cut' and we had to start over, but it's an example of the good rapport we had.

"I always wanted the show to do a script that featured Nichelle and myself. Something where the two of us were thrown onto a planet where there was a great racial problem, only reversed. The fact that I am a Southerner and she is black, and that we're trapped on this planet together could have been a very good story.*

" 'The Deadly Years'—we did that second season, that was an interesting show. I was in makeup from five to six hours. I had to look very very old. I only worked half a day on that show because I was in makeup the other half. I'd sit in the chair for a while, then I'd take a break, go to the john, come back, and they'd work some more. It was a tremendous makeup effort. There were three makeup men working on me all the time, on my hands and on my face. Leonard was lucky on that show. He was blessed by the fact that Vulcans don't age as fast as humans. But I enjoyed it.

"You know, the fans remember these things. The shows that are mentioned to me when I go back east are 'The Trouble with Tribbles,' 'City on the Edge of Forever,' and there was another one, 'Shore Leave.' These are the ones that are mentioned most to me. I've never seen it where fans remember individual episodes of a show before, they remember them by the titles, who was in them, everything.

"I used to have my scripts from the first two years stacked out in the garage. I had all of them, and then I received a letter from a Catholic organization, some nuns back east in Pennsylvania someplace, asking me if I had a script that I could send them that they might auction off for some charity and so I packed the whole bunch of them up and sent them off to them, but at that time I never realized that everybody was so hungry for the scripts. But even if I had, it would still have

---

* As a matter of fact, the idea was one that very definitely *had* been considered. A script version had even been written. And rewritten. And rewritten. The story involved a planet where blacks were the masters and whites were the slaves, but either the premise was too touchy for television or nobody could quite make it work. The script never reached a form where Roddenberry or Coon wanted to put it into production.

been the thing to do. I don't think I have a STAR TREK script left.

"The greatest fan letter I ever received, I still have it somewhere, I opened it up and there was a cardboard inside and pasted on it was a marijuana cigarette. And it said, 'Dear De Forest, you have turned me on so many times, I would like to repay the favor. (signed) One of your female fans.'

"But, I remember, the fan reaction came as a complete shock to me because I had no idea the popularity that STAR TREK had generated. The first time I really became aware of it was on a trip to New York. It was on a Saturday and we said, well, let's go to a matinee. It was kind of a rainy afternoon, so we went right into the theatre, the lobby, and my wife Carolyne said, 'I'm going to the ladies' room.' I said, 'Okay, I'll wait here for you.' There was this vacant candy stand and I was leaning against it and a couple of women saw me and they came over and handed me their programs to sign and I signed them, and a couple more came over and handed me their programs to sign and I started to sign them and after about ten minutes there was a whole mob. I looked up, looking for Carolyne, and I couldn't see her. I was in the middle of a seething, actually a seething, mob. And finally, I saw Carolyne coming up, just her head, coming up the steps from the ladies' room. I literally was surrounded and I couldn't get away and I started to make the move and I couldn't get away and Carolyne waved at me and I waved to her and she pointed like this, 'I'm going to the seats.' They finally had to call the ushers and a security man—the women were getting up out of their seats, mind you, in the theatre and coming into the aisle to get to me.

"This was a complete shock to me. And they were all standing up in the balconies and yelling 'STAR TREK' and 'McCoy.' It was wild. Finally, they got me down to my seat and when I sat down, we were in the middle of a row of nuns, sisters on each side of us. So people are in the aisles and they're passing programs over and the nuns are handing me their programs and I'm signing them. It was such a mess that they were holding the curtain of the show, there was so much noise. This nun that was sitting next to me, she said, 'This must be a terrible annoyance for you wherever you go.' I said, 'It's the first time it's ever happened to me. I wouldn't know.' 'Well,' she said, 'you must remember something. With every little blessing, there comes a penalty.'

"It was equally as bad getting out of there. I wanted to go backstage and say hello to Joel Grey, but I couldn't. The ushers came and got me, surrounded me, got me to the side of the theatre and put me in a cab like a mechanical doll or something. That was the first time I was ever mobbed and it was completely shocking."

Mr. Scott, the Chief Engineer of the *Enterprise*, was played by James Doohan, an actor of no small ability and considerable background in radio and television, as well as motion pictures. At one time, he was known as the busiest actor in Canada, working seven days a week, 9–14 hours a day. "If I didn't have my book full up for the next 6 weeks, I figured I was in a slump."

Like all the members of the STAR TREK family, James Doohan has a sly sense of humor. "I remember some of the practical jokes that were played on me when I was working radio. Things like setting the last three pages of your script on fire or putting a blank page in front of you, things like that.

"Of course, some of the things that happened on the STAR TREK set grew out of mistakes. In 'Catspaw,' we were coming into a dungeon and I tripped down the steps a couple of times. They only recorded one, I think. It's in the blooper reel. I was supposed to be very serious and kind of blank in my mind. I certainly was blank about that final step. I tripped and everyone broke up.

"I got onto STAR TREK through a fellow named Jimmy Goldstone. I had read for him about ten days before I read for STAR TREK. I forget the name of the show, but the producer said I looked too much like the star. I did an English accent too, but I didn't get the job.

"Jimmy Goldstone was flipped anyway, so he called me up about ten days later and said would I mind coming down to Desilu studios on a Saturday morning and reading for this new pilot which was just starting. So I got in there and there was Gene and Bob Justman and Joe D. Agosta, who was head of casting at the time, and a couple of other people I didn't know. And they handed me a script and said, go ahead, do some accents. So I did about five or six accents, Russian, Irish, English, German, and Scottish. And then they asked me to do a couple again. According to Gene I entertained them for about two hours, I thought it was only forty minutes. Anyway, they picked the Scottish, and then we did the pilot. In the pilot I had very little to do. I think I had about three lines. I think they didn't consider they'd be using the engineer very much, and so I had a contract for 5 out of 13 episodes, and as soon as they began working with it they began to feel that they would be using the character much more and that if Leonard and Bill were going to go down to a planet that the Chief Engineer is the logical guy to take care of the ship. You don't put the doctor of the ship in charge. So they began to find out that Scotty was more useful, so I got 13 out of 13, which was very nice. And it just kept getting better and better.

"Actors can put a lot of things into a show. I remember, for instance, I suggested Scotty's dress uniform be a kilt. They immediately grabbed onto the idea. They sent to Scotland for the Scott tartan, which is one of the really old tartans. There are really only about four, and the Scott family is one of the originals. They sent to San Francisco for some other stuff and had the uniform made and it looked pretty good. It was only too bad they didn't have it earlier. There were other episodes when it might have been used.

"Personally, I didn't like the flare legs on the trousers. I didn't like the way they stuck out, I thought that they came on kind of fey. But after a while, it worked out, I got used to it. I think though, that it might have been just as good if they had just had a band of red down the trousers, you know, red for engineering, blue for scientific, green for command, and so on.

"You know, the engine room was just a piddling little thing when they started. They didn't think they'd ever be going to it. Then the found out they *had* to go to it, it helped to create a lot of suspense. The very fact that you were there and did all sorts of things, helped the show a great deal, so each year they added to it . . . Like they added the upstairs section with the ladder leading up to it, and later the Emergency Manual Monitor. Things like that.

"There was a time when I wrote down, from what I knew of science and atomic energy, all the functions of the ship and the reason why certain things worked. Like the force field and the tractor beams where we pulled something in. To me, it seemed that the ship could cone the energy out to a certain distance—the further out, the less powerful it becomes—and all we would do is focus the cone back in, and that would be our tractor beam. Why not? I've got it all written down somewhere. I had to have all of that figured out not just for myself, but also in case the fans asked, how does this work? So I sat down there for a couple of days and figured the whole thing out so I could talk about it—the transporter room breaking down matter into its component parts, the warp drive engines, and so on. Just as an actor, I had to know what my character was doing and *why*.

"I think STAR TREK was one of the greatest creations that has come out of television in the United States, and it really should be brought back. But, of course, only with Gene Roddenberry in charge, because I don't think anyone else can handle it and has the range that Gene has. I don't know of anyone else that has that possible range of understanding. I think there might be more leeway if it were done as a series of movies, once every few months or so. Then you could have a really good STAR TREK movie, and have it as a series—like the way *Planet of the Apes* has been handled. But you see, the problem with these things is that even if they're willing to spend a couple of million on them, you still have to have an executive producer who will make sure that it doesn't come out like trash. That's why it needs a Gene Roddenberry. Because he won't allow it to be trash, Gene has integrity.

"The fans recognize it. That's why the show won't die. I've been to a couple of these STAR TREK conventions, and I think they're great. They're very enthusiastically put on, and I was surprised at the people. You might think that STAR TREK fans are a bunch of kooks, but they're not. It's just their interest that makes them out of the ordinary and makes some people say, 'Oh, STAR TREK nuts.'

"I'll tell you, I don't remember what was first season and what was third season—but the fans, they know exactly what was done and when, but I don't. I can't remember them. They start talking to me about certain scripts, and an actor really forgets certain lines, but they say, 'Oh, but you said so and so and so,' and I say, 'What? What?' I can maybe remember the line, but not the context.

"You know, when I changed my hair, the fans noticed it immediately. I just wasn't happy with it, but I didn't like it combed back either. I thought it looked like hell. But when I went to put it back the old way, Gene didn't like it. He decided I'd have to have a new hairdo, so he sent me to Sebring's. After that it was better, I was able to make it match more easily. It hasn't changed much since then, now it's just a little longer.

"Sometimes, some of the fans created problems. Like one girl was invited on the set and she was there from 8 in the morning to 7 at night, and she would just either stand there and look at you with that dead look in the eyes or she would ask you 50 times a day if you'd like a cup of coffee. And you know, she was there for two or three days. One of the actors got really bugged by it, and he had to go to the executive producer to get that girl off the set. She was driving him crazy, he couldn't work, couldn't plan, couldn't do anything; no matter where he went, she followed him. Fans don't realize that it's very upsetting. When they come in, meet you and talk to you, it's okay, but when they just sit there and they just look at you with that worshipping look—it can really be terrible, like all the actor has to do is look at the fan and she's going to be cured or something. I honestly think that people should not be allowed to stay on a set longer than 45 minutes unless it's business, because it's just too much. Particularly when it's that kind of adulation.

"We had closed sets for a while, then they opened again, then they closed again, and it got pretty bad. The second assistants are very busy and the actors don't like to go to them all the time and say 'Please get rid of this person or that person, they're bugging me.' So, there really ought to be some kind of time limit put on all of these things. But then you'd have to hire someone to go around and say, 'Your time is up and your time is up.'

"I don't think the fans realize sometimes what they're doing. I was moving from one apartment to another apartment and I still had a couple of weeks left in the old place, so I left some stuff there and I went back every now and then to get it, just short trips in my car. One day some kids met me out in the old apartment building saying, 'There's a woman in your patio.' And there was this eighteen-year-old girl, an exchange student who lived in Pasadena or Arcadia, and she'd been waiting there for eighteen hours, all night, she'd been waiting on the patio. It really shook me. So I took her down to the drugstore and bought her a soda and then put her on a bus and sent her home. But it really shook me.

"But those are the exceptions. Most of the fans have been great. There were a group of kids here from Detroit—from the STAR TREK Association For Revival. I gave them some film clips and some autographed things on STAR TREK stationary (which I'm fast running out of) and also some scripts. My point in giving them the film and the scripts was that these kids wanted me to come to a convention they were holding, and so they were going to pay my expenses to get there. Well, I wanted to help, so I said, 'What can I do?' And then I came up with this idea. They could sell some of the autographed scripts, and if I gave them a pile, then that's their expenses and everybody benefits.

"I'll tell you, STAR TREK was always a fascinating show for an actor, especially the content. If it was a choice between another good show and STAR TREK, I think I'd take STAR TREK, even though I may have a better part in the other show. I'd still take STAR TREK. It's one of the best things I've ever worked on."

Ensign Chekov was introduced to the *Enterprise* in STAR TREK's second year. At first, Walter Koenig, who played Chekov, was not a contract player; rather, he was hired on a show-by-show basis. But as he began to fit so well into the STAR TREK ensemble, he became more and more important, until by the third season, he was upgraded to a regular supporting player.

"When the show was still in production," says Koenig, "I was being pushed by *Sixteen* magazine, so I received an enormous flood of letters. At one time, I was getting about 650 letters a week . . . which was about the same as the other people on the show were getting at that time.

"Some of them I got into correspondences with, the ones who were most interesting or most touching or most intelligent; the letters that were a little bit more than 'Would you please send me a photograph?' All girls, I think. They wrote me from all over the country. I remember one girl, I think she was in New York, she kept writing to me and it really seemed to me like she had a lot of problems, but she was an interesting girl. But she was always denigrating herself and putting herself down. There was a big lapse between her eighth and ninth letter, and then finally she wrote to me and told me that she hoped I wouldn't stop liking her, but she was black. Well, that was silly. I wrote to her and said, 'Absurd . . . I'm Jewish, so what the hell does that mean? Why should it make any difference one way or the other?' And she responded to that, and we went on writing for a few months after that.

"I had kids writing me from deaf school too. I used to send them scripts and things. And I got letters from college students; we had long drawn-out debates about what we were doing and what I was doing specifically on the show. Now that the show has moved out of the states, I've gotten letters from all over. I've gotten them from Korea, Viet Nam, Germany, England—the show was very big in England. There were letters from behind the Iron Curtain even. I got some from Hungary or Czeckoslovakia or someplace like that—I couldn't tell, they were in a foreign language.

"I still have most of the letters. I have them out in my garage. Five mail sacks full. I finally had to dispose of some of them though. I just didn't have any more room. All that mail—I never did get used to it.

"We were shooting 'Gamesters of Triskelion.' There were three of us, Bill, Nichelle and myself, and we had just landed on this planet—but we were dislocated, we didn't know where we were, and we were looking around and all of a sudden we hear a voice saying, 'Hello, foreigners' or something like that. And in my zeal, I turned to Bill and instead of saying 'What was that?' I slapped him on the arm like we used to do as kids in New York. And he turned to me and looked like 'Who is this fellow?' and whacked me right back. I had just gotten so much into the scene that I hadn't realized what I was doing.

"I had a thing about that particular episode. Firstly, it was one of the shows that I had a pretty good part in to begin with, but the director was a former song and dance man who was—I can't recall his name—just sort of tap dancing his way through this thing, literally as well as figuratively. I had this big scene where this homely girl comes into the cell with me and says, 'Let me be your mate.' Something like that. We had a very funny relationship set up, because Chekov didn't want to have anything to do with her. Because I was the junior member of the cast, my scenes were relegated to the end of the day, which is quite understandable, I'm not complaining about it, but on this particular day we were pressed for time. So rather than covering me by shooting over her shoulder and covering her by shooting over my shoulder, the director only did it one way—they shot it over my shoulder at her. Which meant if I were to look at her, all the audience would see would be the back of my head. So he suggested I do this—every time I have to deliver a line I do a profile and not look at her, which really didn't leave a lot of room for spontaneity; so I would say something and I'd turn profile, then I'd say something and look at her, and then I'd turn profile and say the line, and I was very disconcerted and very disappointed in that. They never did get around to shooting it the other way.

"The same kind of thing happened to me in another very big scene, and another director who was pressed for time. He shot my scene without even a rehearsal. It was supposed to be a full view, and as it turned out, the most prominent part of me was my left ear.

"But I was very lucky that I was able to be so much a part of the show. There was a set of circumstances that was very fortuitous for me in the second season. George Takei and I were being featured about equally on the show, and then George was cast as Captain Nim in *The Green Berets*. That was filming in Georgia. So he left for ten weeks, and during that time, rather than dividing up the parts between myself and him, they were able to give me more to do, and I got a lot of better shows than I had gotten at first.

"There was one thing that happened that hit me in a funny way. A sad thing, really. I was getting an awful lot of mail, but I was getting it a month after it was sent because it was coming through the United Fan Mail Service. Some of it would go to Paramount first and then the service. And some of it would go to NBC and then to Paramount and finally the service. And finally, I would get it. Anyway, I got a letter from a couple of parents who had a little girl who was ill, quite ill, and she had heard that I had a dog, and she wanted a snapshot of my dog, and the parents asked if I would send her the snapshot of the dog, which I did as soon as I got the letter—but this was three or four weeks after it had been sent. I sent the picture with a little note on the back and I got back a reply from the parents, thanking me, but telling me that the child had passed away. It was really quite sad. But the interesting part of the episode was that they asked me if I wanted this to be publicized, they would be glad to send it over to their local newspaper. But I said no, I didn't want publicity that capitalized on someone else's grief. But it was interesting the way people come to think about TV shows and actors.

"There were nice things that happened too. There was a little girl from Pennsylvania who had been corresponding with me, very sweet girl about 15 and quite bright. She mentioned that she and her mother would like to come out and visit the set and I took it all quite literal and said, 'That'd be great. If you come out, we'll have to say hello.' And that must have sounded like an invitation because they came right out. She was a very lovely kid and the mother had made every effort to make the whole trip happen, it must have meant an awful lot to both of them. Well, I had alerted the rest of the cast, and it was really beautiful. Everybody was just terrific to her. They knew she had come in from Pennsylvania and they were really sweet. Nichelle, Bill, Leonard, everyone—so the kid was in heaven. She and her mother spent the whole day there with us and she really had a ball. She stayed in town for about a week after that, and I took her out to lunch one day. We still correspond. She's in college now, studying literature and drama.

"One of my most depressing moments, one where I felt the most defeated, happened at the beginning of the third season's production. I had talked to Gene Roddenberry. I had gone over to his house, he was extremely generous with his time, and explained that I wanted to know what was going to happen with the character of Chekov, and I was asking in the most subordinate way, I mean, I wasn't being pushy or insistent. Well, he showed me a memo he had received from Mort Werner, the NBC executive, about the character of Chekov, about getting him more involved in the show, getting him in more stories and so on. He wanted to know what Gene was going to do with Chekov as he had gotten a very good reaction from the audience.

"Well, after that, I received a copy of a memo that Gene had sent to his executives that Chekov should be developed more, should get involved with girls, should be proud—but in a good way, and so on. He wanted the character developed. All of this sounded terribly exciting, and I thought, here at last I would get a chance to do something more often than one out of every six or seven shows. But, of course, that was when the show was still scheduled to be shown on Monday at 7:30. That was a marvelous time slot; all the kids would be up and able to see the show—especially the age group that would react best to Chekov. But then the show was moved to 10:00 on Friday nights and I knew that was it for Chekov. And for the show. We all knew it. When Gene left we were all very depressed. It was one of the most depressing moments of the show.

"I always felt that among the people who were in support of me—besides Gene, of course—was Bob Justman. Bob was a gentleman to the core. An extremely nice man. I remember how touching it was when he left the show. This was in the third season. He gave all of us little personal notes, thanking us for cooperation and thanking us for part of his life."

George Takei is one of the smiling-est human beings alive. He radiates energy. As Mr. Sulu, the Helmsman of the *Enterprise*, he was able to discipline and project a great deal of that vitality and maintain the presence of a consistent character, despite the fact that he was one of the least used of the regular cast members. Very few of the scripts gave him chances to show off his acting ability. As George says, "I used to have my lines memorized even before I saw the script. 'Aye, aye, sir,' 'Coming to new course,' and 'Phasers locked on target.'

"You know, it's been eight years since I made my first STAR TREK. I wasn't in the first pilot—the one with Jeffrey Hunter—but I was in the second one. We shot that at MGM. The whole concept of STAR TREK was one that I was very excited about doing. I had never done a series until then, so the idea of working on a continuing character was a real challenge. Of course, Gene Roddenberry was the key to the series; if they tried to do it without him, it would be a mistake. What STAR TREK was, would not be there. But if Gene were to be in charge, I would have no reservation about doing it again.

"I didn't have much to do the first year, so I worked on them to beef up the part. There was one script where I was able to have a little fun. That was 'The Naked Time' where I got to do a little fencing. That was a lot of fun. I really enjoyed that. I knew nothing about fencing at the time. John D.F. Black who wrote the show came on the set one afternoon and he engaged me in conversation and said 'I'm planning something in a script for you and it's going to involve a little fencing. Can you fence?' And I said, 'No, but I can learn.' I was being very honest when I confessed that—but that's what any actor would have said, 'I can learn.'

"So I dashed out and started taking lessons immediately. It turned out I really enjoyed the exercise and the beauty of the whole sport. It was a fun thing, so now it actually has become a hobby of mine. I still work out when I have the time—which isn't as often as I'd like because I'm so busy with other activities.

"The fencing caused a little havoc on the set—there was some concern while we were shooting because I'm a pretty rambunctious person and I was constantly working out on stage. I have a tendency to get involved in what I'm doing and sometimes I forget that other people might not share that same involvement—so who didn't I slice? You know, you'd expect Shatner to grab a sword and fight back, but he didn't; he feigned mock terror and ran away.

"During the second year of the show, I had a chance to play Captain Nim in *The Green Berets* with John Wayne. This meant I would have to be away from STAR TREK for several weeks—in fact, that developed into a real hassle. There was one particular script that was really a nice one, a good one for Sulu. It was 'The Gamesters of Triskelion' and I wanted to do it very much. Roddenberry had showed it to me before I took off for Columbus, Georgia. Well, we had some rain and that delayed the shooting of the picture and they had to change the schedule, so there were more than a couple of weeks of just sitting around. I spent a lot of time hiking—it's beautiful country there—but it was frustrating because I wanted to come back and do that show. So I talked to John Wayne, who was also directing as well as starring, and he thought well, maybe he could let me go so I could dash back to L.A. and do that segment and then dash back to Georgia and resume filming. But this was a great frustration. We were doing some night shots, and they needed one particular shot before I could take off. I had to take the early Sunday morning plane in order to be in Los Angeles for the early Monday morning call. So we were shooting all night Saturday and then we had some mishap with one of the explosions and that took up most of the night. And this one particular scene that we had to have before they could wrap up on the night shots could not be gotten, so John Wayne said, sorry about that, but we need you for Monday night's shooting, we can't let you go. So because of that one shot we couldn't grab on Saturday night, I had to stay over and had to miss out on that episode. It was very frustrating, I had really wanted to do it. As it turned out, they rewrote it for Walter. Ensign Chekov got all of Mr. Sulu's lines. I've got to admit though, that despite my disappointment, I was pleased that Walter was able to do it. All of us shared the common problem of not really having enough to do to satisfy us, so if I couldn't do it, at least another good actor and a good friend was able to benefit from it.

"You know, in the back of your mind, you always have these glimmers of hope that a show will be a smasheroonie, so you do whatever you can to help it. I have relatives in Milwaukee and Denver, and whenever I would go back there, I would always do a little promoting. The year before the show premiered even, I wrote them to let them know and they talked to the local newspaper people and said their relative was coming and would they like to meet him and so forth.

"The thing about a television series is that when you're exposed on a regular basis, it does give you that much more visibility. The fan following is therefore multiplied. I'd been doing things before, but never getting the kind of fan letter response that STAR TREK afforded me. We all had to learn how to cope with it. I answered my mail as best as I could, without encouraging the fans too much. The ones that were really intelligent, very sincerely intended ones, I found to be personally stimulating and I answered them in kind. There are a few people who still maintain that correspondence with me—they write letters of substance, so STAR TREK did afford me some interesting pen pal relationships.

"I had people come and visit me at the studios from quite a long distance. There was a girl who watched STAR TREK in Japan, and was a great STAR TREK follower there. I don't think she came all the way just because of STAR TREK—she wanted to visit America, but she wrote and asked if she could visit the set, and so I showed her around. She didn't speak English, so I had to translate for her. I felt like a Universal Studios tour guide. Miss Japan, who competed in one of those international beauty pageants, also made a special request to visit the STAR TREK set. She didn't speak English either, so I served as a translator for her as well. That was a lot of fun.

"You know, I think the whole actor's thing of 'I want to be alone' is ridiculous. Public appearances are part of our job, and I think most actors enjoy the fan adulation. It's rather a singular kind of privilege to be placed on a pedestal like this. I know that I've been doing some political work, and I know some of the things I am able to do specifically because I'm an actor and can attract a certain following. So there are certain advantages that other people don't have that actors do. Whenever I hear other actors complaining that they don't like the whole thing of being mobbed and so on, I think it's ridiculous. It's part of the career, like it or not, and one has to learn to deal with it. And with it come very special privileges. I enjoy it. And yes, I use it too. But most of all, I enjoy it."

Of all the STAR TREK cast members, Nichelle Nichols, the lovely Lieutenant Uhura, is one of the most lucid on the subject of the show, and science fiction in general; she displays an amazing savvy not just of STAR TREK's appeal, but of its importance as a part of American culture—and from that, she makes the leap to the ultimate considerations of science fiction: "Where are we going and why?"

Nichelle loves to talk about the show, and she can hold an audience spellbound with her descriptions and analyses. For instance, in November of 1972, the International Fantasy Film Convention devoted one of its sessions to STAR TREK. Guests included Nichelle Nichols, Dorothy Fontana, Walter Koenig, George Takei, Majel Barrett and Gene Roddenberry. While waiting in the V.I.P. room, a reporter asked if he could interview a few of the group. Chairs were pulled up in a circle and a casual rap began.

—Forty-five minutes later, the convention chairman reluctantly had to break up the session because the STAR TREK cast was needed to speak to the rest of the convention. But for those forty-five minutes, a true *happening* had occurred. Nichelle Nichols had all but dominated the talk, holding a delighted group of listeners spellbound with her vision of why science fiction— not just STAR TREK—could be one of the great vehicles for spreading human understanding. Above all, she showed that Lieutenant Uhura was capable of a lot more depth than she had ever been allowed to show on the boob tube.

Nichelle is reluctant to talk about the real Nichelle but at another time she spoke on a more personal level about her own experiences. "I think we had the most fun in the first year of the show. It was the best year as far as I'm concerned. It was the best produced, and there were the best directors that we had. We were alive and we enjoyed the scripts and that was when we had the best scripts. We had very few good ones after the first year and a half.

"In the third season, as far as I was concerned, we were just marking time. There were occasionally moments of value, but the things we had set as the tone and the mood of the show, the brotherhood of man and the family of the ship, were completely lost. We started doing silly old cliches like beasties from outer space, where before it had been not beasties, but alien beings, alien only that they were alien to us, different—alien *meaning* different. And I thought that was the beauty of the show at the beginning, and I think that's what Gene Roddenberry most intended and regretted most that the show lost. I do.

"My first job in television was on *The Lieutenant*, with Gary Lockwood. It was a very good role, but it was a feature role, and after I did it, that's when they found out it was my first role on television. I'd done a lot of theatre before that, though. I'd had experience, but I didn't know camera moves, I didn't even know what my key light was—that's how they found out that I had never done television before. The director came over to me and said, 'You're doing a brilliant job. I like the sensitivity that you're getting, but stay in your key lights.' And I said, 'Huh? What?' And finally, he said, 'Don't you know where—haven't you ever done a TV show before?!' And I said no, and they said, 'What?!!' He said 'Cut. Everybody take five.' And he came and put his arm around me and walked down the set and he said, 'Are you putting me on?' And I said, 'No, I'm not.' So after he explained about key lights, they took me around, laughing like hell, and everybody was congratulating me because here this was the third day of shooting and they didn't know it, except occasionally I got out of my key light. The key light is the light that's focused on you, and if you move out of it, you throw a shadow in the wrong place, either across yourself or another actor. They explained a lot of things to me after that and I learned a lot.

"Anyway, after I finished that show, I got a formal legal document from Gene Roddenberry and MGM. It was very long and I couldn't figure it out, and I got scared to death. I thought, what the hell is going on? So I called my agent who already knew about it and it turned out that they were elevating my billing from just a feature role to an introductory co-starring—and that was marvelous. That was my first introduction to Gene Roddenberry. He's very devoted to his friends, to people he likes—and his sense of humor—well, Gene does the whole thing. One day, during the shooting of that show, he went to makeup and had himself made up as a hunchback. He had this big horrible hump put on, and a big nose. He had his eye pulled down, he was hideous. He had this old coat on, and it was the third day of shooting and I didn't know him. I had only met him once, and so he did this right after he found out that I had never done a TV show before. Apparently the director had told him I was doing a good job, and he couldn't believe that I had never done any TV before. So, we were out doing this night shooting, and I turned around and saw this hideous looking man, smoking a cigarette and wearing this old old tweedy English kind of coat. And he kept watching me. And then he kept coming near me. And I began to get a little bugged. And finally I went to the Assistant Director, not to bother the director, and I said, 'Who is that creep that keeps bugging me? He keeps walking over and saying hello, and I don't want to be nasty because I seem to know him from somewhere.' He says, 'I think he's a friend of the producer's.' And I said, 'Really?' And I went back to do my shot.

"Well, I was waiting while another shot was being set up, and this man is stalking me again, and finally I'm just about ready to turn around and ream him out when I noticed something that had fascinated me about Gene Roddenberry, and that is that he always smokes his cigarettes between his middle two fingers. And I looked up, and he said something about my being lovely and I turned to snap at him and I saw that cigarette, and I said, 'Look you—' And then I realized, and screamed, *'Mr. Roddenberry!!'* right in the middle of a take! Somebody else's take. Well, the whole damn set just completely broke up. There was pandemonium for the next half hour, with Assistant Directors trying to pull things together and everybody else just cracking up. Lights had been knocked over and they had to redo the whole damn thing. Gene said he enjoyed that incident more than anything, that it was precious to him. And he remembers it to this day in a very kind way.

"Anyway, then I got that letter from him and I began to realize that this man Gene Roddenberry is quite

a person. He has a great depth to him. I met him sub-
sequently over the next two or three years. I would see
him occasionally on a set or at the studio, and on these
occasional visits, I would stop in to see him or say hello
if I was down for an interview and each time he would
tell me, 'I have something in mind for you. If it comes
about, it will be very very interesting.' Okay, the first
time, the first few times, the first year, you think that's
groovy. The second year, you begin to think that's very
nice of him still to even remember, and you remember
fondly the things that happened on *The Lieutenant*.
And now *The Lieutenant*'s over. And by now it's
'Hello, Gene,' 'Hello, Nichelle.' And sure enough, I
take off for New York for a job, and I get a call from
my agent, 'Get back here, quick!' 'What are you talking
about? I'm not coming back to California!' So they sent
me a ticket and I came flying back for an interview.
What is the interview? I don't know, but as long as
they sent me a ticket—well, he says, 'It's a series that's
going on called STAR TREK.' Well, my agent assumed
that I knew it was Roddenberry, but I didn't. So I went
into the interview—I was competing with four or five
other top actresses—and there was Gene Roddenberry.
I said, 'Gene, I didn't know you had anything to do
with this,' and I gave him a peck on the cheek and sat
down. There were other people sitting there, Joe Sargent, the director, Bob Justman, the associate producer,
and so on. And they asked me to read—Lieutenant
Uhura had not been written yet—so they asked me to
read Spock's part to see how I sounded. So I asked
them to tell me something about Spock. And they started to tell me about Lieutenant Uhura. I said, 'No,
don't tell me about————.' She wasn't even named
yet. Well, they thought that the character of Spock was
closest to what they had in mind for Uhura, so to get
an idea, they would have me read Spock's lines, so I
said, 'If you're asking me to read his words, tell me
what his character is and let me do that character.

Then you can see if I can act or not! Don't ask me to do a character you haven't written, because you don't know if it's going to be exactly this or exactly that. I don't know what she's going to be either. When you find out, then I'll act her.' And they all turned around and looked at each other like I'd just hit them in the head and said, 'You know, that makes sense.' So I read Spock's part and I took on the stoicness of Mr. Spock and did that number. So Gene said, 'Do you think she'd look good in pointed ears? We could call her a Vulcanita.' All this was in fun, of course, but I still didn't know I had the part. They asked me to wait, so I sat down in the outer office and waited. And I waited, and I waited, and I waited, and everybody left. The other actresses had gone in and come out, nobody was left to wait, but me. And I was still waiting and waiting. My agent came by then, he saw me and said, 'Hey, what's happening? Are you still here?' I said, 'Well, they told me to wait.' And he said, 'Okay,' and he left too.

"Well, what had happened was that they'd all gone to lunch. I hadn't seen them leave—that's how the offices were set up—and I waited an hour and a half. Finally Joe Sargent popped in and he said, 'Hi, are you still here?' And I said, 'Yeah, you told me to wait.' And he said, 'Didn't anybody tell you—you got it!' And I said, 'You're kidding!' And he said, 'No.' He put his arm around me and said, 'I understand you haven't done too much television before. But I've heard good things about you. It's going to be a pleasure doing this show with you, big talent.' And I beamed. It made up for sitting so long.

"We started shooting within a matter of weeks. Mine had been the last part cast. Everything else was set. I was the last, because in the second pilot, 'Where No Man Has Gone Before,' the communications officer had been a man. As a matter of fact, it was Lloyd Haynes, who later became the lead on *Room 222*. I guess things happened for the best; if he'd been tied up on STAR TREK, perhaps he wouldn't have done *Room 222*.

"I remember some of the things that happened on the set. One script, I got pretty tired of doing the same thing over and over. We were doing this scene repeatedly and I don't remember what it was, but there was some technical difficulty, and then there was a problem with lines and then it was a problem with blocking and I think Kirk had to come in and I'm supposed to swing out to him and say something like, 'Captain, the Klingons are—' and he says, 'Can't you handle it, Lieutenant Uhura?' And I snap back at him, 'Captain, I'm doing the best I can.'

"You see, everyone was supposed to be losing their tempers in this scene. We kept doing it over and over and it kept going on. Everyone kept blowing his lines and it got kind of silly, couldn't get it right. So, on the next take and I'm stifling a yawn, almost nodding, Bill says to me, 'Am I keeping you up, Lieutenant Uhura?' and everybody cracks up. Up to this time I'm the only one who hasn't blown it yet. So he comes back in on the next take and goes, 'Ahem! Any word, Lieutenant Uhura?' I said, 'Captain, the Klingons, etc., etc.' He says, 'Lieutenant Uhura, can't you handle it?' I said, 'Why shoah, Shugah, Ah can do anything y'all want. Why didn't y'all just tell me all along, honey? Whatevah your little heart desires.' That broke the ice. I thought Bill would just about have a hemorrhage. He really broke up, laughing. And they caught him on camera. I truly didn't know I was going to do that until I actually did it right in a take and the director, whoever it was at the time, yelled, 'Cut! What the hell was that?' But we all got it right on the next take.

"Two of my favorite shows were 'The Trouble with Tribbles' and 'The Tholian Web.' In the latter one, we think Kirk is dead and I see him floating through the walls of my quarters. That was fun to do—of course, I enjoyed anything that I was able to get out of uniform.

Like 'Plato's Stepchildren.' That was the one with the controversial kiss—television's first interracial kiss—but it was a big copout. Bill had to kiss me because these aliens were forcing him to, but they were so concerned about how controversial it was that we played too hard against it. Bill fought it as if he didn't want to kiss me. And the letters came in by the pounds saying, 'I don't care what ship he's the Captain of, if he's got a woman like that in his arms, he's not going to be afraid of kissing her.' I thought it lost all its impact the way we played it.

"I loved it when I got a chance to sing. I have this crazy tremendous range, and when they found out, they used it to as high as I could go. You know, there were people who thought it was an instrument. One of the songs, either Gene Roddenberry or Gene Coon wrote. I did three different episodes where I sang, and in the first one, NBC objected—that was 'Charlie X'—and they said, 'What are you doing? Making this a musical?' And then they saw it and they said, 'Hey! It gives the show a human quality, do it again sometime.' They didn't even wait for an audience reaction.

"On one of the songs we had a very ethereal thing. We had a rendition of it that was out of sight, but it was too now, too hip. It had just the tinge of sultriness and it could have gone wrong. It was called 'Beyond Antares,' I should have recorded it. Anyway, when I took it just a little lower, it had a throaty quality—that was the one that Gene wrote, and what was marvelous about it was that we had Laurindo Almeida and full accompaniment. We had a harp and we had Lucille Ball's music director, Marl Young, he played the harpsichord, and Laurindo Almeida laid in a beautiful beautiful guitar background. I really enjoyed that. I love being in a recording studio.

"You know, I've seen very few of the shows. I don't like to watch myself. Except to criticize. If you start watching yourself too much, you begin overcompensating. You become stagey. Besides, you can start falling in love with yourself. You get into a heavy narcissistic kind of playing and you don't want anything imperfect.

"There was a script where Lieutenant Uhura was supposed to take over the helm because all of the top officers were down on a planet—and then they rewrote it so that she *didn't* take over the helm. They wrote me out. Well, I got furious. I pitched a bitch! This was another copout. To his credit, Gene Roddenberry admitted it: but this was the third season and he wasn't producing. The attitude was that you can't have females taking over a man's ship. But I think Bill would have gotten a personal kick out of it, because it would be the right thing to do. How can you have a mixed crew and suddenly stop in terms of responsibility? In the same light, I resented and balked at having to play the delicate little thing. I refused to do the clinging helpless female. If we were really a starship crew, the whole crew would be well trained and physically fit. They'd know karate and all kinds of defense procedures, and they wouldn't crumble the minute someone gets hit. When you're out in space, in a dangerous situation where the ship might be blown up at any time, you're not going to have some female that goes, 'Ooooh, Captain, save me, save me!' And all those other stupid things that used to bug me like, 'What is it? What do you think it is, Captain? What are we going to do, Captain? Will we make it, Captain?' All those female things, delicate how-are-we-going-to-do-it-without-you-Captain things. Completely unbelievable, and *especially* so from Lieutenant Uhura who is efficient, no-nonsense, stoic, balanced, brilliant. She knows that whole panel and all of a sudden she's supposed to become little lady milquetoast? Ridiculous! Just not so.

"So you battle, because you care, you've got to care about that damn show, you really do. Even in the third year, when I thought I didn't care, I found myself going and telling directors, I'm sorry, but you can't do that—even things that didn't have a damn thing to do with my role, or my sphere. You know, we all did. We'd say, 'Didn't anybody tell you that this is so on the *Enterprise*?'

"I got into difficulty only once with a director, and then it might have been a matter of male ego and my feminine vanity or pride that got in the way. Everyone was working under tremendous pressure, and he yelled at me, and I asked who the hell he was yelling at? I said Uhura wouldn't do it, and he said she would do it, and we couldn't straighten it out. It was one of those kind of things. To his great credit, he came to me when he found out he was wrong, and it was very funny. As he was coming to me to apologize, I was going to him to apologize. And we were constantly saying, 'No, no *you're* absolutely right.' And we stood there trying to apologize so hard, we started fighting all over again! That was Jud Taylor. We stood there and looked at each other and we were still mad and I not letting him apologize and he not letting me. He said, 'Just shut up and let me tell you I was wrong.' And I said, 'Would you just shut up and listen?' And we finally looked at each other and started laughing. All of this happened during lunch, so no one really saw it. It was an empty stage when all this took place. So, after lunch, everybody's waiting and waiting and so we staged a big thing. '*Miss Nichols!* . . .' '*Yes, Mr. Taylor!* . . .' That sort of thing. 'Would you please accept . . .' 'Oh, yes, Jud . . . of course,' And I made cooing noises, 'I will . . .' And we were just oh so polite to one another, and finally he came up to me and we did a waltz. The cast and crew caught on then and broke up. I guess the zany things that went on were why we were so closely knit.

"One of my favorite people was Jerry Finnerman, the Director of Photography. On my very first day there, my very very first day there, I had just done makeup, I was still in my street clothes, and I see this man, and he's got a riding crop and a little beret on and he's kind of walking around the set, but when he saw me, he says, 'Hey you . . .' with the crop yet, and he walked over and he said, 'You're Nichelle Nichols, aren't you?' And I said, 'Yeah,' I didn't know who he was and he thought I did. Or he assumed that I should—but I didn't know who ANYBODY was! Right? So he says, 'Just a minute.' And he walks over to me and takes my face in his hand and he looks at me this way, and he turns it that way and he says, 'Yes, I'm going to do great things with you.' And I said, 'Like hell you are!' And I flew. He's gonna do great things with me, huh? And then somebody said, 'That's your cinematographer,' and I said, 'Oh, my God!'

"But Jerry was beautiful, he realized what it sounded like. He had a great sense of humor, but I guess he was embarrassed about it, so he came very seriously to the makeup room when I returned and he said, 'Would you introduce Miss Nichols and me?' And I said, 'Someone told me who you are and I didn't realize.' And he said he was sorry, he hadn't realized that I didn't know who he was. And he explained about the 'great things.' He said, 'I meant you have great planes to your face, and I want them to highlight your cheeks.' And he really did mastermind my makeup for it. I think he did marvelous marvelous angles. He was always very conscious of me because he said I was his pride and joy. I don't know if he had ever really, really worked with any black people before to this great a degree. He said the coloring, and if you've seen it in color, you know, is very very beautiful.

"We were doing a scene and we had one of *those* directors or Assistant Directors, one of those chop-chop, let's get it going sort, and we were behind time and we were just about ready to shoot and they said Action, and Jerry said, 'Wait a minute.' The director said, 'What's the matter?' And Jerry says, 'I have to fix a light on Uhura.' And the director says, 'Can't we let it go?' And Jerry says, 'No, it'll only take a minute to fix.' So he starts yelling up to one of the gaffers. 'Bring a junior'—that's a type of light—'bring a junior down. Put it across here and—no, lower, lower.' And then he says, 'Naw, that's not right, you've got it on the black—she's *black*. She's black!' Well that's lighting talk, he meant that he wasn't getting enough light on me. And he kept yelling up, 'No, that's not it, she's black, she's *black*.' So there's silence like you've never heard. There was such a hush when he realized what he was saying. And he looked at me and he said, 'Uh—ulp . . . uh, Nichelle—' And I said 'But comely.' And of course, it broke up the whole set, everybody laughed, it broke the tension and everything. And of course we went on about that for months. For the rest of the show. Any time anybody would get upset about something they would pull that on me. Somebody would walk over to me and they would say—especially Leonard or Bill—they'd walk past me and just over their shoulder they would say to me, 'But *comely*.' Which would never fail to break me up, bring me out of whatever I was in a snit about.

"We pulled a joke on Leonard once. In the script, a panel had blown and we were in a desperate situation, a two-seconds-to-destruction kind of thing, and I had to crawl underneath and fix this panel, Uhura being the expert on it, you know. So I put on these overalls and I climbed down there, and they had explained how dangerous it was, not just to me, but to everybody on the ship, everything depends on my accomplishing this. Kirk wasn't on the ship and Spock was in command and he comes the closest he does of ever showing any real emotion by showing real concern.

"So I was doing this and the camera was set up underneath this, they had pulled this board back and the camera was right in my face and here I'm working on this panel and Spock is supposed to come in and say 'How's it going, Lieutenant Uhura?' And I'm sweating a bit and I say, 'Mr. Spock, I don't know if I can do this.' And he says, 'If anyone can do it, Lieutenant, you can.' And that gives me the courage to go on. Well, it was a very difficult shot, we were just about nose to nose, so I had to okay this gag with the director. He thought it was a great idea. So he says to Leonard "I'm going to change a little something here. When you say "If anyone can, you can" stay there, because I want to catch just a tinge of concern that she doesn't see. Wonder if you examine it, you might have to fix it up after her.' And Leonard went to bat for me. He said, 'Well, I see no reason for that. She's efficient in what she does.' But finally, they got it through to him that he should stay there for a moment because he was supposed to leave. So he comes in and I'm doing this panel and the cameras are rolling and I say, 'Mr. Spock, I'm not sure I can do this,' And he says to me, 'Lieutenant, all our lives depend on it, and if anyone can, you can.' And I said, 'He loves me . . .' And then I sang, 'He loves me . . .' And I went into this opera thing, 'Once you have found him, never let him go . . .' And *he* said, 'Carry on, Lieutenant.' He absolutely was frozen. So that was all he could say, 'Carry on, Lieutenant.' That bloody Vulcan, you could never break him up.

"I'll tell you one thing about STAR TREK—and I've worked with a lot of companies—all in all, from Matt Jefferies who did the sets to Irving Feinberg, the prop man, to everyone you worked with, the sound men and the light men, they had a very personal attitude about that show, a very personal pride, a personal sense of ownership. There were times when even a sound man wouldn't let something go by—it may not have had anything to do with sound—but he knew it didn't belong on the *Enterprise*, it wasn't part of the format—and he would speak up. And this fascinated me. Even through the third year, when we had new people (a lot of people by that time had gone on to other jobs) the pride in STAR TREK never stopped. It never stopped, and that's what made the *Enterprise* work."

William Campbell appeared in two of STAR TREK's episodes: "The Squire of Gothos," in which he played Trelane, the penultimate spoiled brat, and "The Trouble with Tribbles," where he was seen as the oily Klingon, Captain Koloth.

As a result of that latter appearance, he almost became a STAR TREK regular. Gene Roddenberry had felt that Captain Kirk needed a regular adversary, a Klingon counterpart with whom he continually bumped heads. When Campbell was called for the part of Captain Koloth, this possibility was mentioned—that he might be hired for as many as thirteen shows per season. Campbell was very excited about it. "After 'The Trouble with Tribbles' was aired, I felt Wow, because I got such a response from playing the Klingon. Even the neighborhood kids teased my wife about being 'Mrs. Klingon.' People were writing to me about the eyebrows and the costume, and the way I played the part. And I thought to myself that whatever the makeup man had done to me must have been distinctive enough that this will go; this Captain of the Klingons will be a good adversary, a good part. Kirk needs him like Flash Gordon needs Ming of Mongo, or Dick Nixon needs Chou En Lai. They respect each other's abilities, even though they're still adversaries.

"I was really disappointed when the show wound down. The one great thing about STAR TREK was there was a marvelous lot of social content there. I could see why they felt they needed a continuing set of villains. I think it must have been very difficult for the writers of the individual episodes; the show had already gone for 52 episodes and each time they had to come up with a completely different set of characters. A continuing villain could have solved a lot of problems—and it could have given them some new story potentials. All the different conflicts with the Klingons could have been shown. All these elements could have been utilized.

"I didn't get into any of the other Klingon episodes, though, because the next time I was approached to do one, I was already involved in something else, so I couldn't do it. They had thought of the part as signing another contractee—and of course, I would have done it for Roddenberry and Coon. Even though the part was a heavy, he was a good heavy, distinctive, you know. The other Klingon, his aide, was the nasty one, and I thought that was a good idea; it gave them depth.

"I got a lot of fan mail after that episode—and the fan response wasn't just in terms of being a Klingon, but it was more or less in regard to the tribbles. The actors weren't really the stars of that show, those little animals were. They really intrigued whoever watched it. One little girl even made a tribble and sent it to me. I received a lot of mail about both STAR TREK episodes I did. And it seems to me that the fans of STAR TREK are unique in that they know every show. And they know who's been on every show and they have their favorites. I've known other actors who've done other episodes, I won't name them, but I've asked, have you ever heard from any of the STAR TREK fans, and they've said no. And I think that proves that the fans had their favorite shows. They're very sophisticated about scripts in the genre. I mean, they can *talk* about them. Which is one of the reasons why I consider those two STAR TREK episodes as high points in my career. I've done a hundred TV shows and somewhere around 16 pictures; either starred in some big ones or co-starred in some big ones, or starred in some moderate ones, like *Caryl Chessman*. In television, though, I played guest star on many shows. But both the STAR TREKs I did, were high points. It's a piece of film that I can be proud of.

"For 'Gothos,' I was contracted by Gene Coon. Now, I had never worked for Gene, but we were friends, and Gene said to me, 'I have a part here for an English fop, and I know you can play it because I've seen your work in other pictures.' But the casting director, Joe D'Agosta, said, 'Gene, Gene, Campbell could never play an English fop. I've never seen him do anything like that.' Gene tried to explain to him that I had played sinister roles and could do this because it was kind of comedic sinister. And Joe just didn't think so, so Gene asked me to read for it. He said, 'Bill, I would never ask you to read, but Joe doesn't think you can do it. I could press it through without Joe, but if I do and it doesn't work, I'll never be able to live with him again because the next time I try to suggest someone, he'll say, "Will you leave the casting to me?" As it turned out, I did the reading under the worst possible conditions, because I had the assistant to Joe D'Agosta, who was not an actor, feeding me the lines. But within one paragraph, Joe said, 'Let's go to wardrobe.' And we went.

"You know, I went into that show with the full realization that 'Squire of Gothos' was my show. Not Leonard Nimoy's, not William Shatner's. I mean, I was the focus of attention. There was an incident, for instance, where I played a judge. The judge was supposed to be an English judge that said, 'And you were called here because you have committed the crime of treason against the government, etc., etc.' And it was specifically an English courtroom. The judge described in the script and the dialogue was all English. My mental image of the judge was with the robe and the little wig that sits on top of the head—as opposed to the French wigs, which are always very long and curly and very

The United Starship *Enterprise* in orbit.

The Bridge

Briefing Room
l to r—Lt. Uhura, Capt. Kirk, Mr. Spock,
Dr. McCoy, Engineer Scott, Ens. Chekov

The Transporter Room

Sickbay

Engineering

"The Ultimate Computer" takes over the Engine Room.

A hit! In a corridor . . .

. . . and on the Bridge

William Shatner

Captain James T. Kirk

Leonard Nimoy

(photo by Stan Burns)

Mr. Spock—First Officer and Ship's Science Officer

DeForest Kelley   *(photo by Stan Burns)*

Dr. Leonard McCoy

James Doohan

(photo by Stan Burns)

Chief Engineer Montgomery Scott

Nichelle Nichols

(photo by Stan Burns)

Lt. Uhura (Communications Officer)

George Takei

(photo by Stan Burns)

Lt. Sulu—Helmsman

Walter Koenig

(photo by Stan Burns)

Ensign Chekov

Majel Barrett

(photo by Stan Burns)

Nurse Christine Chapel

Dorothy Fontana—STAR TREK's story editor for its first two seasons, and one of the shows most prolific writers.
(photo by Stan Burns)

Gene Roddenberry producer, shows off an artist's conception
of a set from his new show, GENESIS II.
(photo by Stan Burns)

The most famous Vulcan of them all—Mr. Spock—who is really only half-Vulcan . . .

. . . and his human mother, Amanda

Sarek, Spock's Vulcan father, in the episode, "Journey to Babel," which brings the two together.

Captain Kirk encounters Sarek for the first time.

T'Pring, Spock's betrothed, and Stonn, the Vulcan she prefers.
"Amok Time"

Surak, an Ancient Vulcan Philosopher from
"The Savage Curtain."

T'pau, a powerful ruler of Vulcan.

Mark Lenard plays a Romulan—seen here with members of his crew, from "Balance of Terror."

Romulan
ship
from
"Balance
of
Terror."

Kang,
Klingon
Captain—
"Day of
the Dove."

A Klingon

Klingon
ships
menace the
Enterprise

Koloth
and
Korax

"I admire
your
mind..."

Keeper—
"The Menagerie."

Balok—
"The Corbomite Maneuver."

Yarnek—
alien from
"The Savage Curtain."

A Mugato, from "A Private Little War."

The Salt Vampire from "Man Trap."

Ruk the Android—"What are little girls made of?"

Dr. Sevrin—
"The Way
to Eden."

The Horta—
"Devil
in the
Dark."

Lal and
Thann—
"The
Empath."

ornate. Well, they sent me to Max Factor and they put the wig on me and I found it was a French wig. I told them that at Max Factor, and the hairdresser there said, 'Well, we'll comb it out and redo it. We know what you want.' So on the day of the scene, the wig box was opened up and it was the French wig, all done up curly. I refused to work the scene in that. Shatner's position in that instance was that I should wear it because who cares? I explained to him that two people should care: one, and for important reasons, is myself, because I'm playing the character; and in order to feel the character I must have the proper paraphernalia. Number two, *he* should care because if I were the star of a show, I would want everything in it to be absolutely perfect. Of course, I'm not blaming Bill for his attitude, he wanted to get the show into the can. I know from the response I received from that show that I was right, because I received three or four very good roles because of that part. It broke me out of the image of being simply a tough guy who could play Caryl Chessman or whatever. Oh, but finally, Gene Coon came down on the set and the question was presented to him. Now, if Gene had said to me, 'Bill, it doesn't matter, go ahead and do it.' I would have reluctantly gone ahead and do it. And as a matter of fact, it *wouldn't* have made any difference. It wasn't the thing that would make or break the episode, and the chances are that few people would have cared. But Gene said, 'Immediately go down and get another wig.' So somebody went and got a wig, it only took twenty or thirty minutes, so they picked up another shot in the meantime. After it was over, I don't think that Shatner felt that I was wrong, he just never felt that it was important. But it was important to me.

"I'll tell you how important that script was to me—I hurt myself doing it and really badly. I mean, I didn't realize it at that time. But we had this sword fight sequence, if you remember, and we did that on the stage.

So they had merely poured sand over the linoleum. And I had on these high French-type boots, they were leather heeled, and in one of the sequences where Shatner and I are running after each other, I did a header and came down on my shoulder. And my shoulder came out of the socket. The pain was excruciating and I jumped up and through it up in the air and it popped back in. Luckily. But by the time I returned home that night, I was black and blue on the entire left side of my body. Of course, they called the nurse down to the set when it happened, but there was nothing she could do for me. I managed to finish that day despite it.

"The unique thing about STAR TREK was that Shatner and Nimoy were really interested in that show. They were aware that I had been given a hell of a role and they wanted to see it emerge, so they stayed on the set, and as a matter of fact, Bill Shatner gave me some marvelous suggestions. The crying sequence at the end was an example. It was very sensitive, but it could have gone both ways. It could have been ranting and raving, or it could be that almost plaintive thing. As it turned out, we shot it both ways, but Shatner said he liked it more subdued, and so did I. That was the shot that was used, and it was better.

"There was a funny thing that happened. We were rehearsing the sequence with Nichelle Nichols and Bill Shatner introduces her, and I say—the line was supposed to be, 'Ah, a Nubian maid. Captured in the sun.' Something like that. So I came up and said—I didn't realize I was saying it, 'Ah, a Nubian slave—' And Nichelle says, 'I'll kick you in the ankle!' It had been a Freudian slip on my part, but she took it very lightly. It was a very funny moment.

"I got a tremendous amount of fan mail out of 'The Squire of Gothos.' A lot of people asked me why I didn't get roles like that more often. You know, nobody hated me at the end. They didn't even hate the character while he was doing it to the Captain and crew of the *Enterprise*, because the way he played it, it was all a game. 'You've got to play my game.' Well, that was his childish petulance, and people picked up on it. So they didn't get mad at him; and then at the end, everyone felt great sympathy for him, that his toy was being taken away. It was a very well conceived character.

"But then, STAR TREK was a very well conceived show. I enjoyed doing it. As I said, it's one of the high points in my career.

"I've never seen a series that hung on like STAR TREK has. Other shows have come and gone. But I've heard more things about STAR TREK than any of them. Like from people in my neighborhood, things like, 'Why doesn't STAR TREK come back, it was such an interesting show,' and so on. I'd like to see them bring it back."

First Season Episodes

THE MAN TRAP

written by George Clayton Johnson

NANCY CRATER	Jeanne Bal (and Francine Pyne)
PROFESSOR ROBERT CRATER	Alfred Ryder
DARNELL	Michael Zaslow
GREEN	Bruce Watson
UHURA'S CREWMAN	Vince Howard

CHARLIE X

written by Dorothy Fontana
from a story by Gene Roddenberry

CHARLIE EVANS	Robert Walker, Jr.
THASIAN	Abraham Sofaer
TINA LAWTON	Patricia McNulty
CAPTAIN REMART	Charles J. Stewart
TOM NELLIS	Dallas Mitchell

WHERE NO MAN HAS GONE BEFORE

written by Samuel A. Peeples

LT. CDR. GARY MITCHELL	Gary Lockwood
DR. ELIZABETH DEHNER	Sally Kellerman
LT. LEE KELSO	Paul Carr
DR. PIPER	Paul Fix

| YEOMAN SMITH | Andrea Dromm |
| ALDEN | Lloyd Haynes |

THE NAKED TIME

written by John D. F. Black

LT. KEVIN RILEY	Bruce Hyde
JOE TORMOLEN	Stewart Moss
DR. HARRISON	John Bellah

THE ENEMY WITHIN

written by Richard Matheson

LT. JOHN FARRELL	Jim Goodwin
TECHNICIAN FISHER	Edward Madden
TECHNICIAN WILSON	Garland Thompson

MUDD'S WOMEN

written by Stephen Kandel
from a story by Gene Roddenberry

HARRY MUDD	Roger C. Carmel
EVE MCHURON	Karen Steele
MAGDA KOVAS	Susan Denberg
RUTH BONAVENTURE	Maggie Thrett
BEN CHILDRESS	Gene Dynarski
JOHN FARRELL	Jim Goodwin
GOSSETT	Jon Kowal
BENTON	Seamon Glass

WHAT ARE LITTLE GIRLS MADE OF?

written by Robert Bloch

DR. ROGER KORBY	Michael Strong
ANDREA	Sherry Jackson
RUK	Ted Cassidy
BROWN	Harry Basch
MATTHEWS	Vince Deadrick
RAYBURN	Budd Albright

MIRI

written by Adrian Spies

MIRI	Kim Darby
JAHN	Michael J. Pollard
FARRELL	Jim Goodwin
LITTLE BOY	John Megna
CREATURE	Ed McCready

(One of the other children in this episode
was played by Dawn Roddenberry, Gene Roddenberry's daughter.)

DAGGER OF THE MIND

written by Shimon Wincelberg (also known as S. Bar
David)

DR. ADAMS	James Gregory
DR. VAN GELDER	Morgan Woodward
DR. HELEN NOEL	Marianna Hill
LETHE	Suzanne Wasson

THE CORBOMITE MANEUVER

written by Jerry Sohl

DAVE BAILEY	Anthony Hall
BALOK	Clint Howard

THE MENAGERIE

written by Gene Roddenberry

CHRISTOPHER PIKE	Jeffrey Hunter
VINA	Susan Oliver
JOSE MENDEZ	Malachi Throne
MISS PIPER	Julie Parrish
LT. HANSON	Hagan Beggs
TYLER	Peter Duryea
KEEPER	Meg Wylie
DR. PHILIP BOYCE	John Hoyt
NUMBER ONE	Majel Barrett

(This was a two-part episode, the bulk of which was made up of the very first pilot episode, "The Cage." Gene Roddenberry wrote a new story around it so it could be used. Note that Majel Barrett had a much more important part in the original conception, but the network balked at a female second in command. Pity.) (This episode won the Hugo Award for the Best Dramatic Presentation of 1966.)

THE CONSCIENCE OF THE KING

written by Barry Trivers

ANTON KARIDIAN	Arnold Moss
LENORE KARIDIAN	Barbara Anderson

LT. KEVIN RILEY	Bruce Hyde
LT. LESLIE	Eddie Paskey

(Eddie Paskey was also William Shatner's stand-in, he could be seen as a background crewman in many episodes. It was standard practice to make maximum use of all the stand-ins this way.)

BALANCE OF TERROR

written by Paul Schneider

ROMULAN COMMANDER	Mark Lenard
ANDREW STILES	Paul Comi
DECIUS	Lawrence Montaigne
CENTURION	John Warburton
ROBERT TOMLINSON	Stephen Mines
ANGELA MARTINE	Barbara Baldavin
HANSON	Garry Walberg

SHORE LEAVE

written by Theodore Sturgeon

TONIA BARROWS	Emily Banks
CARETAJER	Oliver McGowan
RODRIGUEZ	Perry Lopez
FINNEGAN	Bruce Mars
DON JUAN	James Gruzaf
RUTH	Shirley Bonne
SAMURIA	Sebastian Tom

THE GALILEO SEVEN

written by Oliver Crawford and S. Bar David
from a story by Oliver Crawford

BOMA	Don Marshall
GAETANO	Peter Marko
LATIMER	Rees Vaughan
KELOWITZ	Grant Woods
YEOMAN MEARS	Phyllis Douglas
COMMISSIONER FERRIS	John Crawford

THE SQUIRE OF GOTHOS

by Paul Schneider

TRELANE	William Campbell
JAEGER	Richard Carlyle
DE SALLE	Michael Barrier
YEOMAN ROSS	Venita Wolf

ARENA

written by Gene L. Coon
from a story by Fredric Brown

METRON	Carole Shelyne
O'HERLIHY	Jerry Ayres
KELOWITZ	Grant Woods
LT. HAROLD	Tom Troupe
LANG	James Farley
DE PAUL	Sean Kenney

TOMORROW IS YESTERDAY

written by D. C. Fontana

CAPTAIN CHRISTOPHER	Roger Perry
AIR POLICE SERGEANT	Hal Lynch
COLONEL FELLINI	Ed Peck
TECHNICIAN WEBB	Richard Merrifield
TRANSPORTER CHIEF KYLE	John Winston

COURT MARTIAL

written by Don M. Mankiewicz and Stephen W. Carabatsos
from a story by Don M. Mankiewicz

COMMODORE STONE	Percy Rodriguez
SAMUEL GOGLEY	Elisha Cook, Jr.
AREEL SHAW	Joan Marshall
FINNEY	Richard Webb
JAMIE FINNEY	Alice Rawlings
HANSON	Hagan Beggs
TIMOTHY	Winston DeLugo

THE RETURN OF THE ARCHONS

written by Boris Sobelman
from a story by Gene Roddenberry

REGER	Harry Townes
MARPLON	Torin Thatcher
LANDRU	Charles Macauley
LINDSTROM	Christopher Held
TULA	Brioni Farrell
FIRST LAWGIVER	Sid Haig
TAMAR	Jon Lormer
HACOM	Morgan Farley

BILAR	Ralph Maurer
LESLIE	Eddie Paskey
GUARD	David L. Ross

SPACE SEED

written by Gene L. Coon and Carey Wilbur

KHAN SINGH	Ricardo Montalban
MARLA MCGIVERS	Madlyn Rhue
SPINELLI	Blaisdell Makee
JOAQUIN	Mark Tobin

A TASTE OF ARMAGEDDON

writen by Robert Jamner and Gene L. Coon
from a story by Robert Hamner

AMBASSADOR FOX	Gene Lyons
ANAN 879	David Opatoshu
SAR 627	Robert Sampson
MEA 349	Barbara Babcock
YEOMAN TAMURA	Miko Mayama
GALLOWAY	David L. Ross
DE PAUL	Sean Kenney

THIS SIDE OF PARADISE

written by D.C. Fontana
from a story by Nathan Butler and D.C. Fontana

LEILA KALOMI	Jill Ireland
SANDOVAL	Frank Overton
KELOWITZ	Grant Woods
PAINTER	Dick Scotter

THE DEVIL IN THE DARK

written by Gene L. Coon

CHIEF ENGINEER VANDER-BERG	Ken Lynch
HORTA	Janos Prohaska
LT. CDR. GIOTTO	Barry Russo
ED APPEL	Brad Weston
SCHMITTER	Biff Elliott

ERRAND OF MERCY

written by Gene L. Coon

AYELBORNE	John Abbott
KOR	John Colicos
CLAYMARE	Peter Brocco
KLINGON LIEUTENANT	Victor Lundin
TREFAYNE	David Hillary Huges

THE ALTERNATIVE FACTOR

written by Don Ingalls

LAZARUS A/B	Robert Brown
CHARLENE MASTERS	Janet MacLachlen
COMMODORE BARSTOW	Richard Derr
LT. LESLIE	Eddie Paskey

CITY ON THE EDGE OF FOREVER

written by Harlan Ellison

EDITH KEELER	Joan Collins
GUARDIAN	Bartell LaRue
RODENT	John Harmon

(This episode won the Hugo Award for Best Dramatic Presentation of 1967.)

OPERATION—ANNIHILATE

written by Stephen W. Carabatsos

KARTAN	Dave Armstrong
PETER KIRK	Craig Hundley
AURELAN KIRK	Joan Swift
YEOMAN ZARA JAMAL	Maurishka (Taliferro)

Second Season Episodes

AMOK TIME

written by Theodore Sturgeon

T'PRING	Arlene Martel
T'PAU	Celia Lovsky
STONN	Lawrence Montaigne
KOMACK	Byron Morrow

(This episode was nominated for a Hugo Award for Best Dramatic Presentation of 1967.)

WHO MOURNS FOR ADONAIS?

written by Gilbert Ralston and Gene L. Coon from a story by Gilbert Ralston

APOLLO	Michael Forest
LT. CAROLYN PALAMAS	Leslie Parrish
LT. KYLE	John Winston

THE CHANGELING

written by John Meredyth Lucas

MR. SINGH	Blaisdell Makee
NOMAD	Vic Perrin
LT. CARLISLE	Arnold Lessing

MIRROR, MIRROR

written by Jerome Bixby

MARLENA	Barbara Luna
THARN	Vic Perrin

(This episode was nominated for a Hugo Award for Best Dramatic Presentation of 1967.)

THE APPLE

written by Max Ehrlich

AKUTA	Keith Andes
YEOMAN MARTHA LANDON	Celeste Yarnall
ENSIGN MALLORY	Jay Jones
SAYANA	Shari Nims
MAKORA	David Soul

THE DOOMSDAY MACHINE

written by Norman Spinrad

COMMODORE DECKER	William Windom
LT. PALMER	Elizabeth Rogers
ELLIOTT	John Copage
WASHBURN	Richard Compton
LT. KYLE	John Winston
RUSS	Tim Burns

(This episode was nominated for a Hugo Award for Best Dramatic Presentation of 1967.)

CATSPAW

written by Robert Bloch and D.C. Fontana

SYLVIA	Antoinette Bowers
KOROB	Theo Marcus
DE SALLE	Michael Barrier
JACKSON	Jimmy Jones

I, MUDD

written by Stephen Kandel

HARRY MUDD	Roger C. Carmel
NORMAN	Richard Tatro
LT. ROWE	Mike Howden
ENS. JORDAN	Michael Zaslow
STELLA series	Kay Elliott
ALICE series	Rhae and Alice Andrece
HERMAN series	Tom and Ted LeGarde
OTHER SERIES	Maureen and Collen Thornton
	Tamara and Starr Wilson

METAMORPHOSIS

written by Gene L. Coon

ZEFREM COCHRANE	Glenn Corbett
NANCY HEDFORD	Elinor Donahue

JOURNEY TO BABEL

written by D.C. Fontana

AMANDA	Jane Wyatt
SAREK	Mark Lenard

THELEV	William O'Connell
SHRAS	Reggie Nalder
GAV	John Wheeler
LT. JOSEPHS	James X. Mitchell

THE DEADLY YEARS

written by David P. Harmon

COMMODORE STOCKER	Charles Drake
JANET WALLACE	Sarah Marshall
ARLENE GALWAY	Beverly Washburn
JOHNSON	Felix Locker
YEOMAN ATKINS	Carolyn Nelson
MRS. JOHNSON	Laura Wood

OBSESSION

written by Art Wallace

| ENSIGN GARROVICK | Stephen Brooks |
| ENSIGN RIZZO | Jerry Ayres |

WOLF IN THE FOLD

written by Robert Bloch

HENGIST	John Fiedler
JARIS	Charles Macauley
SYBO	Pilar Seurat
TARK	Joseph Bernard
MORLA	Charles Dierkop
YEOMAN TANKRIS	Judy McConnell
KAREN TRACY	Virginia Ladridge
NURSE	Judy Sherven
KARA	Tania Lemani

THE TROUBLE WITH TRIBBLES

written by David Gerrold

NILZ BARIS	William Schallert
KOLOTH	William Campbell
CYRANO JONES	Stanley Adams
LURRY	Whit Bissell
KORAX	Michael Pataki
ARNE DARVIN	Charlie Brill
ADMIRAL FITZPATRICK	Ed Reimers
TRADER	Guy Raymond
ENSIGN FREEMAN	Paul Bradley
GUARD	David L. Ross

(This episode was nominated for the Hugo Award for Best Dramatic Presentation of 1967. It placed second by six votes.) (The complete story of how this episode was written, plus shooting script, is also available as a Ballantine Book, *The Trouble with Tribbles*.)

THE GAMESTERS OF TRISKELION

written by Margaret Armen

GALT	John Ruskin
SHANA	Angelique Pettyjohn
LARS	Steve Sandor
TAMOON	Jane Ross
ENSIGN JANA HAINES	Victoria George
KLOOG	Mickey Morton

A PIECE OF THE ACTION

written by David P. Harmon and Gene L. Coon

BELA OXMYX	Anthony Caruso

JOJO KRAKO	Victor Tayback
KALO	Lee Delano
TEPO	John Harmon
ZABO	Steve Arnold
GIRL #1	Dyanne Thorne
GIRL #2	Sharon Hillyer
SMALL BOY	Sheldon Collins

THE IMMUNITY SYNDROME

written by Robert Sabaroff

REGULAR ENTERPRISE CREW, NO GUEST STARS

A PRIVATE LITTLE WAR

written by Gene Roddenberry
from a story by Judd Crucis

NONA	Nancy Kovack
TYREE	Michael Witney
DR. MBENGA	Booker Marshall
APELLA	Arthur Bernard
KRELL	Joe Romeo

RETURN TO TOMORROW

written by John Kingsbridge

DR. ANNE MULHALL	Diane Muldaur

PATTERNS OF FORCE

written by John Meredyth Lucas

JOHN GILL	David Brian
MELAKON	Skip Homeier
ISAK	Richard Evans
DARAS	Valora Norland
ABROM	William Wintersole
ENEG	Patrick Horgan
SS LIEUTENANT	Ralph Maurer
SS MAJOR	Gilbert Green
NEWSCASTER	Bart La Rue
FIRST TROOPER	Paul Baxley
GESTAPO LT.	Pater Canon

BY ANY OTHER NAME

written by D.C. Fontana and Jerome Bixby
from a story by Jerome Bixby

ROJAN	Warren Stevens
KELINDA	Barbara Bouchet
HANAR	Stewart Moss
TOMAR	Robert Fortier
LT. SHEA	Carol Byrd
DREA	Leslie Dalton
YEOMAN LESLIE THOMPSON	Julie Cobb

THE OMEGA GLORY

written by Gene Roddenberry

CAPTAIN RONALD TRACY	Morgan Woodward
CLOUD WILLIAM	Toy Jensen
SIRAH	Irene Kelley
GALLOWAY	David L. Ross
LESLIE	Eddie Paskey

DR. CARTER	Ed McReady
WU	Lloyd Kino
YANG SCHOLAR	Morgan Farley

THE ULTIMATE COMPUTER

written by D.C. Fontana
from a story by Lawrence N. Wolfe

DR. DAYSTROM	William Marshall
COMMODORE WESLEY	Barry Russo
HARPER	Sean Morgan

BREAD AND CIRCUSES

written by Gene Roddenberry and Gene L. Coon
from a story by John Kneubel

MERICK	William Smithers
CLAUDIUS MARCUS	Logan Ramsey
SEPTIMUS	Ian Wolfe
FLAVIUS MAXIMUS	Rhodes Reason
DRUSILLA	Lois Jewell
ANNOUNCER	Bart La Rue
MASTER OF GAMES	Jack Perkins

FRIDAY'S CHILD

written by D.C. Fontana

KRAS	Tige Andrews
MAAB	Michael Dante
ELEEN	Julie Newmar
KEEL	Cal Bolder
DUUR	Kirk Raymone

| TEER AKAAR | Ben Gage |
| GRANT | Robert Bralver |

ASSIGNMENT: EARTH

written by Art Wallace
from a story by Gene Roddenberry and Art Wallace

GARY SEVEN	Robert Lansing
ROBERTA LINCOLN	Terri Garr
CROMWELL	Jim Keefer
COLONEL NESVIG	Morgan Jones
SECURITY CHIEF RAWLINGS	Lincoln Demyan

(This was a very strange episode. It was not
only a STAR TREK episode, it was also a pilot for
a new series. However, it didn't sell.)

Third Season Episodes

SPECTRE OF THE GUN

written by Lee Cronin

WYATT EARP	Ron Soble
SYLVIA	Bonnie Beecher
MORGAN EARP	Rex Holman
SHERIFF BEHAN	Bill Zuckert
DOC HOLLIDAY	Sam Gilman
MELKOT VOICE	Abraham Sofaer
MELKOT MASK	by Mike Minor
VIRGIL EARP	Charles Maxwell
ED	Charles Seel
BARBER	Ed McReady
MELKOTIAN BUOY VOICE	James Doohan
RANCHER	Gregg Palmer
RIDER	Richard Anthony

ELAAN OF TROYIUS

written by John Meredyth Lucas

ELAAN	France Nuyen
PETRI	Jay Robinson
KRYTON	Tony Young
EVANS	Lee Duncan
WATSON	Victor Brandt
KLINGON	K. L. Smith
GUARDS	Dick Durock
	Charles Beck

THE PARADISE SYNDROME

written by Margaret Armen

MIRAMANEE	Sabrina Scharf
SALSH	Rudy Solari

THE ENTERPRISE INCIDENT

written by D.C. Fontana

ROMULAN COMMANDER	Joanne Linville
TAL	Jack Donner
ENTERPRISE TECHNICAL OFFICER	Richard Compton
ROMULAN TECHNICIAN	Robert Gentile
SOLDIER	Gordon Coffey
GUARD	Mike Howden

AND THE CHILDREN SHALL LEAD

written by Edward J. Lakso

GORGAN	Melvin Belli
TOMMY STARNES	Craig Hundley
PROF. STARNES	James Wellman
MARY	Pamelyn Ferdin
RAY	Brian Tochi
STEVE	Caesar Belli
DON	Mark Robert Brown
TECHNICIAN	Louis Elias

SPOCK'S BRAIN

written by Lee Cronin

KARA	Marj Dusay
MORG	James Daris
LUMA	Sheila Leighton

IS THERE IN TRUTH NO BEAUTY?

written by Jean Lisette Aroeste

MIRANDA	Diana Muldaur
MARVICK	David Frankham

THE EMPATH

written by Joyce Muskat

GEM	Kathryn Hays
LAL	Alan Bergman
THANN	Willard Sage
DR. LINKE	Jason Wingreen
DR. OZABA	Davis Roberts

THE THOLIAN WEB

written by Judy Burns and Chet Richards

REGULAR ENTERPRISE CREW, NO GUEST CAST

FOR THE WORLD IS HOLLOW AND I HAVE TOUCHED THE SKY

written by Rik Vollaerts

NATIRA	Kate Woodville

ADMIRAL WESTERVLEIT   Byron Morrow
OLD MAN   Jon Lormer

DAY OF THE DOVE

written by Jerome Bixby

KANG   Michael Ansara
MARA   Susan Howard

PLATO'S STEPCHILDREN

written by Meyer Dolinsky

ALEXANDER   Michael Dunn
PARMEN   Liam Sullivan
PHILANA   Barbara Babcock
ERACLITUS   Ted Scott
DIONYD   Derek Partridge

WINK OF AN EYE

written by Lee Cronin

DEELA   Kathie Brown
RAEL   Jason Evers
EKOR   Eric Holland
COMPTON   Geoffrey Binney

THAT WHICH SURVIVES

written by John Meredyth Lucas
from a story by D.C. Fontana

LOSIRA   Lee Meriwether
D'AMATO   Arthur Batanides
LT. RAHADA   Naomi Pollack

LET THAT BE YOUR LAST BATTLEFIELD

written by Oliver Crawford
from a story by Lee Cronin

BELE	Frank Gorshin
LOKAI	Lou Antonio

WHOM GODS DESTROY

written by Lee Erwin

MARTA	Yvonne Craig
GARTH	Steve Ihnat
CORY	Key Luke
ANDORIAN	Richard Geary
TELLARITE	Gary Downey

MARK OF GIDEON

written by George F. Slavin and Stanley Adams

ODONA	Sharon Acker
HODIN	David Hurst
KRODACK	Gene Kynarski
ADMIRAL FITZGERALD	Richard Derr

THE LIGHTS OF ZETAR

written by Jeremy Tarcher and Shari Lewis

LT. MIRA ROMAINE	Jan Shutan
LT. KYLE	John Winston
RINDONIAN	Libby Erwin
CREWMAN'S VOICE	Bud da Vinci

THE CLOUD MINDERS

written by Margaret Armen
from a story by David Gerrold and Oliver Crawford

PLASUS	Jeff Corey
DROXINE	Diana Ewing
VANNA	Charlene Polite
ANKA	Fred Williamson
MIDRO	Ed Long

THE WAY TO EDEN

written by Arthur Heinemann
from a story by Michael Richards and Arthur Heinemann

DR. SEVRIN	Skip Homeier
ADAM	Charles Napier
IRINA	Mary Linda Rapelye
TONGO RAD	Victor Brandt
HIPPIE #1	Deborah Downey
HIPPIE #2	Phyllis Douglas

REQUIEM FOR METHUSELAH

written by Jerome Bixby

FLINT	James Daly
REENA	Louise Sorel

THE SAVAGE CURTAIN

written by Arthur Heinemann and Gene Roddenberry
from a story by Gene Roddenberry

ABRAHAM LINCOLN	Lee Bergere

SURAK	Barry Atwater
COLONEL GREEN	Phil Pine
ZORA	Carol Daniels Dement
KAHLESS	Robert Herron
GENGHIS KHAN	Nathan Jung
YARNEK	Janos Prohaska
YARNEK'S VOICE	Bart LaRue
DICKERSON	Lt. Arell Blanton

ALL OUR YESTERDAYS

written by Jean Lisette Aroeste

ATOZ	Ian Wolfe
ZARABETH	Mariette Hartley

TURNABOUT INTRUDER

written by Arthur Singer
from a story by Gene Roddenberry

DR. JANICE LESTER	Sandra Smith
DR. COLEMAN	Harry Landers

"To boldly go where no man has gone before . . ."

"Peace. Live long and prosper."

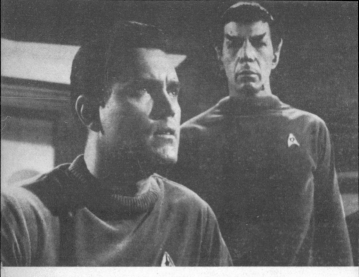

First Pilot: Captain Christopher Pike and Mr. Spock.

Captain Pike's First Officer, known as "No. 1."

Second Pilot: Captain James T. Kirk—

—and his First Officer, Mr. Spock.

The Bridge

"Tomorrow is Yester-day."

"What are Little Girls Made Of?"

"The Changling"

"Mark of Gideon"

"Miri"

"Miri"

"All Our
Yesterdays"

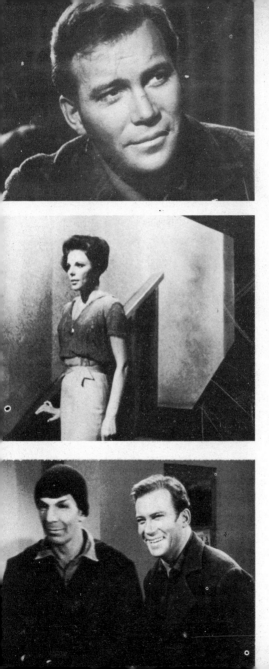

"City On the Edge of Forever"

"The
Deadly
Years"

Chekov
and
Kirk

"Journey
to
Babel"

"The Immunity Syndrome"

"Journey to Babel"

Spock
and
Amanda

Spock at
his sta-
tion on
the Bridge

"Amok Time"

The state of *plak-tow* from "Amok Time"

Three dimensional chess

Spock
and
Kirk

"This Side
of
Paradise"

"Balance
of
Terror"

"Is There
in Truth
No
Beauty?"

Spock
and
McCoy

"Charlie
X"

McCoy

"The
Deadly
Years"

"Journey
to Babel"

"Charlie X"

Scotty

Uhura

Nurse
Chapel

Chekov

Uhura

Sulu

"The
Naked
Time"

"Mantrap"

matte shot
for
"Menagerie"

"The Tholian Web"

"I, Mudd"

"Where No Man Has Gone Before

"Mirror, Mirror"

"Gamesters of Triskelion"

"Operation
Annihi-
late"

"The Enemy
Within"

"Mark of
Gideon"

"Return
of the
Archons"

"Bread
and
Circuses"

"That
Which
Survives"

"The Naked
Time"

"The
Tholian
Web"

"Balance of Terror"

"Arena"

"For the World is Hollow and
I Have Touched the Sky"

"Day of the Dove"

"Journey to Babel"

"The Apple"

"City on the Edge of Forever"

"Journey
to
Babel"

"Whom
Gods
Destroy"

"Devil
in the
Dark"

"That
Which
Survives"

"Mirror,
Mirror"

"Court
Martial"

"Amok Time"—T'Pring at seven

T'Pring as adult

The challenge

Spock
and
T'Pau

The
challenger

Duel to
the
death

It must —

— have
been —

— a
blooper —

PART THREE

The Star Trek Phenomenon

SAVING STAR TREK

Once upon a time, there was a lady named Bjo Trimble, and she loved STAR TREK so much—she still does—that she could not bear to see it die after just two seasons.

So she wrote a letter to NBC in late 1967 telling them that STAR TREK was a good TV show and they should keep it on the air. Then she asked a few of her friends to do the same.

About a million of them did.

Bjo (pronounced Bee-jo) was one of STAR TREK's first fans. She wrote to Gene Roddenberry, the show's producer and creator, almost immediately after the first few episodes had been telecast, and asked if she could meet him. Of course, he was delighted to. At that time, neither the cast nor crew had any idea of the eventual public response to the show—and they were all a bit scared about whether or not the series would be a success. STAR TREK was, quite frankly, one of the biggest gambles in TV history.

Gene Roddenberry was impressed with this perky little redheaded lady, and gradually she became the fan liaison for STAR TREK. She felt that there was much that the fans could do to show their involvement with the show. Perhaps a letter campaign . . .

The idea was *not* pulled casually from a hat. Bjo already had a pretty good idea of the intensity of reaction to STAR TREK, she was handling some of the show's fan mail for Roddenberry—but in addition to that, she herself had been a science fiction fan for a number of years. And that was her real advantage.

Let me explain this.

First, forget all previous definitions of the word *fan*. To use the word in any of its more common connotations would be a misnomer and a disservice. If you approach science fiction *fandom* with the traditional definitions, you'll never understand it.

Most people who react to science fiction, react to it as they would to anything else—like mystery novels, stamp collecting or masturbation—it's an interest. But it's not their *only* interest and they can go on about their lives with only an occasional bump to their consciousnesses.

Not so the science fiction *fan*. There's something about science fiction—it stretches the mind. After you've spent a few afternoons with Heinlein, Asimov, Sturgeon and Clarke, everything else is mundane. Dull. After you've spent an evening saving the Earth, exploring the galaxy, discovering immortality, probing the depths of the mind, touring the far future and achieving *The Answer to it All*, who cares about the dishes or the six o'clock news? Once your mind has been thoroughly boggled, you want to keep that sense of wonder—you don't want to lose the wider horizons that science fiction has given you.

It's not enough for the *trufan* to escape for just an hour or two into an alternate universe. He doesn't want to be a tourist. He wants to be a resident. So he sets out to build his alternate worlds for real, and makes them so totally convincing that he alters a portion of the actual realtime continuum. He makes it come true.

Creating alternate realities and making them real enough to live in is the business of science fiction writers; they do it for a living. The science fiction fans do it for fun.

A ˉfan collects books, collects magazines, collects cover paintings and still pictures from films, collects comic books and original artwork, collects film clips and old props and anything else even remotely related to his central interest.

And he writes. Incessantly. A fan writes his own amateur fiction, most of it pretty bad, and inflicts it on his friends. But an SF writer has to start somewhere, and many of them start out as fans. It's when a fan becomes so good at making his realities believable that others are willing to pay for the privilege of sharing them that he becomes a pro.

Other fans become critics. A fan critic is the hardest kind of all—he does it because he likes it. He'll write reviews of new movies and analyses of old ones, he'll write complex criticisms of the latest novels, and even more involved critiques of other reviewers. He'll do in-depth studies of individual writers in the field and he'll write long articles about ideas and machines and the overall shape of the universe. He'll write about *any-thing* that suggests itself to him.

And then he'll publish it.

A *fanzine*—look it up, it's in the dictionary—is an amateur magazine, generally mimeographed, sometimes dittoed, occasionally offset-printed with full color covers, and looking better than the prozines. The fan publisher pays for it himself and generally edits it himself too; all the articles and artwork are voluntary, and generally the fan sells just enough copies to other fans to break even on the whole thing. If he generates any ego-response, then the effort was worth it and he starts planning another issue.

Fanzines are probably the most important avenue of communication between fans. Besides being ego-builders, a good fanzine also garners status for its publisher. Most fanzine editors trade copies of their zine for copies of other zines, a semi-incestuous practice which results in interminable comments and reviews on each other's zines. However, the reviews also create what might best be called "The Dandelion Effect."

An editor sends one copy of his fanzine to another editor, who reviews it and publishes the address of the first editor. Anyone who reads the review and is interested in obtaining a copy of the first fanzine can then send for it by mail. Depending on the nature of the zine and what it publishes, it is possible to build a circulation of several thousand. But at that point the fanzine becomes a very expensive hobby. Fanzines generally are not profit-making operations.

The real interest is in writing and publishing and in being responded to by others.

And that kind of interest results in Amateur Press Associations—and there are many of them. Each member of an APA prints up to fifty or sixty copies of his zine (as many as is required) and contributes them to the distribution, which is collated and then mailed, or delivered by hand. In return for his one zine, each APA-member gets forty or fifty in return, many of them with public comments to him about his latest APA-zine.

Organized (you should pardon the expression) fandom touches about five thousand people in the United States.

*Dis*organized fandom reaches a lot more. I make no guesses at the number—but every really *intense* fan is merely a nucleus at the core of ten or twenty other human beings, whose interest in science fiction is not quite so rabid, but who enjoy the contact with someone whose interest is.

Fandom is like a small town spread out across the United States—and throughout the rest of the world too. There are science fiction clubs in almost every major city; if there isn't a club, there is at least a nucleus of fans.

The lifelines of fandom are the U.S. mail and the telephone system. Fandom depends upon communication—communication is the name of the game. What is being communicated is often less important than the fact that the communication exists.

Fans have large address books—no, make that files. Fans have large postage bills—twenty or thirty dollars a month just to keep in touch is not uncommon. Fans are—well, fans.

In *The Crying of Lot 49*, by Thomas Pynchon, a woman named Oedipa Maas discovers a vast underground network of secret communications, a sort of second postal system, which spans the country and touches all sorts of sub-worlds and tangential cultures. It reaches into computer companies and gay bars and stamp collectors' homes and used book stores and organizations of Iowa Masons and drug addicts and anywhere else that other levels—*separated* levels—of cultural activity have developed. Fandom is something like that. Without the secret recognition signs though. (Mention the name Heinlein, that's enough.)

Science fiction fandom can touch a large number of human beings in a very short time. It's a seemingly amorphous grapevine with no discernible structure at all—until you get into it. Then you find that the apparent lack of structure is really the chaotic overlaying of hundreds of lesser structures, interrelated and interdependent. Big structures appear in fandom only when massive amounts of energy are directed into the system—then the fans organize and channel that energy, they focus it and distribute it.

If the input is STAR TREK, then what is the output?

A letter campaign to save the show.

And more than that.

Science fiction fandom has existed in the United States for more than forty years. Properly, it began with Hugo Gernsback's magazines and the Science Fiction League. It's a healthy and viable subculture and will probably go on for decades. But a few years ago, it gave birth to a giant—or maybe a monster—called STAR TREK fandom.

The midwife was Bjo Trimble.

Bjo Trimble is a pert, redheaded little ogre of a woman with incredible talent, vitality, enthusiasm, ability and aggressiveness. She writes, she paints, she cartoons, she designs clothes, she does professional makeup for movies, she does offset layouts and paste-ups, she compiles indexes, and if someone were to invent a new art form tomorrow. Bjo would be a master of it by next Friday.

All human beings are unique—but Bjo is uniquer than most. She has a husband, two daughters, a houseful of cats and books and breathtaking artwork, and a dragon in the basement. (Honest.) When a door-to-door canvasser asked her what the most important appliance in her home was, she replied without hesitation, "The typewriter." (She does not have an automatic dishwasher—she *does* have four typewriters.)

Bjo Trimble is an organizer—and one of the best. If Bjo can't do it, it can't be done.

She and STAR TREK fandom were designed for each other. There probably isn't anyone else who could have done what she did—at least not half so well. It was largely because of her efforts that the STAR TREK Phenomenon developed as it did.

Bjo is a science fiction fan. That doesn't mean that she participates in *all* the activities that were listed above, but she is familiar with them. Because of her fannish activities, she doesn't have just an address book. Not even address files. No, Bjo Trimble has *mailing lists*.

When she got the idea of a "Save STAR TREK" letter campaign, she had about eight hundred people she could contact. Most of them were science fiction fans themselves and many of them had mailing lists of their own.

Chain letter—? Uh uh. More like chain reaction.

But at this point, Bjo can tell the story herself:

"We decided to try—on a fairly small scale, really—a sort of letter writing campaign to convince NBC to pick up the show again.

"I had seen a good deal of the mail coming in, not only to STAR TREK, but other shows as well, and most of it struck me that the people were writing the wrong thing to get their point across. Like for instance, letters that started off, 'You big dumb shit, put the show back on!' And obviously, nobody is going to finish reading a letter like that.

"So, I wrote up a list of dos and don'ts, which are now being copied by similar campaigns for other shows, on how to write a reasonable and intelligent sounding letter to get your point across. One of them was that you should put your letter in a legal-sized envelope, because it looked more businesslike; don't put 'Gene Roddenberry' or 'STAR TREK' on the outside because then it would go straight to the fan mail department and not be opened by the NBC studios. Address the NBC people directly—and, of course, we listed their names and addresses—and then, on the *inside*, that's where you start in about wanting the show saved. NBC couldn't afford *not* to open these letters—without outside identification, they had no way of knowing if they were important or not.

"We mailed out these flyers listing all this information to about eight hundred people—the mailing list of the last big science fiction convention, so we were reaching right away much of science fiction fandom. My main point in the covering letter was, 'See how many other people you can reach.' And people would then write back and say, 'Send me more flyers, I can run them through my local company paper.'

"One man xeroxed his letter and sent it through all the departments of the largest Polaroid division. And Polaroid turns out to be one of the holding companies that owns the NBC corporation. Employees above a certain level own stock in the company, so that provided a little irony because they were writing in to NBC as *stockholders*.

"MENSA, which is a kind of social club for geniuses, copied our letter entirely in their official newspaper, and that went out to about six thousand members of the organization.

"Several college newspapers either duplicated the letter or told people where to write.

"The *Kansas City Star Tribune* phoned us and we gave them an hour and a half interview about what we were doing, and got hundreds of letters in response because they reprinted our address in the article.

"High school kids would write in for more letters and pass them out to friends and so on. Several high school newspapers repeated the information.

"One employee of NASA wrote us from Texas. And a SAC officer, out of the main SAC base, wherever that is, wrote and asked for fifty copies. This kind of thing went on for weeks.

"Thousands of letters later, and somewhere around four or five hundred dollars worth of postage, we found we had created a monster. We were sending out as many flyers as we could afford, about eight or ten letters a day, or whatever we could afford postage for.

"Gene Roddenberry gave us a great many film clips and so on, odds and ends of things around the set, to sell to fans and friends, so that we could defray some of the expenses of the campaign. Well, the stuff went like wildfire and I knew then that fans—all STAR TREK fans, not just our friends—would dig the chance to buy this kind of stuff.

"I told Roddenberry this, but at first he didn't believe me. And then after we took several cartons of STAR TREK trivia, a Spock shirt, some Spock ears, a tribble, some scripts, some film clips and so on, to a convention, he was convinced. We had to fight the people off of the stuff. The auction of this material brought in over four hundred and seventy dollars. (By the way, it was for the TOFF fund, to bring a Japanese fan over to the United States for the next World Science Fiction Convention.)

"Roddenberry was impressed by this evidence of the show's impact, and we had done some research on other costs and kinds of merchandising, and that's how STAR TREK Enterprises was born. We set it up for him. We made up a mailing list from the fan mail and from the letter writing campaign and that was the list we used when we sent out the first catalogues. STAR TREK Enterprises sold scripts, decals, film clips, insignia stickers, color postcards, writer's guides, memo pads, letterheads, cast biographies, bumper stickers, flight deck certificates, and monthly newsletters.*

"But all that came later. First, we had to get STAR TREK renewed. That was our central concern.

"Our campaign kept building and building as word of it got around. This was early 1968 already, and there had been protest marches against NBC in Los Angeles, New York and San Francisco. All in all, I'd say we sent out about four thousand flyers to people all over the country.

"Were we having any effect? Well, we began hearing rumors. NBC had called Gene Roddenberry's office to ask, 'What are you people doing down there?' And, of course, Gene said, 'Who? Me?' NBC was sure that Roddenberry was behind it all. We had his blessing, of course, and his help, but he wasn't *actively* behind the effort. It was entirely a fan enterprise. We were trying to reach as many people as possible and get them to write NBC if they cared at all about STAR TREK.

---

* Although Bjo Trimble has moved on to other things, STAR TREK Enterprises is still doing business. You can get their latest catalogue by writing to: Star Trek Enterprises, P.O. Box 38429, Hollywood, Ca. 90038. Tell them where you heard about it.

"One of the things we stressed in our flyers was individuality. A lot of people had said, 'Oh, write me a letter and I'll sign it.' Or, 'Can't I just mimeograph something off?' I came down very hard on this, I felt it wouldn't help us at all—and my theory was borne out by the fact that a letter writing campaign was recently tried for the country-music program, *Hee-Haw*. And it failed. And when asked why it failed, one of the studio executives replied that it looked as if it had come from an extremely small group of people who were trying to force an issue, because *all* of the letters were the same. That was why I very carefully didn't even write a sample letter. We were following along blindly thinking that if enough people wrote in to NBC, they would have to notice us. As a result, all of our letters were individualistic, and I think that was an important point in our favor.

"At last, Gene Roddenberry's secretary, Penny Unger, heard that the mail to NBC had topped one million pieces, and we were all pretty jubilant about that. Other shows had been renewed because of letter writing campaigns in the past, and in those cases, it had taken a good deal fewer letters, so when we heard that more than one million people had written in, we felt pretty good. One NBC official was reported to have said that a hundred and fifty thousand letters would have done it.

"At any rate, NBC came on the air with a precedent making announcement one night, right after STAR TREK—I wish I had a tape of it—that the show *had been* renewed and would everybody *please* stop writing in. This was pretty indicative that we had flooded them way too much with mail.

"Of course, STAR TREK fans, being what they were, promptly turned around and flooded NBC with thank you letters, still written on legal-size paper and envelopes and nothing to identify them on the outside. NBC had to open these letters too! An anguished vice-president called Gene Roddenberry and pleaded, 'Gene, how do you turn them off! Please!'

"You see, all those letters *had* to be opened. NBC had to hire extra girls just to handle that sheer bulk of mail, to open it and sort it and tabulate it, and the costs started adding up. Anyone who's ever run a business can tell you, office hours can be very expensive. Just the sheer job of opening thousands of pieces of mail a week—just *opening* it—requires more man hours and more office hours than the average business can afford.

"A few weeks later, NBC told *TV Guide* that they had gotten two hundred thousand pieces of mail. And in subsequent years, that number has steadily dropped. Recently, NBC was admitting only to a hundred and fifty thousand, and more recently, only fifty thousand letters. But I know we generated more than that.

"I was at a party, business people mostly, and a man who was fairly high in the computer business was there with a friend, also in the computer business—this friend had been working with NBC at the time of our campaign. He heard someone mention my name, Bjo, and he walked over and asked, 'Bjo Trimble?' I said, 'Yes. . .?' I'd never met this fellow before in my whole life, but he started laughing. 'You have no idea,' he said, 'how many people would like to meet you—especially at NBC. Your name is very well known.'

"I said, 'Why?'

"And he said, 'Well, you broke down the machines at NBC in New York.'

"I said, 'No, I didn't—I never even touched them.' Anyway, he explained that—and I don't understand computer work—in some way, in trying to tabulate the load of mail—apparently they were trying to break it down to find out what kind of people were writing in—the overload of mail was so much that the machines couldn't handle it. He was one of the people called in to repair them, and the talk was all over the place that more than one million letters had come in. So this is how that one million letter figure was verified by an entirely separate source. So, I know—and NBC knows—that there were over one million letters. Whether or not they want to admit it, that's how many there were. NBC claims that the whole thing was engineered by a hard core of fanatics—but there just aren't that many science fiction fanatics in this country. Most of that mail had to come from STAR TREK fans—and even if people were writing in two or three letters apiece, that's still more than the hundred and fifty thousand minimum.

"Actually, we probably touched a lot more than a million people—we'll never know for sure. You see, in that one million letters, petitions were counted only as one letter. I myself have seen petitions with from three hundred to eighteen hundred names on them. And one boy, with a remarkable amount of enterprise, in a small Texas town of three thousand people, managed to get over two thousand names on his petition. He must have gotten everything short of the family pets to sign. And there were a lot of petitions.

"Eventually, we had an NBC man from Burbank come out and talk to us on the STAR TREK set one night, and he asked us if we would tell them how we had done it. How had we reached so many people so fast? And how had we gotten the information to them about who to write and how to address the envelope and how to phrase the letter politely? Of course, we didn't tell him. We might have to do it again someday.

"The mail campaign was a lot of fun—and we made a lot of friends through it. Quite frankly, it expanded our knowledge and dealings with people by a great deal, so in spite of the fact that it was expensive getting all those flyers run off and mailed out, it was well worth it. It was worth it to have proven the amount of power that people have if they work together to accomplish something."

STAR TREK'S FANS

Not all the letters went to NBC.

STAR TREK received a considerable amount of fan mail itself.

For instance, there was one little boy who had evidently learned business form. His letter had his address and the date at the top, Desilu-Paramount's address, and the identification, "To STAR TREK." Then, it started out: "Dear Mr. Trek . . ." And went on from there, a very personal letter.

Then there was the woman who wrote a seven page letter, in which she very carefully explained that she was a happily married woman and this was not prurient interest, *but* she pointed out that red-blooded people have all of their extremities pink, and since Spock was supposed to be green-blooded, she wanted to know—with reference to particular extremities—if they were green.*

Bjo Trimble handled STAR TREK's fan mail for a while. "We opened all the mail," she said. "Whether it was marked personal or not. After a while, you got the feeling of being a voyeur—especially after reading seventeen page letters to William Shatner describing in *great* detail what certain women had in the way of daydreams about him. And you know, you really wonder, if they're making it up out of their own mind, and if they are then they've got a great future in dirty books—and if they *aren't*, then what kind of literature are they reading and where are they getting it? I

---

* Yes, *they*. Idle speculation around the set had it that the particular extremity this woman was inquiring about was forked . . .

haven't read very many more red-hot things than we opened in the STAR TREK fan mail. It was amazing. Really.

"We got one marvelous letter from a woman who pointed out that she was not at all prejudiced, and she really believed in equality and all of this, and since we had a Russian, which she sort of agreed with, and a Scotsman and an Oriental, there was really no need to have Nichelle Nichols . . . and so we sent her an autographed picture of Nichelle and our thanks . . .

"One little boy had a birthday coming up soon and sent a full page letter listing all the things he wanted. He wanted a bicycle and a catcher's mitt—and he named the brands, by the way, on all of these things—he wanted a suit of clothes, he wanted a scout uniform, he wanted one each of everything there was on the entire *Enterprise*, props, uniforms, one of the panels from the bridge, and he ended the thing with '—and twenty-five dollars for incidentals which I haven't thought of yet.' We sent him an autographed picture of Mr. Spock. You wonder at the crass nerve of some of these people, but he pointed out that we—meaning the entire *Enterprise* crew—had a good deal more money than he did and could afford this for him for his birthday.

"There was one boy who wanted a *working* phaser sent to him—but *not*, in case his little brother asked for one too, to his little brother. We kind of wondered how that family was getting along . . .

"One kid wanted one of Dr. McCoy's hypodermics that *worked*—and he wanted it *full*. And he named the stuff he wanted it full of. And it was the cordrazine or whatever that sent McCoy off into the twentieth century in 'City on the Edge of Forever.' I don't know—I think he was going to become the biggest pusher in his neighborhood or something . . .

"We got letters with—what I hoped were inadvertent—innuendos. One girl wanted William Shatner to come to her graduation and stay overnight at her house and go with her to the prom. She pointed out that this would give her a good deal of status among her girl friends—especially his staying overnight at the house. And then ended her letter with, 'In case you'd like to know what you're getting into, here's my picture ...' We're still not awfully sure if she understood what she was saying or not ...

"And we got one little group of kids from Colorado who had decided that—after seeing 'Mirror, Mirror,'—that Kirk needed a 'Captain's Woman.' They wanted Stefanie Powers (*The Girl from U.N.C.L.E.*) to play the part. And after about the fifteenth letter from the fifteenth different child on this point, I finally wrote back to the two ringleaders and I said, 'I'm not awfully sure you understand what a "Captain's Woman" is, but she's not a very nice lady and I suggest you talk to your mother ...' We never heard from them again. It really tickled us though, we kept getting these letters: 'Kirk needs a "Captain's Woman," ' and I kept thinking he'd probably agree ..."

There were other letters too.

After "The Trouble with Tribbles" was telecast in 1967, for a while, almost every letter received included a request for one of the tribbles. (These were little fuzzy creatures that bred like crazy till Captain Kirk was up to his neck in them.) "Surely you have so many of them ..." was the general theme, "you can certainly spare one or two. I know you must have millions, I saw them on the show." Nope. Only five hundred.* But how do you explain that to twenty million fans?

---

* What happened to the original tribbles? Well, a few of them went to the fans, others went to the children of the cast and crew—but most of them were donated to a good cause. In April of 1969, I co-produced a live television auction to raise money to keep Los Angeles' educational station, KCET, Channel 28, on the air. STAR TREK Enterprises (then known as Lincoln Enterprises) donated some of their decals, catalogues and photographs, as well as film clips. Ballantine Books donated fifty copies of *The Making of Star Trek*, by Stephen Whitfield, which Gene

Some of the letter-writers thought that the tribbles were actually alive. They wanted to know what animals were used and where they could get one. And one gentleman was highly outraged that STAR TREK had been mistreating living creatures by cooping them up in a hot storage compartment, then dropping them onto a soundstage floor and photographing them under hot lights. Had the animals been properly fed, watered and cared for? He didn't think so.

In point of fact, any time any kind of living animal is used in film work, there are very strict production codes to prevent their mistreatment. The days when a film producer could stampede a herd of horses off a cliff just for an exciting shot are long past.

One of the main focuses of the fan mail, of course, was Mr. Spock.

Leonard Nimoy's characterization of the half-alien, half-human First Officer touched a particularly responsive chord in a lot of little girls—and a lot of big girls too. The pointed ears and arched eyebrows suggested great strength and masculinity with a healthy hint of controlled *evil*. But Spock's conscious suppression of emotion, as well as his unavailability as a sexual object, made him (in the words of one of these young ladies) "A safe rape. You could love him without risking your virginity."

Actually, it may have been more than that. Deep

Roddenberry and D.C. Fontana (STAR TREK's *story editor*) autographed. And Irving Feinberg, the show's propman snuck into Paramount and brought out a couple large bags of tribbles. This material was collated into about fifty separate packages and sold off at prices ranging from $5 to $25. James Doohan was the auctioneer for the tribbles and he brought in more than four hundred dollars. (It's next to impossible now to get one of the original tribbles, but "authentic" ones are still being manufactured and sold. They're as identical as possible to the originals. Write to Tribbles, Box 526, Hollywood, Calif. 90028 for information. Tell them I said it's okay.)

down inside, each of these little girls—and the big girls too—believed that she was the one who could warm up Mr. Spock. If she could be given half a chance, she could get through to him.

—And if she couldn't, well then that was just proof that no one could.

Mr. Spock, as a character, touched the *right* emotional chords. He suggested the Devil. He echoed of satyrs and Pan and elves and other unholy things—but he suppressed it. He suppressed the half of him that was human and prey to earthy desires. His self-control was an almost visible thing. His knowledge was never carnal, his being was totally rational, and a fan could approach his character on the mental level without ever having to worry about reacting physically.

And that was just right for the fans.

That many of STAR TREK's most rabid fans were teenagers was no coincidence. It was Mr. Spock that they were focused on. They identified with him and the central conflict in his life—the continuing need to control himself in an emotional environment. Most of them felt the same way themselves. Adolescence is one of the most difficult times in a human being's life. The child is having to decide what kind of an adult he is going to be. His body is changing rapidly and forcing the decision on him by giving him adult capabilities. There is no escape from this messy business of emotions and love and mating and—scariest of all, *sex.*

Mr. Spock had the answer though. Suppression. Control. Logic is the god, and emotions don't exist; relegate them to the dark underside of the mind and never never let them show. This is one of the reasons that science fiction has such an appeal to teenagers; when the adolescent has trouble accepting his transition to adulthood, he casts around for alternate worlds to live in, worlds where these difficult things don't exist or are suppressed. In Mr. Spock, they found not just an answer, but a role model.

If rabid STAR TREK fans are "Trekkies," then within that group is a subcult of "Spockies." Girls—and some boys—who focus not on science fiction, not on STAR TREK, but only on Mr. Spock. The fan mail proved this over and over. It was not all Leonard Nimoy's appeal that attracted the fans to him, but the concept of the character he played. The alienness.

For many viewers, this was their first glimpse of another kind of reality—one where things from space are not automatically monsters. This was their first real meeting with something from another planet—and it was *friendly*. They wanted to know more.

For instance, after the episode 'Journey to Babel," the fan mail poured in at an incredible rate. But it was not for Spock. The show had dealt with Spock's parents, played by Jane Wyatt and Mark Lenard—and for two weeks, the letters to Mark Lenard topped even those coming in to Leonard Nimoy.

Later on, in the third season, the phenomenon was repeated again, when an ancient Vulcan philosopher showed up in "The Savage Curtain." Again the fans were intrigued—and again they wrote in. They demanded to see more of Surak, who was played by Barry Atwater.

Clearly, it was not just Spock alone—although he played a large part in it—it was the whole Vulcan concept: cool, rational beings, in complete command of themselves, non-violent, curious and super-intelligent. Whatever emotions they had were under control—or else channeled and heavily ritualized, as for instance, the seven-year sexual cycle, which, when it did occur, was irresistibly strong. Nimoy's performance added a dimension of enormous, *unused* strength, and of dry humor occasionally. But probably, the keynote appeal of Vulcans was their controlled strength.

The majority of STAR TREK's fans, however, were not so limited in their involvement as the "Spockies." Most of them were primarily intrigued with the show's format: the idea of a giant starship exploring the galaxy, each week touching upon strange and exotic new worlds, experiencing fantastic adventures and meeting incredible beings, was clearly one of the most dazzling formats in television. Also one of the most difficult. Former producer, Gene L. Coon believed it to be "the hardest show in television history to write for."

Unlike other television series, STAR TREK demanded more involvement from its viewers. A certain familiarity with advanced technology was implied, but the show had so *many* devices and wonders that it simply could not present all of them in every episode. Phasers and spaceships can be taken for granted by an uninitiated audience, but try and remember—how many episodes did you have to watch before you began to *understand* the transporter? Or the ship's computer? Or the sick bay? —Or Vulcans?

The background of the show was too broad. A whole new culture had to be presented. The only way to do it was cumulatively, from show to show. It took at least four or five weeks of steady viewing to gain a degree of familiarity with Gene Roddenberry's universe, but there were always new discoveries to be made and you had to watch regularly to keep up with them. At the end of the first year, only the broad outlines had been sketched, the details still had to be filled in.

Both as television, and as science fiction, STAR TREK had its weaknesses, but despite whatever drawbacks it had, it still succeeded in fulfilling the functions of both of those mediums. As television, it entertained, and as science fiction, it stretched the mind. STAR TREK widened a lot of horizons—right out to the edge of the galaxy. And maybe even a little bit beyond.

And the fans responded.

If STAR TREK demanded an involvement, the fans were more than willing to meet it. STAR TREK fandom grew in direct response to the show. It grew slowly at first—the phenomenon wasn't really recognized as a social force in its own right until STAR TREK had already been on the air for two years. And few people realized the extent of the phenomenon until the show was already off the air. (If they had, it might not have gone off the air, but that's another story.)

Trekkies have often been compared with Groupies. In one respect, the comparison is apt. Groupies follow rock stars around, hoping to share in the fame and magic of the superstar experience. Trekkies respond to STAR TREK the same way—but much more intensely. And in that respect, the comparison with Groupies is unfair. For one thing, being a Trekkie involves a hell of a lot more work.

All that a Groupie has to do is devote herself slavishly to her particular rock idols, collect their albums and newspaper clippings and attend their concerts and try to get in backstage. The responsibilities of a Trekkie are much more demanding.

A Trekkie not only keeps careful tabs on everyone involved with STAR TREK, she—(generally, Trekkies are adolescent or post-adolescent girls, but not always)—she collects film clips, publishes fanzines, writes her own STAR TREK stories—usually with herself as heroine, she keeps scrapbooks, she sews up costumes and uniforms for herself to match the ones on the show, she learns how to make herself up as a Vulcan, she corresponds endlessly with other Trekkies, and so on . . .

And there are the conventions.

There are at least a dozen science fiction conventions every year. The World Science Fiction Convention, at which the International Hugo Award for excellence in science fiction is presented, usually commands an attendance of two thousand or more fans and writers from all over the world. Major regional conventions usually have attendances of at least five or six hundred, and even a small local convention can depend on fifty or sixty people from the surrounding area, minimum. And there are somewhere in the neighborhood of two hundred of these local conventions a year. Although the main focus of all of these conventions is science fiction, comics or movies, STAR TREK is usually well represented.

There are always a few Trekkies who show up to trade their film clips and wear their costumes and sell their STAR TREK fanzines. They flash each other the Vulcan Peace Sign and exchange such logical salutations as, "May you live long and prosper."

If a convention holds a masquerade ball, there will always be at least one or two STAR TREK costumes. If there is a huckster room, there will be at least one or two people selling STAR TREK memorabilia. If there are any panel discussions on science fiction and the dramatic arts, STAR TREK will always be mentioned.

This is not to imply that all science fiction fans are Trekkies, or vice versa. On the contrary, the two groups are quite distinct. Science fiction fandom existed long before STAR TREK, and science fiction fans regard STAR TREK as just one more science fiction TV show, moderately enjoyable and better than most. On the other hand, Trekkies regard STAR TREK as the *raison d'être* of science fiction, as if all the rest were merely preparation and STAR TREK the proper pinnacle of accomplishment.

This dichotomy is mainly a matter of attitude. There is no civil war between the two groups. Fans are generally a pretty tolerant lot: "I won't pee on your tree if you won't pee on mine."

Science fiction fandom has seen a lot of changes in the past thirty years. The development of the STAR TREK phenomenon is just one more in a succession of violent wrenches to the fannish consciousness. The subculture has gone through at least eight or nine generations of fans, and science fiction aficionados have seen a lot of their dreams come true and many of their predictions realized. Fandom itself has almost risen to respectability along with science fiction.

Many of the older fans still remember that science fiction began as a "junk" literature, and it has a long heritage of pulp fiction in its history, stretching back beyond Buck Rogers and *Thrilling Wonder Stories*, back to before World War I when Hugo Gernsback was publishing "scientific fiction" stories in his *Modern Electrics Magazine*.

To many of the more seasoned SF fans (anyone who has been around for five years or more) STAR TREK is just the contemporary form of "junk." That is, at the moment, it's the lowest common denominator in science fiction. Its appeal is on the gut level and its stories tend more toward action than idea. It is science fiction for the masses. Hence, many of the older fans are a bit skeptical of the hardcore Trekkies.

Nevertheless, STAR TREK's science fiction, while not always believable, still attempted to stress a maturity of approach against a generally credible background. Despite the restrictions of television production, every effort was made to keep the special effects and other production values as accurate as possible. If STAR TREK is now "the lowest common denominator," then that just demonstrates science fiction's amazing capacity for growth. In the B-pictures that were being made in the fifties, and even the early sixties, like as not, the spaceships were stock shots of old V-2's—and later on, Saturn V's and other missiles. Alien planets were usually Griffith Park.

Until very recently—i.e. post-STAR TREK and post-, *2001: A Space Odyssey*— TV and motion picture handling of science fiction (with rare exceptions such as George Pal's efforts) was thirty to forty years behind science fiction in the written form. It was still rooting around in old-fashioned space opera, bems (bug-eyed monsters) and the like. STAR TREK represented an extraordinary leap, and most of the science fiction world recognized it.

STAR TREK may very well be the spiritual descendant of Buck Rogers, but the difference is a couple of orders of magnitude—especially in sophistication and credibility.

Science fiction fans have a slogan-derived acronym to express their attitude toward fannish activities: FIAWOL—it means, "Fandom is a way of life." Conversely, other fans, who don't take the thing too seriously, insist on FIJAGH: "Fandom is just a goddamn hobby."

Both are correct, of course. It just depends on the individual's attitude.

Fandom—any fandom—is a subculture, and subculture means "way of life." But in order for a subculture to be viable, it has to be rich enough in structure and detail to be consistent. Otherwise, it's not a subculture at all; it's a fetish, a compulsion, an obsession.

Science fiction fandom has long since demonstrated its viability as a subculture. Whether or not STAR TREK fandom can also do so remains to be seen.

Unfortunately, this distinction seems to have escaped some of the more fanatic Trekkies, some of the organizers of fan clubs and publishers of fanzines. Because STAR TREK appeared to take place within a viable and consistent culture, some hardcore Trekkies believe that a permanent fandom can be engendered simply by adopting the STAR TREK culture—or as much of it as was shown or implied—wholeheartedly. The difference between a culture and the illusion of one eludes them.

These are the people who have forgotten that STAR TREK was only a TV show. They've so immersed themselves in it that they've lost touch with reality.

Some cases in point, some good, some bad; judge for yourself which of these are head cases:

One woman had her marriage break up because of

STAR TREK. She lost her job because of her over-involvement in fan activities and later she left her husband to be a full time Trekkie.

A young boy of about sixteen has exploited his natural resemblance to Leonard Nimoy by cutting his hair and shaping his eyebrows into a Vulcan style. He almost always affects a blue velour shirt and has adopted so many of Mr. Spock's mannerisms and gestures that they are no longer an act and have become part of his own demeanor. To all extents and purposes, he *is* Spock. Recently, he has teamed up with a Shatner look-alike of the same age . . .

For a while, there was a group of girls who were practicing black magic rituals designed to make their favorite STAR TREK stars fall in love with them. They were stopped only when warned that every hour of black magic practiced takes a year off one's personal beauty.

And there's a woman who's trying to compile a list of *all* STAR TREK fans and fanzines in the United States. Either she intends to publish the ultimate index of the ultimate fanzine, one or the other. Other *Trekfans* are busy writing their own STAR TREK novels—although they have no hope of ever having them published—because they don't like the books that James Blish is doing.

In Los Angeles, a fellow named Roger Heisman has managed to glom onto the actual *Enterprise* shuttlecraft, the full-size mockup that was used in several episodes, particularly "Galileo Seven." He has it on his front lawn and is trying to restore it, inside and out. (The interior of the shuttlecraft never had an actual set inside it; Heisman is building one.) He has also made himself a STAR TREK uniform and props such as phasers and communicators. His props are so accurate as to be indistinguishable from the originals. He has also tried to build himself a bridge set.

Along the same lines, in Poughkeepsie, New York,

Michael McMaster and Art Brumaghim have actually built their own bridge set and a transporter room to actually make their own STAR TREK movie. The set covers a half-circle, from Mr. Spock's science station to Mr. Scott's station to the right of the elevator. There is a captain's chair and a pilot console. They have also made costumes and props identical to those used on the show. The effect was so accurate that they even fooled Gene Roddenberry with it. At a STAR TREK convention in Detroit in October of 1972, McMaster handed Roddenberry a photograph and asked him if he could identify what was wrong with the picture. Roddenberry stared at it for a while and finally said, "Well, the Captain is wearing glasses—" And then he realized what he was saying and took a closer look. "This isn't my bridge set—!" McMaster and Brumaghim's effort was truly a labor of love; their plans were based entirely on the floorplan of the bridge in *The Making of* STAR TREK, and microscopic study of film clips ordered from STAR TREK Enterprises.

There are other fans who have attempted the same kinds of effort, but not on so vast a scale. Many of the female STAR TREK fans confine their efforts to building costumes that they can wear, costumes based on various episodes or characters. Others form STAR TREK clubs and act out various episodes.

This author's personal favorite is the sweet little old lady in Southern California who has tape recorded every single STAR TREK episode—for the express purpose of later dubbing in her own voice over the leading lady's.

These people are "STAR TREK nuts" but most of them are *good* "nuts" because they can still relate to the rest of the world—and they've channeled their interest into constructive outlets; building, writing and creating. Others, like the black magic crew, having gone off the deep end, do great damage not only to themselves, but to others as well. And in the truly *extreme* cases, this kind of fanaticism is pitiable. For instance, one girl ran away from home to go to Hollywood and try to move in with Leonard Nimoy. She chased after him for months, in general making his life miserable. In the process she managed to interfere with shooting schedules, personal lives and the nerves of everybody she came in contact with.

There's an explanation for this kind of reaction. It involves, first of all, the medium of television and the star system. Week after week, television brings the actors into the individual's home, forces a kind of pseudo-intimacy, creates the illusion of friendship where no relationship exists at all. The people on the tube are giving off signals of "I like you, you're a part of my tribe and my family," but it's only an act—and when a fan meets the actors and tries to respond to those perceived signals of intimacy, he or she slams up against the brick wall of "Who are you? You're not in my tribe or family. I don't even know you." It's very frustrating. Television creates the illusion that one has shared a meaningful experience with the actors, but in real life, the fan finds that the actors have not experienced it the same way.

All stars run into this—there's only one William Shatner; there are millions of William Shatner fans. All of them know who he is, but to him, they're all a sea of blurred faces. He can't even begin to make the effort. He has to concentrate on being William Shatner the actor first, because in the long run that's the best way that he can serve *all* of his fans. The same applies to any man or woman who becomes a star.

But being a star also means being conspicuous. It means standing just a little bit taller than everybody else—means being *noticeable*.

And when you're noticeable, you're a target.

You can't know who's aiming at you or with what; they're lost somewhere in that mob—but they can see you and they're projecting all of their hopes onto your existence. Your life is theirs. They're using you as a focus for their fears, their hostilities, their prejudices, hangups and neuroses. When you're a star, you're a magnet for all of that.

If it were possible for a star to somehow stop being a *star*, to step down and just be an ordinary human being and relate like any other human being, the fans wouldn't like it—they'd react negatively. Fans don't want their idols to be human. An idol must be first of all an *idol*. He must be bigger then life. The fans don't want to know about his warts. They only want to worship.

In twentieth century America, the movie star still reigns supreme as the number one god in the pantheon. This is the guy who lives the life style you'd like to, but can't—so he lives it for you. Steve McQueen races motorcycles, and Liz Taylor keeps a yacht in London, and John Wayne has a ranch in Arizona, and Frank Sinatra has his own private helipad in Palm Springs. A fan's hunger to delve into the personal lives of the stars is not because he wants to see them reduced to being just people, but because he wants to know that even when they brush their teeth or drink their beer, they do it with *style*. The more personal detail the fan can come by, the more closely he can identify with his larger-than-life hero.

There's a big wide world out there—and it's full of excitement. The stars and the show become the vehicle for the fans' identification with that exciting world.

STAR TREK not only proved this, it expanded on the relationship by a couple of orders of magnitude. Instead of merely a world, STAR TREK made its fans aware of a whole galaxy, a universe, made them realize that Earth was merely one speck of matter in a tiny corner of space and time. There's all the future and all the past—and all of space stretching in all directions. The concept is almost frightening. You need something to hang onto; you certainly need a couple of strong au-

thority-images to identify with. The *Enterprise* filled
the need for a stable frame of reference, and Kirk and
Spock (and the rest of the crew) provided the emotional
reassurance. The way the show was set up, STAR TREK
made it almost safe to confront the rest of the universe.

The interesting thing about the STAR TREK fan
phenomenon is that just when it should have died
away—it began to grow.

Many of the really extreme Trekkies began to fade
after the show went out of production, after the sets
were torn down, the cast and crew dispersed to other
projects and there was no longer any hope of getting
STAR TREK resurrected just one more time. Some of
these Trekkies grew up, others just grew older, but the
effect was the same—they lost interest and moved on to
other things.

To those who had any connection at all with the
show, it seemed that this outward movement was the
beginning of the end. Now that there were no longer
any new STAR TREK episodes being produced, the intensity of the fans' devotion would undoubtedly die
away. How wrong they were.

For almost immediately, STAR TREK went into syndication.

What this meant was that the 79 episodes that had
already been filmed were to be rerun—*endlessly*—on
local stations all across the country. Syndication is the
sale of a package of episodes to a single market, i.e. a
television station. That market can use those shows in a
variety of ways, but the most usual is to "strip" them.
"Stripping" means running one episode per weeknight,
and this was the practice that was generally used with
STAR TREK.

Now, in 1966 STAR TREK had been on Thursdays at
8:30. In 1967 it moved to Fridays at 8:30. In 1968, although it had been scheduled to appear on Mondays at

7:30 (we'll talk about that later), the show eventually
came on at 10:00 Fridays. What this meant in terms of
viewers is obvious. There weren't any—at least not
enough to justify a fourth season. The scheduling of the
show at 10 p.m. on Friday nights was an asinine thing
to do in the first place. It seemed as if NBC were trying
to ignore the show, pretend it wasn't there, and had
shuffled it into a dark corner where they hoped eventually it would just die away. By their actions, it looked
as if they were trying to kill STAR TREK. 10 p.m. was
just too late an hour for a whole generation of eager,
would-be STAR TREK fans.

Apparently, the local station managers had more
sense. When they got their hands on the STAR TREK
reruns, they knew what to do. They scheduled them for
5:00 and 6:00 and 7:00. Never any later. They knew
which audience they wanted to reach—and reach it
they did.

All the teens and pre-teens who had never seen STAR
TREK before suddenly discovered a whole new universe
of excitement; it was the same thrill of discovery that
the first generation of Trekkies had experienced only
three years before, and it was happening all over again.

As of this writing, the show has been syndicated to
146 markets. That's one mark of its popularity. Another is the fact that almost everywhere it has been
scheduled, it has wiped up the ratings race. More than
one station manager has been delighted to discover that
he has captured the lion's share of the local viewing audience with STAR TREK.

Between the hours of 4:00 and 8:00 p.m. are when
teens and pre-teens do most of their viewing. That's
valuable commercial time—time to schedule a show
that they will be sure to watch, time to sell commercials
specifically oriented toward their consumer needs.
Teenagers are one of the most volatile consumer forces
in America, one that advertisers are constantly trying to

reach. If they're watching STAR TREK, then that's the vehicle to reach them by.

The result of this is that not only did STAR TREK find a whole new audience, but that same new audience discovered STAR TREK fandom. Because the show is out of production though, these new fans have to be less actor-oriented and more story-directed. They have to be; there's very little else for them. They envy the older fans who were lucky enough to be a part of the initial excitement.

Although it seemed logical to expect that the movement would have died away with the show, it was an erroneous assumption. As Mr. Spock would have said, "Totally illogical." Because once a social structure forms, it does not easily disband. Once the links are put into place, they tend to remain in place.

Example: Bjo Trimble. Before her letter campaign, she had a mailing list of about eight hundred people who were interested in science fiction. *After* that campaign, her list had grown to twelve *thousand*. And one simply does not throw away a mailing list. If a fan is interested in STAR TREK, he might also be interested in J.R.R. Tolkien, and science fiction conventions, and *Planet of the Apes,* and fanzines and related memorabilia.

And Bjo Trimble was not alone. There was S. Cornelie Cole in Texas, and Carol Lee in New York, and the Basta sisters in Detroit, and others too numerous to mention.

These are the people who published STAR TREK fanzines, and ran STAR TREK fan clubs and wrote letters by the score. Especially intense were the fans who did *not* live in New York or California. These were the people who didn't have the convenient access to the studios or the stars. To them, the excitement was distant—unless they provided their own excitement by *making* their own. All they had was their intensity— and be damned if they were going to give that up.

Their precious links with others all over the country had been formed mostly through the mail and over the telephones (hundred dollar phone bills were not uncommon.) Ostensibly STAR TREK was the reason for all that communication—but just because STAR TREK was gone was no reason to stop communicating. The links had been established, they were going to be *used* whether STAR TREK was still around or not. A whole new world of friendship had been opened for a great many people who hungered to stretch their horizons. Anyone who thought it would be easily dismantled just by the cancellation of a TV show was a poor judge of human nature.

A couple of examples here to prove a point:

Leonard Nimoy was on a promotional tour one time. When he walked into his hotel room in Chicago, the phone rang. He answered it—it was Susan from Colorado. He chatted with her for a bit, then hung up. A few minutes later, the phone rang again, this time it was Diane from Miami. He chatted with her for a while, then begged off because he had to get ready for an appearance that evening. A few moments later, the phone rang again. This time, it was Gail in New York. Intrigued, Leonard asked how they all knew where he was. Oh, replied the girl. Susan from Colorado called Diane in Miami who called her in New York, etc.

On that same tour, he ended a phone conversation in one city, flew to another, only to find the same girl waiting on the phone for him at his new hotel room. She had found out his whole itinerary and was prepared to talk him across the country.

This is the STAR TREK grapevine in action. A more subdued example, but one more far-reaching in its consequences, is the incredible film-clip caper.

To properly appreciate this, you have to understand that there are a limited number of 35 millimeter film clips from STAR TREK floating around. While STAR TREK Enterprises was in business, they sold sets of these film clips to fans. The clips could be mounted in slide holders and projected exactly as any other 35mm slide. The clips are in full color and are literally a piece of the show.

These are actual clips of unused STAR TREK footage. Shots of the *Enterprise,* of Kirk and Spock, of alien beings and strange planets, of weird sets and weirder characters—anything and everything in fact that had ever appeared before the cameras. These are the beginnings and endings of shots, the parts that are edited out, these are duplicate work prints, outtakes, unusable sequences and other assorted sweepings from the cutting room floor. They're of no worth to anybody—except a STAR TREK fan.

(Want to play STAR TREK Trivia? Two Trekkies and a pile of slides. Each one picks a slide and has to identify it—what show is this from, who are the actors involved, what characters do they play, and what's going on in this scene? A real Trekkie can identify the episode by the characters in the scene, the cut of a costume, or even the lighting of a background. Miss three times, and obviously you're just a Klingon imposter.)

These film clips are in great demand by the fans—after all, being able to project Captain Kirk or Mr. Spock onto a wall-sized screen can be almost as exciting as an episode itself. STAR TREK's visuals were almost always dramatic—if you've ever seen them projected, rather than just on a TV screen, you know what I mean. And if all you ever had was just a small black and white TV set, then a color slide is even more overpowering.

The interesting thing is that these film clips came out of Paramount in batches—and were being released in batches by STAR TREK Enterprises. For example, in late '69, they were still only working on the episodes of late '67. That is, when the show went off the air, they were only halfway through the second season.

But one of the people who keeps tabs on STAR TREK

Fandom noticed a funny thing. There were slides from the third season floating around. And there shouldn't be. Not yet. STAR TREK Enterprises hadn't gotten that far.

For a while, this was a minor mystery among certain circles—where were these film clips coming from? Certainly from no source that anyone knew or would admit to. Not even the big-name fans, the presidents of fan clubs, or wheeler-dealers knew.

Finally, one of the sources was pinned down, a teenage girl who admitted how she had gotten her clips. When STAR TREK went into syndication, each local station began cutting bits and pieces out of each episode, so as to make more time for commercials.*

This little girl had gotten a phone call from one of her friends in another city, who had heard about it from a friend in still another city. (And so on.) It seems that somewhere, some little Trekkie had approached the local station in her area, gotten friendly with the film cutter, and asked what he was doing with the pieces he was cutting out of the STAR TREK shows. He told her that he was throwing them away. They were no good to anyone. She got friendlier then and said, "Oh, don't throw them away. Save them for me. I collect them." Just how friendly she had to get in order to accomplish this goal is not known. (But I suspect that very few film cutters resented this attention.)

In any case, she then proceeded to phone all of her friends in other cities where STAR TREK was being syndicated. And shortly thereafter, other film cutters at other local stations found themselves being approached by pretty (and sometimes not-so-pretty) young girls

---

* I know. I cringe too at the thought. Some of these cuts were horrendous. Whole episodes were emasculated by the ill-timed dropping of a single scene. Unfortunately, this was necessary to make that all-important commercial time available—otherwise the station couldn't afford STAR TREK in the first place. Fortunately, most of the episodes held up well; they were able to withstand even that amount of abuse.

who were only too eager to be friendly in return for
one small favor . . .

And then they called their friends in other cities . . .

STAR TREK has been syndicated in 146 markets. You
figure it out.

The extent of the STAR TREK phenomenon can be
partially gauged by the number of fanzines and fan
clubs devoted exclusively to the show.

For instance, the fanzines.

All it takes to produce a fanzine is one fan and a
typewriter. And some enthusiasm. Journalistic ability is
no prerequisite at all, but a good mimeo is. A fanzine is
judged as much by its reproduction as by its content.

The average fanzine is published at the whim of the
fan. That makes it about as regular as a spastic colon,
and gives it about the same life expectancy as an Italian government. Which is to say, not very and not long.

But despite all this, fanzines have one saving grace.
They're fun.

In general, a fanzine is a fairly accurate reflection of
what is going on in its writer's mind—whether the
writer intended that or not.

Further, as an avenue of communication, a fanzine
functions as a scatter-gun. It allows a writer to communicate not to just one person at a time, but many people. And a fanzine is a time machine too—the writer's
words are being preserved on paper and thus sent into
the future so that other fans, months and years removed, can share their feelings and reactions.

STAR TREK fanzines are all of this. Generally, they
drip with enthusiasm for STAR TREK, its cast and crew.
The articles tend to be analyses of the show in general
or reviews of specific episodes, articles about individual
cast members or the characters they play, fan-written
STAR TREK adventures, and occasionally interviews or
news reports. STAR TREK fanzines also contain excited
reports of STAR TREK activities at recent conventions,
and in the days when the show was still in production,

often published articles by fans who had been lucky enough to visit the actual sets.

The fanzines began shortly after STAR TREK appeared on the air. As the Trek-fans discovered science fiction fandom, they began to adopt more and more of its conventions. (Pun intended, but more about that later.) Articles about STAR TREK in science fiction fanzines turned into STAR TREK fanzines with occasional science fiction articles.

As the STAR TREK phenomenon developed and grew, more and more of the Trekkies, many of whom had never heard of science fiction fandom before STAR TREK, began to put out their own zines. They paid little attention to either tradition or structure—but then again, few fans do—substituting enthusiasm instead. In science fiction fandom, however, gross displays of enthusiasm are considered neo-fannish, hence *gauche*. But because of the nature of the two fandoms, they must share the same space-time continuum.

Some of the fanzines that have been published include *Eridani Triad, Pastaklan Vesla* (A Horta Press Publication), *Spock's Showcase, Terran Times, The Nimoyan, Retrospect* (Spotlight on Leonard Nimoy), *Deck 6, Faunch, Grup, Babel, Vorpal Sword, Anti-Matter,* Spock's Scribes' *Storyteller, Impulse, Leonard Nimoy Power, LNSTFCCF* (Leonard Nimoy Star Trek Fan Club of Concerned Fans), *Masiform-D, Nimoyan Digest, Nuts and Bolts Work Sheet, Pentathlon, Spockanalia, Star Date, Star-Fleet Communications, S. T. Phile, T-Negative, Kevas & Trillium, The Voyages, The William Shatner Letter Exchange, Gonomony, Guardian of Forever, Kraith Collected, Log of the U.S.S.* Enterprise, *NCC 1701, LNAF* (Leonard Nimoy Association of Fans), *Nimoyan Federation, Overload* (A Scotty zine), *Quadrant, Star Base Omega, Star-Borne, Stargram, Star Trek Song Book, Tholiam Web, Triskelion,* and *A Taste of Armageddon.* (No, I do not know where you can order any of these.)

To be perfectly fair, there's quite a bit of overlap in the production of these fanzines. Some of them are produced by the same groups of people. However, also being fair, this list is by no means complete. The 45 fanzines listed above are probably only the tip of the iceberg, the better distributed fanzines. Each fanzine only indicates a nexus of fans and fannish interests. The existence of one fanzine implies the existence of others.

STAR TREK fanzines, of course, are of limited interest—except, of course, to those who are STAR TREK fans. One of the side effects of fannishness, however, is that as the degree of enthusiasm increases, the critical facilities seem to decrease. The more enthusiastic of STAR TREK'S fans seem to be blind to the show's faults—as well as to reality.

A lot of the female STAR TREK fans spend much of their time writing new STAR TREK stories—generally, there is a teenage girl in the story somewhere, a personification of the author, who acts out her wish-fantasy with the appropriate STAR TREK character. For instance, a young Brooklyn girl wrote a complete STAR TREK script about McCoy's long lost daughter. And when she comes aboard the *Enterprise,* Kirk falls in love with her. At one point, he even decides to quit the service to marry the girl. Unfortunately, at that moment, the *Enterprise* is attacked by a Klingon warship and Kirk rushes to the bridge, forcing the girl to realize that Kirk is already married—to his ship. End of story.

The author of this effort even went so far as to have the script mimeographed in the exact format that Paramount Studios used for the real STAR TREK scripts. The result was an almost-convincing fake.

Other fans, less ambitious, limited themselves to short stories—but again about the *Enterprise* and its crew. Almost every Trek-zine has at least one of these efforts, usually several.

Other STAR TREK fans, determined to be pros someday, are writing their own STAR TREK novels.* At the time of this writing, however, the only publisher authorized to print STAR TREK *fiction* is Bantam Books. They have an exclusive arrangement with James Blish (a noted author and critic in his own right) to do story adaptions of many of the STAR TREK episodes as well as an original STAR TREK novel (with another in the works).

So far, Blish has done nine STAR TREK books. Bantam has sold about four million of them, an average of five hundred thousand copies each. And the books continue to sell as fast as Bantam can print them.

This author met James Blish in England in 1971 and asked him about his STAR TREK books, how he felt about them. What he said stuck in my memory, and when I began to conceive of this book about STAR TREK, I wrote to him asking if I might repeat his comments here. He replied quickly and graciously:

". . . When I was first offered the job, I had misgivings, because it looked purely mechanical from my side. At the time, I had a regular job and my writing was all moonlighting, as had been the situation for many years, and I felt that I'd be better off working on my own characters and ideas. But I had a use for the money, so I went ahead. I enjoyed the work more than I had expected to—some of it was actually fun, such as contriving explanations for situations which couldn't have been shown in the dramatized form—but when I finished the first book, I had almost decided not to do another.

"Then the fan mail began to come in, and it has kept

---

* I know of one that has been mimeographed and is being sold through the mails. I should point out here that it is an illegal effort. Paramount Pictures owns the rights to STAR TREK, and any *unauthorized* use of the STAR TREK characters is a violation of the copyright laws. A novel published and sold through the mails is an infringement on the rights of both Paramount and Bantam Books. The practice is to be discouraged; it is equal to stealing.

on coming in, averaging three letters a day over nearly five years. I have received more letters about the ST books than I have about the entire body of my original work, despite the fact that almost all of my other books are still in print.

"I've analyzed this mail in one of the ST prefaces. Here it's sufficient to say that most of the writers, in addition to urging me to go on, said that prior to STAR TREK they either hadn't encountered any science fiction, or hadn't liked what they had seen (mostly, I gather, monster movies). Many of them asked me to recommend other books, not only of my own, but by other writers; and while I couldn't even begin to answer all the mail, I did and still do answer requests of that kind.

"The conclusion seemed inescapable to me that STAR TREK had opened up a whole new audience—mostly very young—for science fiction, and that it was a far larger audience than any the genre had ever had before. This seemed to me to be eminently worth fostering, for all of us as well as for myself, so—despite some sneers from older fans and even a few writers—I changed my mind and went ahead. There are now eight books of script adaptions and one novel (*Spock Must Die!*) and it looks like I'll continue until all the scripts have been used up, and maybe even two books beyond that. It depends, of course, on how well the sales hold up, but I plan to stay with it as long as the audience does."

By far the most impressive aspect of the STAR TREK phenomenon is the STAR TREK convention.

Science fiction conventions are nothing new, there

have been science fiction conventions for more than three decades; the old time fans have seen the style in conventions change just as the styles of science fiction have changed—but through all the changes, one thing remains the same, the attendees continue to be the young and enthusiastic. Starry-eyed and caught up with the sense of wonder, the average con-goer is in his late teens or early twenties, probably wears glasses, is an only child, and in some way, somehow is out of the ordinary in either appearance or mental processes. A goodly proportion of them have I.Q.s higher than average, many are in the genius range.

A fan's mind is like a hundred-year attic—with a new wing added every six months. It's filled with fascinating artifacts and objects, some gathering dust in long unused corners and waiting for the right stimulus to call them forth again, others still glittering in their plastic wraps, never having been opened, simply deposited out of the way on the off chance that someday they might be needed. A fan is a textbook of the interesting and arcane. Three fans are an encyclopedia. Ten fans are a whole library. And if you can gather enough fans together, say two thousand, you will have gathered all the knowledge of the universe in one place. It's called a convention. (What you do with it then is up to you.)

Star Trek's first episode was presented to the attendees of the 1966 Worldcon in Cleveland, Ohio. (Worldcons are traditionally held over Labor Day weekends, and are generally the biggest convention of the year.) The audience of science fiction fans of all ages gave it a standing ovation.

As the show came to be aired and Star Trek fandom began to develop as an entity, many of its members came from outside fandom. At first, science fiction fandom was the only "organized" outlet for their enthusiasm—so they flocked to the science fiction fan clubs hoping that they would be Star Trek fan clubs. Unfortunately, they weren't. SF fandom would have appreciated the influx of new blood except for two things. First, the phenomenon was growing so fast that there were too many Trek-fans to be assimilated, they threatened the long-time traditions and structures of whatever group they joined. The interest of the Trekkies in STAR TREK was so all-consuming that it threatened to swamp everything in sight. They didn't want to hear about Asimov's laws of robotics or Heinlein's method of grokking. They only wanted to talk about Kirk and Spock and the *Enterprise*. And to them, that was the sum total of science fiction.

Naturally, some of the SF fans reacted negatively. Their identities were being threatened. What they held dear was being ignored in favor of what was to them, merely a laudable effort. The science fiction fans still *watched* STAR TREK. They simply didn't believe it was the most perfect creative effort any form of science fiction had ever seen.

So when the Trekkies came to the cons, they were coming as a special interest group—to be tolerated, but not necessarily honored. They were entitled to the same rights and privileges as any other special interest group—say the Mythopoeic Society, or the Creative Anachronists, or the Count Dracula Society—but they were not the stars of the con, not by a long shot.

—At least, not until a group of New York Trek-fans got the idea of putting on a convention to be *only* about STAR TREK. They scheduled it for January of 1972 and planned it to be a quiet little weekend for about 600 people, a "relaxi-con" if you will.

Nearly 4,000 people showed up.

After 3,300 paid memberships, the committee stopped counting. After that, it was free, and at least another 500 people came in.

The STAR TREK con was an imitation of a science fiction convention—only filtered through Gene Roddenberry's universe. All the films shown were STAR TREK episodes, all the panels were about aspects of the show, and the biggest celebrities were Gene and Majel Roddenberry, D.C. Fontana, and Isaac Asimov. Most of the hucksters were peddling STAR TREK film clips, fanzines and other memorabilia. Most of the costumes at the masquerade were derived from the series—and all of it was a hell of a lot of fun for the people who were there.

(A side note here. A lady who attends World SF Conventions regularly, compared the STAR TREK Convention to the most recent Worldcon. "Much nicer," she said. "The people are a much gentler breed of fan—and *polite!* It was a pleasure, really a pleasure.") (Perhaps it's because STAR TREK remains their central interest, not fandom. Or perhaps it's because they simply don't know each other well enough yet ... Most science fiction fans know each other too well.)

That first STAR TREK convention was so successful that a second one began planning almost immediately. And a third. And a fourth. And others ... Detroit in October. New York in February. Los Angeles in April. New Orleans in June. And so on.

While there is some degree of overlap in the planning of these things, each convention generally represents a different group of STAR TREK fans. For instance, Equicon, planned for Los Angeles (Easter of '73) is being organized by a Hollywood-based group. In their enthusiasm, they have sought out nearly every human being in this corner of the galaxy who ever had anything to do with the show. Because they want to put on the biggest and best STAR TREK convention ever, they have explored the possibility of rebuilding the bridge set of the *Enterprise,* retrieving the shuttlecraft, and assembling the original cast of the series. Because the convention is scheduled for Los Angeles, most of the cast and crew will attend.

These conventions are a joyous celebration of STAR TREK as a way of life. They are fun because STAR

TREK was fun. At first glance—especially to the mundane outsider—the whole thing might seem kind of nutty. But it isn't.

The subvocal message of STAR TREK was optimistic—there *will* be a future. And it will be a good one. We will all live in it together. We will all accept each other as equals.

With rare exception, the STAR TREK fans are trying to bring that kind of future about by living in it now.

And that's not so nutty at all.

PART FOUR

Star Trek Analyzed—The Unfulfilled Potential

Good television is produced by good teams. A good team needs a strong Captain, one who not only knows what he wants to do, but one who is respected, admired, and liked by his crew. Gene Roddenberry is such a producer. Above all, the team works to Gene Roddenberry's plan. Dorothy Fontana, story editor on STAR TREK, once said—and this is an important clue to *why* STAR TREK worked—"When Gene wasn't available and we had a problem that had to be solved, we tried to ask ourselves, 'How would Gene do it?'"

That Gene Roddenberry had the basics correct is undeniable. Proof of it is the fact that STAR TREK has affected the face of modern science fiction as thoroughly as any book or movie before it.

Some forerunners: Hugo Gernsback created the pulp science fiction format—today's SF magazines are the direct descendants. Isaac Asimov thought up the three laws of robotics—thereby changing the concept of robots for all time to come. John W. Campbell created a particular kind of "hard-core" science fiction as typified by the kind of stories he purchased for *Astounding,* then *Analog* science fiction. Stanley Kubrick set a new standard for visual science fiction with his motion picture, *2001: A Space Odyssey*; his accomplishment is a landmark against which all others will be judged.

Just as Kubrick changed the face of motion picture SF, so did Gene Roddenberry establish a new level of quality for television science fiction. No more *Time Tunnel,* no more *Voyage to the Bottom of the Sea,* no more *Lost in Space.* In effect, *Gene Roddenberry was saying,* "Let there be a believable and realistic format,

203

a background against which to tell fantastic and dramatic adventures. Begone with your childish fantasies—from this point on, television science fiction will *mature!*"

STAR TREK didn't always reach this goal, of course—but at least, it was always trying.

Let me digress for a moment to make a point. STAR TREK is the visualization of such a basic concept that it is a whole genre of science fiction: the spaceship exploring new worlds.

While Gene Roddenberry did not create the original concept, he fleshed it out so completely that all future motion picture or television attempts to explore this area will be forced to solve many of their problems the same way that STAR TREK did.

Just as it is impossible to write a science fiction story about robots without being aware of Isaac Asimov's massive body of work in the area, it will be impossible to do stories about interstellar explorers without recognition of the ground covered by STAR TREK.

Example: you're a producer, you're going to make a series about a spaceship and its crew. Start thinking: how big a ship? Who are the crew? Male? Female? Mixed? How many? What are their duties? What does the bridge look like? What will the weapons be called? What do they look like? How do they work? What kind of communication system will you have? What do the hand units look like? What do the crew's uniforms look like? And what kind of adventures will they have? No matter what you do, you will be repeating STAR TREK's original questions, and no matter what your answers are, the comparisons will be unavoidable. STAR TREK covered the area too well.

Remember a movie called *Forbidden Planet?* It was made in 1956, long before STAR TREK was ever conceived, and starred Leslie Neilsen, Walter Pidgeon and Anne Francis. The picture is about a military spaceship that lands on Altair IV looking for survivors of a lost mission. They find one survivor, a scientist, and his eighteen-year-old daughter. They also find the artifacts of a highly advanced civilization, and a strange powerful force that kills in the night. The movie could almost be an episode of STAR TREK.

The men who made that movie had to solve the same problems as Gene Roddenberry did with STAR TREK. Some of the solutions were different, some were disturbingly the same. If you were to view *Forbidden Planet* today—it holds up surprisingly well—not knowing whether it had been made before or after STAR TREK, you might be struck by too many resemblances between the two. It is easy to suspect that one was influenced by the other. The Captain of the ship is too Kirk-like, especially in his relationships with the other characters, particularly the ship's doctor. The hand props of the picture, and the suggested technology—all of these imply a vast culture with science to match. But most of all, the attitudes of the central characters are indistinguishable from those of the crew of the *Enterprise*. Leslie Neilsen's J.J. Adams and William Shatner's James T. Kirk would be equally at home on each other's spaceships.

A more current example of STAR TREK'S overall *completeness* is shown by the problems encountered in the writing of a post-STAR TREK television effort, a 90-minute script called "The Winds of Space." It is a pilot for a new series (not yet sold) written by Dorothy Fontana and due to be directed by Douglas Trumbull and Michael Gruskoff, the team who made *Silent Running*. The story is about a different spaceship and a different crew (three men, one woman, one drone)—but the same basic format problems have to be solved. The only difference is the shape of the answers. At one point in the writing, Dorothy Fontana felt so uncomfortable about having to repeat some of STAR TREK'S answers that she called Gene Roddenberry to talk to him about it.

Is the weapon a phaser or a stun-gun? Is the device a communicator or a hand-mike? Is the craft a shuttle or a scout? Is it a different name or a different answer?

The genre has already been too fully fleshed, too completely developed. The existence of certain conventions is taken for granted. Good answers don't change unless the context does.

In developing STAR TREK as he did, Gene Roddenberry accomplished a feat of no small magnitude. Whatever else one may say about STAR TREK and how well it accomplished its goals, one cannot deny that it established *a new genre for television*—a genre as distinct and rigid as the Western, the Cop show, the Private Eye, the Doctor series, and the situation comedy. Gene Roddenberry developed "the STAR TREK format."

And any further series about men in space will have to pay the price in the similarity they will bear to the original.

STAR TREK wasn't the first place the concept of men exploring the galaxy appeared—but then again, Shakespeare wasn't the first writer to deal with Troilus and Cressida. Shakespeare just did it a little bit better. And so did Roddenberry.

The difference is that when Shakespeare was through with *Troilus and Cressida* it was recognized as the last word on the subject and no one else attempted it. Roddenberry's STAR TREK, however, will stand not as a landmark—only as a challenge. The series will be recognized as the best statement of the form only until someone betters it. And it will be bettered. Someday. Television demands that it continue to top itself.

And that's just one more measure of the basic strength of the whole format. The Western format endures because it's a good background for stories. Same for the hospital series and the cop show. The STAR TREK format is too good, too universal for writers to leave alone.

The problem is that it's also one of the most *demanding*.

Science fiction demands, above everything else, *believability*.

Without it, the writer is only telling a fantasy. With believability comes immediacy, and an increased concern for the fate of the story's characters. But science fiction extracts a high price for believability.

The format requires visual production values—usually these are expensive. The format requires a high level of technology—and familiarity with same. The format requires characters that can understand and move through their environment easily—and that demands a high level of competency from the writer.

In a sense, the writer has to be a god. He has to create a whole world and all of its peoples. He has to know all of its physical laws and all of its geography. And if, as Shakespeare has said, "All the world's a stage," then the writer must also be a director and all the actors for the world he creates. He has to play all the roles, answer all the questions, confront all the crises, and in the end be responsible for the solutions to all the problems he has created for himself.

And if he doesn't do a good job of it—then the reader or viewer is going to feel unsatisfied and cheated.

This is especially true in television. Gene Coon, line producer for STAR TREK, and the only man other than Roddenberry who could make the show work on a regular basis, has said, "All of your production problems can be solved best *in the typewriter*. They can be solved a lot cheaper and faster than they can on the set."

Corollary to this is the fact that television's best producers often start out as writers. Both Gene Coon and Gene Roddenberry began their television careers as writers. In a sense, STAR TREK owes its success to the fact that it had good Genes.

If there is one individual who can make or break a show—whether it be a Broadway play, a multi-million-dollar motion picture, or merely a two hundred thousand dollar episode of a television series—if there is one individual whose effort is somehow more important than any other's, *it is the writer*.

No matter who else is involved in the project, the writer's effort is still the primary one. If the script is no good, there isn't a director or actor in the world who can save it. A great director can make a competent effort look like a good one, a great actor can make a mediocre part seem important—but in no case can they create what wasn't there to begin with. If it isn't in the script, then no amount of stylistic trickery or special effects can keep a bad play from being just that: a *bad* play.

STAR TREK had its share of bad episodes. In almost every case, the blame can be traced to the script. To be sure, there were episodes where some of the acting might have been less than competent, or where a director might have been especially clumsy, but if the story was *good* it generally seemed to pass unnoticed.*

It was primarily when the script was bad that STAR TREK had a poor episode.

For example:

"The Omega Glory" A thinly disguised anti-war statement. "Yangs" and "Kohms" fight an endless series of battles until the good Captain quotes the pledge of allegiance at them.

"Spock's Brain" A group of mysterious women

---

* I cite as an example of this, my own script, "The Trouble with Tribbles." Despite the fact that the production of it was unnecessarily rushed, few people have ever commented on (what seems to me) some rather hurried performances. In fact, the episode is generally regarded as one of STAR TREK's best. I believe (I'm not at all modest about it) that this is due to the overall *correctness* of the story being told.

steal Spock's brain out of his head to run their electric Mah-Jongg set. Dr. McCoy puts it back. Surprisingly, it still works.

"The Alternative Factor" Lazarus A and Lazarus B take turns flashing in and out of existence aboard the *Enterprise,* confusing Captain Kirk by seeming to be one person who can't make up his mind whether he wants to be reasonable or psychotic. Finally, in desperation, Kirk shoves both of them out an air lock.

"Spectre of the Gun" They didn't have a science fiction script—but they needed a story in a hurry—so Kirk, Spock and McCoy get to relive the gunfight at the OK corral.

And so on.

There were other bad episodes, but these four were just about the worst offenders.

Following the line of reasoning above—that the writer is ultimately responsible for a bad show—then we would have to point the finger and cry "J'accuse" at the writers of these four efforts.

—Except that one of them was written by Gene Roddenberry, and another was written by Gene Coon under a pen name.

And these were the two men who knew more about STAR TREK than anybody else.

So, who are the villains?

Why did STAR TREK have any bad episodes? If even the two top producers of the show could be responsible for weak scripts, then the cause of STAR TREK'S occasional (and in the third year, frequent) failures must be something other than just an occasional poor writer. Part of the answer is that STAR TREK was doing the equivalent of half a motion picture every six shooting days and there just wasn't time or money to do everything they wanted to do. There isn't time to polish the scripts like they should be polished.

So there are the two villains—*time* and *money*. There isn't enough of either. It is the television *produc-*

tion system itself that is responsible for failure to realize potential. Which probably comes as news to nobody, but hopefully the networks might be listening ...

STAR TREK's first season was generally regarded as its best. About this, Gene Roddenberry says, "When I do a concept for a show, if four or five or six stories don't come to me pretty fast, I know that somewhere I'm in trouble on that concept and I put it aside and start looking at it again.

"One of the interesting things about STAR TREK, talking about stories, is that I came up with—in the final premise—about 22 story ideas, and we recently made a count and I believe 15 of them were actually used in the series. I did not take screen credit for all of those stories because it was just stated in a paragraph, and the development came from someone else. During the first two years many of the scripts you saw came out of those stories. I had the same thing in *Genesis II* that I'm doing now. I sat down and in two days wrote 20 stories and when that happened I knew I was onto something.

"I think one of the mistakes of many I made on the show was that I probably should have continued that system. In between every year, I should have sat down in the show's hiatus and come up with 20 or more stories, of which maybe 10 or 12 would have set the stage for the next season. It would have saved us a great deal of time because it means instead of a writer coming and you talk a story with him and he goes home and thinks and in three or four days you talk it some more and maybe waste two or three weeks getting a story ready, he could have come in and said, 'Yes, I dig this one. There's some changes I see and so on, but wow, thematically, I think it's great,' and I say, 'Go on, we're off to work.' "

—Interestingly enough, a variation of this system has been tried on certain other shows. The producer and story editors, working with the individual script writers, hash out each story completely so the writer knows *exactly* what story he will be writing before he ever goes near a typewriter. Those who've worked this way swear by it—especially because it's fair to all parties involved.

But in 1966 through 1968, television was more firmly locked into a pattern which tended to work against the production of quality shows. A director had to shoot ten minutes of usable film per working day, he had only six days in which to make a one hour episode. (Actually 56 minutes after commercials and credits are subtracted; today that total is down to 48. More commercials, longer credits, and a tendency to show previews of the next episode have eaten up the time.)

Budgets are limited too—far more than the layman would think. For STAR TREK, a large part of each budget went for special effects—sets and actors were expensive too. There aren't many stores in Hollywood that sell authentic Rigelian furniture, it all has to be built. And every actor has to be costumed. On any other show, say a Western or a Private Eye series, much of this kind of background detail could be drawn from stock, or if necessary, purchased. But with STAR TREK, it all had to be designed and built.

As Gene Roddenberry says, "We were creating a whole new world every week. But, with the limited budget we had to work with, we could only afford to show a very small part of that world." Everything shown in every episode had to be *built*. If it was part of the *Enterprise,* then it could be used again in future episodes, and so every dollar spent for in-ship improvements was an investment in the overall look of the show.

As a result, the *Enterprise* gradually became more and more detailed. For instance, the engine room as portrayed by the end of the second season was quite a bit more complex and detailed than it had been the first time it was shown. In "Mirror, Mirror," for example, a small set on stilts was built. It was called the "Emergency Manual Monitor." It had a window in its rear wall through which the original engine room set could be seen. The effect was as if the actors were in an additional control room overlooking the main floor. It was a particularly well thought out set device and the result was quite convincing. It opened up the engine room by increasing its apparent depth.

If STAR TREK had been telling only shipboard stories, quite a detailed spaceship could have been constructed and shown. But unfortunately, the network wanted lots of "planet" stories. Hence, most of STAR TREK'S expenses were *not* for reusable items. The *Enterprise* had already been built. The phasers, tricorders and communicators had already been designed. The costumes were established. Aside from the occasional piece of detail work required by a specific script, most of the money had to be spent for development of items that could not be used again—and there was never enough time or money to do the job as thoroughly as it should have been done.

The average script allowed for the construction of three sets and some corridors, very little more. It allowed no more than five or six speaking parts—and rarely were more than three of them *major* parts. (The limitation of how much story you could tell in 48 minutes was a factor here too.) If there was any particularly difficult special effects or costume work—such as an alien Gorn, or a crew of Romulans—all the other budgets had to be cut accordingly.* (Fortunately, things like corridors, jungles and cave walls can easily be redressed to look like an additonal set.) The show rarely used more than twenty extras to suggest a crowd—or even a whole population.

* Klingons were easy aliens to do. All they needed were costumes, mustaches and swarthy makeup. Romulans were more expensive because they had pointed ears and fancy helmets that had to be built. Andorians and Tellarites were very expensive

While this restriction was a seriously limiting one—it was not a fatal flaw. There were many successful episodes that managed to work within these restrictions. In some cases, these restrictions even worked to strengthen a particular show—by forcing the writer to concentrate on the immediate story and not waste time on extraneous material.

Examples:

"The Doomsday Machine" (by Norman Spinrad) A retelling of Ahab and the whale. The only guest star was William Windom, and most of the action took place aboard the *Enterprise* or on a ship identical to her.

"Amok Time" (by Theodore Sturgeon) Once every seven years, Spock has to swim upstream to spawn. This script involved an arena on the planet Vulcan, four additional speaking parts, and a handful of extras.

"Journey to Babel" (by Dorothy Fontana) The *Enterprise* is ferrying a group of interstellar ambassadors, including Spock's parents. Although this story takes place entirely aboard the starship, there were a considerable number of aliens portrayed, requiring a good deal of costume and makeup work.

The typical STAR TREK script was never really a fully fleshed drama, per se. There are few television series that are. Rather, it was a story told in visual shorthand. Only the basic fragments are presented, details are merely suggested, and the viewer is left to fill in the gaps for himself.

Most television dramas depend on this kind of shorthand for their success. It has been called "the willing

---

because of the amount of makeup time required. Andorians with their blue skin and Tellarites with all their facial appliances presented problems of time and money. Any makeup problem can be solved eventually—but in television, it has to be solved this week. That STAR TREK's aliens were so often so unbelievable is tribute to Fred Phillips, the show's makeup man.

suspension of disbelief," but there is more to it than that.

Film as a story-telling medium has been in existence for more than sixty years—ever since Tom Edison filmed *The Great Train Robbery*. Three generations have grown up with visual communication an ever-increasing part of their lives. Film is the primary means of storytelling in the world today. With increased film viewing comes increased sophistication in film techniques. The original *King Kong* had women fainting in the aisles in its premiere engagement—today it's shown on television and rated suitable for children. In just thirty-five years the same film has gone from horror story to fairy tale. And the animation techniques that were so startling in 1935 are merely routine today.

Filmic devices and conventions quickly become easily recognized by a sophisticated audience. "Yes, we know all that already," they are saying. "Let's go on with the story." Hence, movies become faster and faster paced, packing ever more story into shorter and shorter bits of time. Long involved explanations aren't necessary any more. The audience doesn't care how you have set up the situation—they want to see what you are going to do with it after you've got it.

The motion picture *Destination Moon* was made in 1951. Fully half of it was spent in detailing and justifying the construction of an atomic rocket with which to journey into space. Only the last half of the film portrayed the actual trip.

Sixteen years later, *2001: A Space Odyssey* compressed all the same information into the space between one frame of film and the next. An ape learns to use a bone as a tool. He tosses it into the air—and the bone becomes a Pan Am spaceship carrying Dr. Heywood Floyd to Clavius crater and Tycho Moon Anomaly One. That picture *starts* with a trip to the moon.

In George Pal's *Destination Moon* (and also his later

film, *Conquest of Space*) there were long involved explanations of the condition of weightlessness and why it involved a need for magnetic boots. In Stanley Kubrick's *2001: A Space Odyssey* there were none—in fact, all the dialogue in that picture was kept to a minimum, with a corresponding lack of explanations. None were needed anyway. Far more than any other film, *2001* depended on its incredible imagery to tell its story. The visually startling centrifuge set, around which Keir Dullea ran interminable wind-sprints was never explained as being necessary to provide a simulated gravity environment. Sophisticated audiences were able to accept it without the explanation.

When Douglas Trumbull made *Silent Running* just a few years later, his American Air Lines space freighter obviously had some kind of artificial gravity. Making such an assumption obviously simplified many of his production problems—but at no time was it necessary to explain it to his audiences. They were more concerned with the story *within* the environment rather than how the environment had been set up.

Television works on a more limited scale than the motion picture. A *much* more limited scale. It is impossible to accomplish ten million dollars worth of amazement for a mere two hundred thousand (per episode)—but the same principles of storytelling hold true for both media.

Thus television must concentrate on the more immediate and personal story. What can't be shown must be suggested, and the audience will simply have to imagine the details that the producer can't afford to portray.

A motion picture depends on the same kind of suggestion on a much larger scale—but on that scale, enough is shown so that the audience is *helped* in their imagining. In television, the skimpiness of the suggestion is more obvious.

But—in no way can this be any kind of a justification for an unconvincing story.

Television is at its best in telling the immediate and personal story. What this means is that the kind of conflict that would be an epic on a motion picture screen must be stripped to its bare essentials in order to fit on the 21-inch TV screen.

Cecil B. DeMille or David Wark Griffith might have been able to use two mighty armies of ten thousand men each to portray a decisive battle of the American Civil War on screen. Joe Pevney or Marc Daniels (two of STAR TREK's directors) had to content themselves with one soldier from each side in a face to face meeting—but that could be a much more *intense* kind of story. And a better one for television.

STAR TREK'S best stories were those that were about *people;* one or two individuals caught in a trying situation.

Examples:

"Charlie X" (by Dorothy Fontana, from a story by Gene Roddenberry) Charlie has been raised by aliens, now he has to learn how to be a mature human being—unfortunately the aliens have given him superpowers in order to help him survive, thus depriving him of the *need* to mature. His whole problem, thus, is how to relate to humans. He can't of course—for Charlie it's too late.

"The Corbomite Maneuver" (by Jerry Sohl) The *Enterprise* encounters an immense alien vessel. Kirk must save his ship and prove that Terrans *are* friendly. He bluffs that the "corbomite" in the *Enterprise*'s hull will explode and destroy both ships. After he makes the bluff work—basically a duel of personalities—Kirk returns to aid the disabled alien.

"Devil in the Dark" (by Gene Coon) That rock-monster lurking down in the mines is only a mother Horta trying to protect her eggs. Spock discovers this through the Vulcan mind-meld. McCoy is able to patch up her injuries with a glob of silicon cement. ("I'm a doctor, not a plasterer.") You can get more personal than mother-love, but not much.

"Balance of Terror" (by Paul Schneider) A thinly disguised retelling of *The Enemy Below,* a submarine-vs.-destroyer duel. Here, it was the *Enterprise* vs. the Romulans. But, it worked because of the intensity of the subconflicts aboard the *Enterprise.*

"The Squire of Gothos" (by Paul Schneider) Trelane, a very playful fellow of extraordinary power, has captured Kirk, Spock, McCoy, Sulu, and Uhura. He teases them until his parents show up and tell him it's time to come in now.

All of the above mentioned stories are from STAR TREK's first—and generally most successful—season. All of them are quite good as individual episodes, but they are also representative of the overall "feel" of that first season.

In general, most of the scripts written involved highly personal conflicts for members of the *Enterprise* crew. Thus the stories were kept to a manageable scale.

If the show could have kept to that same kind of personal story, its high level of quality could have been maintained throughout the succeeding seasons. Unfortunately, there were several things that tended to work against STAR TREK as time progressed. These elements of decay can happen to any TV show. They can be identified as *Format* and *Formula.* Format becomes Formula via *Hardening of the Arteries* and *Erosion.*

All of these elements of decay stem from the basic problem of the television production system itself, a system which the networks have set up to suit themselves, not the viewers that they are ostensibly serving. The networks are *not* entertainment-oriented—they are profit-oriented. To a network vice-president, a TV show is little more than "product." He might as well be ordering sausages from the delicatessen—he doesn't want it good, he wants it Tuesday. Artistic validity is simply not a consideration. Arbitrary network standards outweigh story demands—as a result, many stories happen because the writers and producers are literally trapped into doing them. There simply aren't any alternatives to an order from the network. Except resign—and that's happened too.

Consider what a format is.

When a producer says, "Hey, I'm going to make a show about Captain Hornblower in outer space!" the studio wants to know, "Yes, but what is your format?" Meaning: Tell us the details. *How* are you going to do it.

At this point the producer has to sit down and figure out how he is going to tell his stories—what set of situations, characters, equipment, background, and physical laws of the universe will give him the broadest possible base for the stories he wants to tell?

"Well, I need a Captain and a spaceship and a crew. The spaceship should be able to travel faster than light so it can visit other planets, but it takes too much time and money to show it landing on a new planet every week, I need—yes, a transporter beam ... and let's see, we'll need a big crew so we can tell stories about individuals aboard the ship ... oh, now who sent him out? We ought to know what his orders are . . ." And so on.

A format is a guide for whatever is to come later. It's a flight plan for a series. But just like any other kind of flight plan, the slightest error will magnify itself over a period of time if it isn't corrected or compensated for. The errors in a show's original format will repeat themselves until they become so noticeable as to be annoying. Twenty-six repetitions a season make a mistake very hard to live with.

Actually, *mistake* isn't quite the right word. Let's say "element of conceptualization" instead. That is, something that seems quite workable in the first two or three stories may turn out to be a very rigorous trap by the thirteenth or fourteenth episode.

The transporter room is a good example. It was one of STAR TREK's best ideas—a teleportation device so that the Captain and crew of the starship could "beam down" to a planet whenever they chose. Thus, the special-effects crew was relieved of the responsibility of having to show either the starship or its shuttlecraft landing on a new planet each week. A golden flicker mixed with a dissolve and an over-dubbed reverberated whine is not only cheaper—it's more versatile and impressive.

Unfortunately the use of the transporter set up conditions of its own that were not foreseen in the initial postulation.

For the transporter to work, the individual had to have a "communicator"—a gold-and-black clamshell device that served as an all-purpose walkie-talkie. The transporter would "lock on" the human being holding device and "beam" him up.

And that was the error. If the transporter had been designed for the express purpose (pun intended) of getting our heroes into the story faster, then it also allowed them to get *out* of it just as quickly.

Any time Captain Kirk got himself into real trouble, all he needed to do was call the *Enterprise* and holler, "Scotty! Save my ass!" and Scotty would beam him up so fast the air would crackle. Knowing that, then there certainly would be no suspense whenever Kirk was captured by the giant Yang-yangs or the Creeping Blorch. Both he and we knew that it wasn't permanent.

Therefore, one of three things had to happen to keep Kirk in a story where he was personally menaced:

He would run into aliens of such superior ability that they could nullify his transporter beam. Thus he got captured.

He would run into aliens of such inferior ability that they would knock him over the head and take his communicator away from him without knowing what it was. Again, he got captured.

Or—contact between the Captain and the *Enterprise* would be cut off by some arbitrary force created by the writer for this specific purpose, thus *trapping* Kirk in the story until contact could be restored—usually not until just before the last commercial.

Individually, any one of these alternatives might have been part of a good story—indeed, they all were, as witness "The Squire of Gothos," "Tomorrow Is Yesterday," and "Errand of Mercy," respectively.

However, by the time we get to the fifth or sixth repetition—"The Apple," "Bread and Circuses," "A Private Little War," "The Gamesters of Triskelion," "A Piece of the Action," "The Omega Glory," "Spectre of the Gun," "The Paradise Syndrome," and "Plato's Stepchildren"—the cumulative effect is the focusing of attention on the mechanism used to prevent Kirk from being rescued. We become aware of the format's degeneration into formula. We begin to realize that "Plato's Stepchildren" is the same story as "The Gamesters of Triskelion"; the only difference is in the details. We've become too familiar with the device for it to be effective as a dramatic tool any more—now it's a cliché.

The extreme use of any device will wear it out. The rapid degeneration of this particular element of the STAR TREK format only points up which writers were (at that point in their scripts) creatively bankrupt. Rather than looking for another way to solve the problem, they fell back on old tricks. Pretty soon, that same old trick got boring.

The real answer, of course, was simply to *avoid* situations or stories that required Kirk to be overpowered. Gene Roddenberry says about writing in general: *"Every story starts with a need. A need for something to happen or something not to happen. That need must be closely and deeply associated with the main character. Perhaps he needs a thousand dollars to pay off a gam-*

bling debt to keep the mob from killing him. Or perhaps he needs *not* to have himself placed in the electric chair tonight at 12:01 a.m. and the switch pulled which will execute him for a murder he never committed. Whatever need you propound for the character in your story, it is absolutely necessary that that need get more and more pressing, also more and more difficult to fulfill, as the story progresses. In a good story, you finally get the reader or viewer clawing at the pages or the screen in his anxiety to get fulfillment since he has become the hero and feels all the jeopardy, frustration and agony which is building and building toward the story climax. When the need is resolved in the story climax, the reader or viewer feels fulfillment."

Now, returning to the contention that the real answer was not to let Captain Kirk be placed in positions where he would be overpowered. To do so *once* is a valid story. To do so *twice* might even be valid. To do it more than that, you begin to undermine the character of Captain Kirk—what kind of a Captain is this anyway? He keeps letting himself get clonked on the head and captured. You'd think he'd learn.

The writers that let Captain Kirk continue to be trapped this way were creating an *artificial* need. Remember the artificial excitement of having the actors fall out of their chairs while the camera was shaken?— this is the same kind of thing, but a little more sophisticated. Oh, it's adventure all right, but it isn't real drama.

Gene said that the need must be "closely and deeply associated with the main character." Trapping a character into a situation and asking him to solve it does *not* fulfill this requirement—being in a situation does not mean that the character will automatically care about it "closely and deeply." In such a situation, the hero's *primary* need is to escape, not to solve the problems of anyone else. But a hasty writer will "solve" this problem by arbitrarily constructing a white rat's puzzle-box test: Captain Kirk must solve the problem posed in order to win his reward, i.e. escape.

This kind of writing—and it is very *bad* writing—stems from a weak or hasty understanding of the STAR TREK format, a failure to think its implications out to their logical conclusions, and overall, being *defeated* by the requirements of television rather than being *challenged* by them.

These white-rat puzzle-box stories are the illegitimate offspring of the forced marriage of two extremely different forms: the hero-in-danger story and the "Mary Worth" story.

You see, as it's set up, the *Enterprise* IS a cosmic "Mary Worth," meddling her way across the galaxy, solving problems as she goes. But drama—*real* drama—requires that the hero be forced to make a decision, an *important* decision. Unfortunately, to the networks, that means that the hero must be *placed in danger*. Period. (Shows like *The Waltons* are exceptional—in more ways than one. But they take a long time to develop a loyal audience and networks are notoriously impatient.) Thus, in the typical story, the hero is trapped into somebody else's problem (on STAR TREK, a cultural one) and must solve it to escape.

The result is a series of puzzle-box episodes. Unfortunately, these kind of stories are generally unimportant ones. We don't really care about them. We know the hero will escape—that's why he's the hero. Thus our only reason for watching the show is to see *how* he does it. Ho hum. Unless the situation is particularly good, or the escape is particularly imaginative (*a la Mission Impossible*) it's just so much chocolate pudding for the mind. Instead of "The End," the film might just as well say "So what?"

One of STAR TREK's episodes that *worked* was "City on the Edge of Forever." It was written by Harlan

Ellison (with some rewriting by Gene Roddenberry) and won the Hugo award for the best science fiction drama of 1967. The story involved a portal to the past; Dr. McCoy, accidentally under the influence of an overdose of cordrazine (a very strange drug) jumps into the portal and is transported into Earth's history, specifically 1930 America. Kirk and Spock must follow him in order to keep him from changing the past and all the events that stem from it—including the establishment of Starfleet Command and the construction of the *Enterprise*.

But, once in the past, Kirk meets and falls in love with Edith Keeler—a woman who is also strangely out of her time; although native to the era, her ideas and dreams are those of a later age. She talks of peace and world-wide wealth, and even of ships to the stars. But Kirk soon discovers to his horror that the event in the past that must not be changed or altered in any way is Edith Keeler's impending death. If she should be allowed to live, she would form a pacifist movement that would eventually result in America losing World War II to Hitler's Germany. This is the problem that Kirk must solve in order to escape the trap of this story.

Essentially, this *is* a puzzle-box kind of story. The time portal is only a device to trap Kirk into the situation. He must solve it to escape. But this story works—and if we examine *why* it works, we'll see why most puzzle-box stories don't. This one is the exception that tests the rule.

First of all, in the writing of this story, both Harlan Ellison and Gene Roddenberry recognized that the problem as it is set up is basically unsolvable. Captain Kirk cannot save both. He must lose either his ship or his woman. Of course, his decision must be to save the *Enterprise*. Edith Keeler must die and James Kirk must lose her.

The situation that Kirk is trapped into is not an arbitrary one—it is *his* situation. He is not solving someone else's problem to escape, he is solving his own. Thus, the important decision that he must make at the climax of the story is one that will affect him *deeply*.

—And that's the second reason for the success of this story. The *need* in it is "closely and deeply associated with the main character." Captain Kirk is truly affected by these events. In a puzzle-box story, his need to escape would have been primary. But in "City On the Edge of Forever" that need becomes secondary to a much stronger conflict.

Which leads into the third reason. The time portal, as it is used in this episode, is more than a trap. Although it does function to separate Kirk from any kind of support from his ship, its primary purpose is to propel Kirk into a *more important* conflict. Rather than a trap, it is a vehicle to get the Captain into the real story: the decision between Edith Keeler and the *Enterprise*.

In the hands of a lesser writer, this would have been a lesser story. The conflict would have been arbitrary, it would have been one that did not affect Kirk (or any other crew member) deeply, and the time portal would have been used as a trap.

A perfect example of this is "All Our Yesterdays," in which Kirk, Spock and McCoy are once again trapped in the past—only this time, the past is not Earth's, but some other planet's. And it's not Kirk that falls in love, it's Spock. (Ho hum.) There's no further decision to make. It is forgone that Mr. Spock will return; he is giving up nothing more than a chance encounter. The story deals with an arbitrary trap and an arbitrary solution. No matter who they meet, their primary need remains one of escape.

Thus, in the puzzle-box story, real drama is defeated before it ever has a chance to get started—all of the relationships are secondary. Neither Kirk nor anyone else has any real need to explore the relationships that might develop with any of the people they will meet in the process of escaping. For all the personal involvement that is required, they might just as well be hacking their way with machetes through a jungle.

Referring back to the original format of the show, Gene Roddenberry felt that STAR TREK would be stronger if there were a high degree of personal involvement by one or more characters aboard the ship in every story told. In this, he was correct. Personal involvement was a very basic "element of conceptualization" in STAR TREK's original format. But it was also one of the most misused.

Personal involvement—*if it is superimposed onto the primary conflict of the story*—is little more than a dramatic device. Like the last device we considered, it can be worn out too.

The involvement of a familiar character in a conflict heightens the tension we will feel as the story approaches its climax. There is a stronger identification with the story, thus there is more involvement on the part of the viewer with the crisis to be confronted.

But when a device is superimposed on a weak story —and when it is done continually—the cumulative effect is to focus the viewer's attention on the device and not the story. Again, the overuse of this device is a symptom of creative bankruptcy.

Given a weak story, how do you make it stronger?

James Blish, a noted science fiction author in his own right and author of nine STAR TREK books, says quite simply: "Analyze the basic conflict. Ask yourself, 'Who does it hurt?' That's your story."

A weak writer, however, takes the easy way out. "Well, you see, Kirk falls in love with this girl . . ." Or, "Well, you see, Spock falls in love with this girl . . ." Or "Well, Scotty falls in love with this girl . . ." Or "Well McCoy falls in love with this girl . . ." Or "Chekov falls in love with this girl . . ." Oh "Well, you see, Uhura . . ." Never mind.

Once, or even twice, this story might be interesting. "City on the Edge of Forever" was Kirk's love story. "This Side of Paradise" was Spock's adventure of the heart. They should have stopped there. Kirk shouldn't have been allowed to fall in love again for at least thirty episodes. Same for Spock. And the other characters should have had other kinds of stories told about them—not love stories. The cumulative effect is that the ship is crewed by 432 incurable cases of satyriasis. (Or nymphomania, as the case may be.)

But not only is a love story the easiest story to tell—just show a man and woman talking meaningless dialogue and smiling at each other—it also seems to be the only story that some writers can tell. (I have no quibble there, but they tell it so *badly*.)

There are other kinds of personal involvement that are every bit as strong. In "Operation—Annihilate!" Kirk finds that his brother has been killed in part of a planet-wide plague of insanity. In "The Conscience of the King" Kirk is one of the last two survivors who can identify an interplanetary war criminal. Kirk had lost many friends to the man twenty years before, and one of the members of his crew had lost his family. In "Court Martial" Kirk's whole career as Captain of the *Enterprise* is at stake. In none of these stories is there the kind of love interest that would work against the believability of the series as a whole. And that's important.

We can't ever fade out on a happy ending of Kirk with his arms around the girl; nor can any other character in a series fall in love, for that matter. Not without changing the format; *because* the following week, we'll want to know what happened to the girl. Where is she? What happened to her? Why isn't she back? The fact that she *isn't* back just proves that there wasn't that high a degree of personal involvement after

all. She was just a one-night stand. That's why she has
to either die or go away—then we can believe the hero
really loved her, and we're not in any danger of having
to change the format.

The need for a heroine in every story is a leftover
convention from the era of romanticism. There, the
hero killed the dragon, slew the giant, conquered the
trolls, defeated the orcs, and saved the kingdom—and
his reward was the beautiful princess who immediately
agreed to be his wife. (Love was never a consideration.
Of course, she loved him—that was her job!)

Frankly, it's a stupid convention—it reduces women
to objects. The subliminal message is that a woman is
merely a reward for a job well done. Superimposed on
a science fiction series—especially STAR TREK—the effect is unreal. No, surreal.

We are continually shown that women are responsible members of the *Enterprise* crew. Lieutenant Uhura,
for instance, is fourth in command, right after Mr.
Scott. Obviously, in the STAR TREK universe, equality
between men and women is a reality—except for Captain Kirk. More often than not, when he solves a particularly difficult problem, he is rewarded with a particularly luscious tidbit whose function in the story is just
that—to be Kirk's reward.

There are a lot of variations on the theme, but eventually it begins to grate like Johnny one-note on the
kazoo. A story does not *need* a heroine. It needs a
problem for the hero to solve. His reward is the solving
of the problem. To then give him objects (a chest of
gold, a medal, a woman) reduces the magnitude of his
bravery and places the emphasis of the story on the object to be gained, not the problem to be solved.

Kirk should be a starship Captain, not a cosmic
womanizer. Certainly he will have love affairs, but for
goodness sake, couldn't they be mature affairs between
two real live human beings? That means they should be
kept in proportion to the rest of his life—as a Captain,

he's going to have more problems than women. And the same should apply to every other member of the crew.

(As a sidelight here, one of the subplots in "Balance of Terror" involved Kirk officiating at a wedding between two of his crew members. This seemed a particularly fascinating development. We should have been seeing more of the in-ship relationships. Weren't there any man-wife teams of scientists aboard? There should have been—certainly all those people didn't remain celibate for five years . . .)

The love story kind of involvement was particularly overworked during the third season—during that set of shows, *everybody* had a chance to fall in love at least once, and all the major leads got two or three chances.

During the second season of STAR TREK, a different kind of involvement was experimented with—"Well, who are we going to *almost* kill this week?"

In "Amok Time" Kirk gets killed—no, he doesn't; we just think he is for a while. In "The Changling" Scotty gets killed—no, he doesn't; he gets brought back to life. In "The Apple" Spock keels over after being shot by a poisonous plant—no, he's immune to its effects.

And in the third season: Kirk gets killed in "The *Enterprise* Incident"—no he doesn't; it's just a trick on the Romulans. In "For the World Is Hollow and I Have Touched the Sky" McCoy gets clobbered by a computer—no, not quite. And in "The Tholian Webb" Kirk is missing and presumed dead for half the episode. Ho hum.

Again, just as with the others, once is valid, even twice—but more than that and the device becomes recognizable, repetitious and worn-out. We know that these characters are not going to be killed: they're the heroes. So stop cheating us and start telling some real stories.

The almost-death is a fantasy, a fairy tale. We kill the hero and then double-talk him back to life. A *real* story would work within the conventions of the format, exploring the relationships that are created thereby and confonting the conflicts that develop.

Examples:

Two of STAR TREK'S very best episodes were "Amok Time" and "Journey to Babel." Both of these stories presented a good deal of Spock's background as well as the history and customs of the planet Vulcan. Both of these episodes were true dramas. All of the conflicts and relationships were honest, they were developed out of what we already knew. They were expansions and explorations.

On the other hand, an episode like————(you fill in the blank) is mostly a cheat. An alien or group of aliens takes over the ship for their own purposes until Captain Kirk tricks them into defeat. It was titled "Who Mourns for Adonais?" and "Plato's Stepchildren" and "Catspaw" and "Spectre of the Gun" and "And the Children Shall Lead" and "By Any Other Name" and so on.

All of these were variations of the same theme. The only time it worked, however, was in "The Squire of Gothos." In that episode, the alien was shown to be a super-powered child—which is the only justification for that kind of a power trip anyway. After all, if your aliens have that much power, why do they want the *Enterprise* anyway? The only possible reason could be as a plaything—in which case, your alien is only a super-child. Trelane, the Squire of Gothos.

In general, the story of the aliens taking over the *Enterprise* is a phony. It's an artificial menace—it doesn't truly explore any of the character relationships and it doesn't add much to the overall STAR TREK concept. And like all the others, it's only a valid story once or twice. More than that and it's just a big Ho Hum.

Dorothy Fontana once remarked that one of the biggest problems in telling some of the stories was the size of the ship's crew. What could you do with all those extra people when you didn't need them?

In "I, Mudd", for instance, we're told that Harry Mudd's five hundred identical beautiful girl androids beamed up to the ship, grabbed everybody and beamed them down. But we've never shown any of this. It was too expensive to show. So, as it was written, the script was about Kirk, Spock, McCoy, Uhura, Scotty and Chekov. The rest of the crew was out of sight and out of mind.

In "By Any Other Name" we're shown that the alien Kelvans have the power to reduce human beings to plaster dodecahedrons. What happened was that neither Dorothy Fontana not Jerry Bixby nor Gene Coon could figure out a way to get all the extra crewpersons out of the way, so Dorothy and Gene went in to see Gene Roddenberry and as they explained the problem to him, he was toying with a Mexican onyx dodecahedron which he had on his desk as an ornament. (To save you a trip to the dictionary, a dodecahedron is a twelve-sided solid with equal and regular sides, each side a perfect pentagon.) Gene began to muse aloud, "Suppose the aliens could freeze the pattern of each person into a solid block like this . . ."

Dorothy Fontana admits that the solution is basically an unsatisfactory one—it's arbitrary—but at the time, nobody could come up with a better idea and they did have to get the script to the soundstage on schedule . . .*

All of these "elements of conceptualization" resulted in dramatic devices that over a period of three years and 79 episodes were used and re-used till they were so familiar as to be offensive.

* In the concept that Dorothy is developing with Doug Trumbull and Mike Gruskoff, "The Winds of Space," her spaceship has a crew of only four. Plus one robot-drone. "Plus," she says, "anyone we need to create trouble and suspense. Naturally, the *Spinnaker* will transport colonists, scientists and others."

The blame lies with the network, NBC.

—Uh, well, now that's not quite fair. NBC is just a set of initials. The real villain is not really a villain; he's just a man who didn't understand what he had when he said, "Let's buy this show called STAR TREK."

His mistake was a simple one—but was deadly. Instead of saying, "This is a dramatic series," he said, "This will be an action-adventure series."

And therein lies the problem.

That's the kind of story Gene Roddenberry had to produce—action-adventure stories.

That's the kind of story that the writers had to write.

And that's why the viewer kept getting variations of "Kirk in Danger." (If not Kirk in danger, then someone he loves is in danger, or someone he's responsible for—but always, someone in danger. Helluva way to run a starship.)

Some of the writers rose above this: Theodore Sturgeon with his delightful "Shore Leave" script; Harlan Ellison and his award-winning "City on the Edge of Forever"; Gene Coon's clever "Devil in the Dark."

But many of the show's writers *failed* to meet this challenge.

Look, it's too easy to create dramatic tension by putting someone in danger, then throwing obstacles in the path of his rescuers. The viewer *knows* he's going to be rescued, so essentially it's a phony device—unless it is used to open up a bigger, more important story.

But it wouldn't happen in a twenty-third century starship with the annoying regularity that it did on STAR TREK. Considering a real-life example: out of the ten Apollo space missions, there has only been *one* space disaster; the rest of the missions have come off pretty much as planned. Considering the total Apollo lunar program, only three astronauts have died—and that was while they were still on the launch pad in a preflight check-out. If it only happens once—or even twice—out of every nine missions in real life, then it certainly shouldn't happen any more often in a series that depends so much on scientific accuracy for its believability. And considering the way that technology continues to advance, it shouldn't happen *at all* by the twenty-third century. If it does, it would be a major story by itself, not a lesser part of some other one.

But putting someone in danger is the *easy* story to tell. To a hack writer, that's what action-adventure means.

Of course, if you want to haggle definitions, it's impossible to have a real adventure without *some* danger. That's why STAR TREK should never have been an action-adventure series. It should have been, first and foremost, a *dramatic* series, with excursions into the action-adventure format.

If STAR TREK had been truly a dramatic series, then the essential STAR TREK story would not have had to have been "Kirk in Danger," but "Kirk Has a Decision to Make." The decision is the core of every dramatic episode. It is why an audience will stay tuned for 48 minutes of story.

So. If we reconsider all those devices inherent in the original format, or developed as the series progressed, we'll see that many of them were little more than ways to portray Captain James T. Kirk, or some other member of the crew of the *Enterprise*, in danger. They are devices to create artificial excitement.

Real excitement can be generated by a cast of two on a blank stage. All you need are two good characters in strong opposition. Period. Drama.

But television is hastily produced. There isn't time, there isn't money—and most of all, there isn't talent enough. Not every member of the Writer's Guild of America is a Hemingway, or even an Ellison—let alone a Fontana or a Roddenberry.

If a writer is to make a living in any given year, he

has to get all of his assignments at once during the February-March "buying season." Then he has to write those scripts, and there isn't the time to "Mother Hen" each one. He can't visit the sets, he can't be available for consultations, he doesn't expect to be the one to make last-minute changes—he's already working on his script for another TV show. The system keeps him from giving each story the care he would like to. So he relies heavily on the "format" and it's used—and used—and used— (Fortunately, the Writers Guild of America is working to change the system, but it takes time, it takes time, and in the meanwhile, a lot of bad writing is coming down the pike.) Until it becomes a *formula.*

A "formula" story is the pat story, the easy story, the one that gets written by the book. It's a compilation of all the tried and true tricks. It's six devices in search of a plot. It's a hero-vs.-villain story. It's generally a waste of time.

With STAR TREK, it might work something like this: The *Enterprise* approaches a planet. Something happens. Anything. Kirk, Spock and McCoy get captured by six foot green women in steel brassieres. They take away the spacemen's communicators because they offend the computer-god that these women worship.

Meanwhile, Scotty discovers that he's having trouble with the doubletalk generator, and he can't fix it—the *Enterprise* will shrivel into a prune in two hours unless something is done immediately. But Scotty can't get in touch with the Captain—

Of course, he can't—Kirk, Spock and McCoy have been brought before the high priest of the cosmic computer, who decides that they are unfit to live. All except the Vulcan, who has interesting ears. She puts Spock into a mind-zapping machine which leaves him quoting poetry (17-syllable Japanese haiku verses) for the next two acts. McCoy can't do a damn thing for him, "I'm a doctor, not a critic!" Meanwhile, it's been more than two hours since Kirk's last piece of ass and he starts getting twitchy. McCoy can't do anything for him either. So Kirk seduces the cute priestess—there always is at least one.

On the ship, sparks fly from Chekov's control panel and everybody falls out of their chairs. Uhura tries opening the hailing frequencies, and when she can't, admits to being frightened. Scotty figures only fifteen minutes are left. Already the crew members are starting to get wrinkled as the starship begins "prunifying."

Down on the planet, Kirk, Spock and McCoy are being held in the dungeon—why is it always a dungeon?—until the girl he has seduced decides that she has never been laid so good in her life and discards all of her years-long training and lifetime-held beliefs to rescue him, conveniently remembering to bring him his communicator and phaser. Abruptly, Spock reveals how hard he has been working to hide his emotions and then snaps back to normal. Thinking logically, he and Kirk then drive the cosmic computer crazy with illogic—naturally, it can't cope; its designers never having been as smart as our Earthmen—and it shorts out all its fuses and releases the *Enterprise,* just in time for the last commercial. For a tag, the seduced priestess promises Kirk that she will work to build a new civilization on her planet—just for Kirk—one where women's lib and steel brassieres will be illegal.

Sound familiar?

It should. It's a compendium of all the bad plot devices that ever wore out their welcome on too many STAR TREK episodes. Probably, a competent script could be built on this formula plot—eliminating some of the facetiousness, of course. But it wouldn't be a very good STAR TREK episode. Because there's nothing really new or interesting about it. Kirk doesn't have much of a decision to make; it's all excitement and very little story.

If it were a real drama, it could be described in one

sentence. The sentence begins with: "Kirk has to decide between . . ."

And ends with:

". . . saving the woman he loves or allowing the past to be changed."

". . . risking his ship or saving Spock's life."

". . . being a diplomat or being a soldier."

Those three sentences were the basis of three good STAR TREK stories. But "Green Priestesses of the Cosmic Computer" has no such internal conflict. It's all formula.

Formula occurs when format starts to repeat itself. Formula occurs when format does not challenge writers—or when writers are giving less than their best. Formula occurs when a show becomes creatively bankrupt. Flashy devices can conceal the lack for a while, but ultimately the lack of any real meat in the story will leave the viewers hungry and unsatisfied.

Formula occurs primarily when a show has been trapped in a format which does not allow full exploration of the given situation. Thus, the producers and writers are condemned to repeat only that which the format does allow. And action-adventure is nowhere near as broad as drama.

There are two ways by which Format turns into Formula.

One is *Hardening of the Arteries,* the other is *Erosion.*

Considering the first process of decay as it applies to a television series, every time something is postulated or established in a continuing series, from that episode on, every writer who works with the format must be aware of that condition. If it is shown in the STAR TREK universe that the galaxy has an edge which blasts spaceships to smithereens, then you cannot write any episode about the *Enterprise* going into intergalactic space unless you explain how the starship gets around the galaxy's energy barrier.*

Thus, hardening of the arteries is the process by which a television show gradually limits itself by setting up conditions which will affect all episodes that will come after. Producers are always a little bit wary about expanding on their formats because of the danger of this happening—the happening—they might inadvertently set something up that could backfire and severely limit them in the future.

A few examples from STAR TREK:

The Prime Directive—also known as General Order Number One. This, according to the STAR TREK Writers' Guide, third revision, is "a wise, but often troublesome rule which prohibits starship interference with the normal development of alien life and societies." It was first postulated in an episode entitled, "The Apple" in which Kirk and crew must violate the directive and destroy an Eden. The justification was that this Eden was an artificial condition which was already interfering with the normal development of this particular culture. It rapidly became clear that the Prime Directive was to be more honored in the breach than otherwise.

But the Prime Directive also showed up in "A Private Little War," "Patterns of Force," "A Piece of the Action," "Bread and Circuses," and other episodes. This is why it was such a troublesome rule—it was troublesome to the writers who had to work their stories

---

* Frankly, I think the idea of a definable "edge" to the galaxy is a load of peanut butter. It's like trying to bisect a sneeze. And the idea of an "energy barrier" around the galaxy—Hoo! It is to boggle the mind.

However, Sam Peeples, who wrote the second pilot script, "Where No Man Has Gone Before," verified the *possibility* of such concepts before he wrote the script. Sam is a member of First Fandom, a long time SF buff and a recognized contributor to the field. He does not make stupid mistakes and he even forced down Isaac Asimov on this particular question. So, it could be possible.

around it. In all of these episodes, Kirk eventually *had to* interfere with the so-called normal development of the alien society. Sometimes he was putting it back on its proper course after someone else had tampered with it, "Bread and Circuses," "Patterns of Force," for example.

The STAR TREK Writers' Guide summarizes the rule like this: "It can be disregarded when absolutely vital to the interests of the entire Earth Federation, but the Captain who does violate it had better be ready to present a sound defense of his actions."

Which means, translated into English: The Prime Directive is a great idea, but it's a bloody nuisance. Let's forget about the whole thing.

The Prime Directive gets in the way of telling "Mary Worth" stories. It keeps the *Enterprise* from being a cosmic meddler. And that's too much of a limitation on the format. It keeps Kirk from being a moralist because he can no longer say, "This is right and this is wrong" to the people of Eminiar VII and Vendikar in "A Taste of Armageddon." In fact, he can't even blow up the computer that controls their simulated war if he subscribes to General Order Number One.

Nor can he destroy the Landru computer on Beta III in "Return of the Archons." Nor is he allowed to upset the status quo on Triskelion in "The Gamesters of Triskelion."*

This is a very idealistic rule—but it keeps getting in the way of the story. Therefore, it has to be disregarded. Regularly.

In the third season, it was totally ignored. Forgotten. They had problems enough without it.

By far the most serious hardening of STAR TREK's arteries, however, was on a much more subtle level. The

---

* Originally, this episode was called "The Gamesters of Pentathlon." It must have been too expensive that way, so they knocked two points off the symbol and changed the name to "Triskelion."

relationships between the characters sometimes solidi-
fied to the point where occasionally they could not
break out of a set pattern of responses. The result was
that relationships began to dictate the shape of some of
the stories. Conflicts would be distorted so as to create
specific but tangential scenes for individual characters.
One character in particular—Spock.

Spock was one of the great strengths of the show—
but he was also one of the biggest crosses it had to
bear. His popularity tended to overshadow that of the
rest of the show. The network, and a good many fans,
would have been just as happy if the show had been
called, "The Mr. Spock Hour."

(An interesting note here. The network had had
qualms about Mr. Spock's alien-ness long before the
show went on the air. At one point, they even put out
an advance publicity brochure with his ears and eyebrows airbrushed back to normal. But later on, after
the show became a hit, not a single network executive
would cop to being wrong. Harlan Ellison tried to track
the order down for an article he had been planning to
write, and was present as the order was traced all the
way down the line, and each time the buck was passed
a little farther. Finally, they tried to pin the blame on a
guy they caught in the art department holding an air-
brush. They wanted to fire the poor dope on the spot!
And all he had done was follow orders that no one
would admit to giving!)

Because of Spock's importance as a drawing card,
more and more stories began to focus on him. Many of
these were valid stories to tell, "Journey to Babel," and
"Amok Time," for instance. But sometimes—

Although the character was almost always kept in
dramatic proportion to the overall story, he began to
play pivotal parts in *too many* episodes—at the expense
of other characters in the series. The cumulative effect
was that Lieutenant Uhura was only good for opening
hailing frequencies, and Sulu could only sit at the helm

and occasionally fall out of his chair. Chekov was little more than a Captain Kirk in training, but with a Russian accent. And Christine Chapel was the ideal woman—silent and dutiful.

In the course of a season, it should be possible to focus on every regular character at least once. This episode will be Uhura's story, that one will be Chekov's, this one is Sulu's, that one is Chapel's.

But in the course of three seasons there was never an episode which dealt in depth with Mr. Sulu. Chekov fared a little better, but there never was a script that was specifically about Lieutenant Uhura. Nurse Chapel was lucky, she was important in two or three episodes.

There was only one episode especially about Dr. McCoy ("For the World Is Hollow and I Have Touched the Sky") and only one or two about Scotty ("Wolf in the Fold," and "The Lights of Zetar.") There *were* episodes where any or all of these characters played pivotal parts, but the episode that was particularly an individual's own was the rare occurrence.*

In general, it all went to Kirk and Spock.

It had to go to Kirk, he was the lead. Besides, the Captain is the man with the ultimate responsibility; he would be the focus of any conflict. And the Kirk-Spock relationship was basically a good one. Kirk's adventurousness and sense of humor contrasted nicely with Spock's cool aloofness. They were a good team. But far too many of the stories used Spock when any other character might have functioned just as well. The

---

* There was supposed to be an episode called "Joanna." It was to be about Dr. McCoy's daughter, but the third season producer felt that McCoy was Kirk's peer, and therefore not old enough to have a grown daughter, so the episode was changed to "The Way to Eden," and the focus become Chekov's Russian girl friend. Dorothy Fontana had written the first version of "Joanna," but quit when it became "The Way to Eden." That episode was written by Michael Richards and Arthur Heinemann with teleplay by the latter.

overuse of Mr. Spock enlarges him all out of proportion to everything else on the *Enterprise.*

The basic format of the show, as we have seen, was "Kirk in Danger." This meant that Kirk—and whoever he worked best with—had to solve a problem. It was natural to write the story about Kirk and Spock.

If the format had been a dramatic one, "Kirk Makes a Decision," the stories could have focused on any individual crew member. Kirk would not have had to place himself in dangerous situations—the danger could have been to someone else, but still Kirk's responsibility. As long as the climactic decision remains the Captain's, he's still the most important character and he's still the star of the show.

But the format *wasn't* dramatic. It was action-adventure. The story was "Kirk in Danger"—and this led to the further petrification of the STAR TREK format into formula.

—And this is the most deadly of all the criticisms that have ever been leveled against STAR TREK:

A Captain, whether he be the Captain of a starship or an aircraft carrier, simply does not place himself in danger. Ever.

A Captain is too important an officer, his training is too expensive, his skills are too vital to the running of the ship to be risked. A good Captain is like a good general, he stays in his command and control center *and delegates authority.* He tells other people what to do—it isn't necessary for him to do it himself.

An aircraft carrier captain doesn't fly the planes himself. An army general doesn't hit the beaches until they've been secured. And a spaceship Captain won't do it either. The first time he tries it—well, maybe that's a special case. The second time he goes beaming down into the thick of things, he's going to be hauled up before a review board. The third time, he's going to be relieved of command and a more responsible man will replace him.

And to take Mr. Spock, *his second in command,* with him. is a compounding of the offense!

Should anything happen to them, the *Enterprise* would be deprived of her two top officers. It simply doesn't make sense that these are the two individuals who would risk their lives regularly.

And yet, as pictured on STAR TREK, not a week went by that Captain Kirk and Mr. Spock didn't end up in front of the business end of a gun, club, phaser or other tool of destruction at least once.

The real reason for this, of course, is that these are the two top stars of the show. Period. They're getting paid to be the stars. Therefore, the stories have to be about them. It doesn't make sense to pay top money to William Shatner and Leonard Nimoy and then have to hire someone else to be the stars of the stories. If you're going to do your stories about someone else, then you might as well make them the stars in the first place. No, your stories have to be about Kirk and Spock.

This is the one *major* problem in the STAR TREK format, the one difficulty that forces the show into a set of formula situations week after week—the focusing of attention on two characters who should not logically be placing themselves in physical danger, *but must do so regularly.*

This is the real pity of hardened arteries—the show ends up telling and retelling only variations of the same story because it has so limited itself it can't tell any other kind of story.

There is a solution for STAR TREK—but it involves a major change in the show's format. Considering it, however, it would be a logical extrapolation of the starship's use of its manpower:

In addition to all the other members of the *Enterprise* crew, there should be a "Contact Team," a specially trained crew of men and women whose sole purpose was to deal with alien cultures and civilizations. Kirk and Spock would stay on the bridge—as their jobs should require them to do—and monitor the duties of the team. Kirk would make his decisions by remote control, after being carefully advised by his medical, science and engineering officers.

The Contact Team would risk their lives—but that would be part of their jobs and they would be aware of the risks involved. They would not be allowed to beam hastily back up from the surface of a strange planet because of the possibility of biological contamination of the ship. One of their members would have to be a medical expert, constantly monitoring the alien environment that these individuals are exploring—not until he gave the okay, would they be allowed to return to the *Enterprise*. And even then, an in-ship quarantine would be necessary. This team would be frankly expendable, there would be a high turn-over in its members—so the show *could* use mostly guest players instead of having to hire new regulars.

Probably, the best place from which to draw this Contact Team would be the *Enterprise's* own Security Forces. These are men who are trained in combat anyway and should be alert to the slightest possibility of danger. That's probably why they were aboard in the first place—but because they weren't used as such, but rather functioned as an inboard police force, they gave the ship a kind of totalitarian feeling.

A good man to place in charge of the Contact Team would have been Ensign Chekov. As originally postulated, he was meant to be a brilliant young officer of great potential. This would give him a chance to show off some of that potential, a chance he was rarely given otherwise.

All this is theoretical, of course. STAR TREK is no longer being produced—and any analyses of the show at this point can be only be Monday morning quarterbacking. Almost everybody has 20-20 hindsight. But still, it's nice to think about.

And besides, maybe the guy who produces the *next* outer space series will read this book . . .

The last process of STAR TREK's decay to consider is Erosion.

As postulated, the original format was excellent.

It was workable and many fine stories resulted, especially in the first season.

But the second season was not quite as good. And the third season—well, to be honest, it was generally abysmal.

Of course, a great deal of this deterioration is due to what went on behind the scenes. For instance, neither Gene Roddenberry, Gene Coon, nor Dorothy Fontana were working on the show during the third season (although Dorothy Fontana did work on one script).

In addition, there were many writers involved in STAR TREK's third season who were not as familiar with the show—or with science fiction in general—as they should have been. For instance, in STAR TREK's first two years, many of the scripts were written by "name" science fiction writers: Harlan Ellison, Norman Spinrad, Robert Bloch, Theodore Sturgeon, Richard Matheson. Other scripts were written by men who had proven themselves at least once in the science fiction field with either a novel or short story collection: George Clayton Johnson, Jerome Bixby, Jerry Sohl, and Max Ehrlich. And one of the scripts was based on a short story by Fredric Brown.

During the third season, the only one of these men to do any script work was Jerome Bixby. None of the others returned, some by choice, some because the third season producer did not feel comfortable working with them or did not like their submissions.

Although this could be considered a serious error in a science fiction television show—not using any *science fiction* writers—it is not necessarily a fatal one. A good writer should be able to handle almost any medium. Gene Roddenberry has said he would rather work with a "good writer" than one who is just familiar with his specific area.

But the non-use of any science fiction writers—even in an advisory capacity—is an indicator of the show's decline.

All that the viewer had to go on, however, was what he saw on his television screen. But that was enough—

Erosion in a TV series is the wearing down of the original concept, the destruction of it piece by piece as various elements chip and crack it away: carelessness in production, lack of pride in what one is doing, network restrictions, writer apathy, front-office feuds, and so on.

For instance, in the very first episode telecast, "The Man Trap" (by George Clayton Johnson) black crewmen, as well as Orientals, were very much in evidence aboard the *Enterprise*, and in a variety of costumes to indicate the wide range of jobs and skills represented aboard the ship. One of the most subtly startling and *correct* moments of the whole season came during that episode. The Salt Vampire could make itself appear to be an attractive member of the opposite sex to whomever it had selected as its victim. McCoy saw it as a lost lover, Janice Rand saw it as a handsome crewman, but Lieutenant Uhura saw the creature as a tall and virile black man. There was something very *right* about that scene—probably the implication that Lieutenant Uhura is more than a token Black, she is a real woman. (Yeah . . . !)

Blacks and Orientals were important in other episodes. And other minorities as well. This was more than just progressive thinking on the part of Gene Roddenberry—it was a necessary part of the STAR TREK concept. The ship *had* to be interracial because it represented *all* of mankind. How can the human race ever hope to achieve friendship with alien races if it can't even make friends with itself?

However, as the series progressed, especially in the last half of the second season and most of the third, this concept began to erode away. With the exception of the regular characters, the rest of the crew of the *Enterprise* began to erode from their multi-racial makeup into a White Anglo-Saxon Protestant (WASP) regime.

I doubt that it was a conscious decision on anyone's part—it was probably just carelessness. In the rush of production (in an industry dominated by white actors) the use of blacks and other minorities was forgotten. Yet there are few roles in STAR TREK'S 79 scripts that specifically call for either a white-skinned or black-skinned man. Any of the parts written could have been played by an actor of any race, provided he was human—and extra-terrestrials should have been welcome to audition too.

This kind of erosion must have happened in the casting sessions—and it is a kind of thoughtlessness. To break out of one's preconceived ideas always requires a conscious effort. As an aside here, let me point out that the proportion of blacks and Orientals on STAR TREK was not a fair or accurate representation, at least not of the human race in general. The white race is in the minority—less than a third of the world's population. Most of the rest are black and yellow. It's a probable assumption that this proportion will not change significantly in the next two hundred years. We should have seen some of that reflected in STAR TREK'S casting. (The network, however, specifically forbade the use of any Chinese crew . . .)

What we did see *was* progressive—it was far more than most other television shows of that time were attempting. But STAR TREK should have begun to use more and more members of minorities, not less. Despite the fact that most of the world's technology is presently dominated by white-skinned human beings, it will not always remain so. The stars and the planets will not be colonized by the Ku Klux Klan.

Another kind of erosion, a more serious kind, came in the quality of the scripts. The decline could almost have been charted on a curve. We've already seen how the stories began to petrify into formula efforts and the relationships of the characters as well, but at the same time, individual characterizations were being eroded. Characters were being taken out of context and superficial or dishonest motivations were being superimposed on them.

For instance, in "The *Enterprise* Incident," Mr. Spock plays a love scene with a Romulan female. In the first draft of this, Spock never touches her—his most tender line is, "I admire your mind." The Romulan woman, understanding the Vulcan mind, understands this as the compliment that Spock intended. By the time the scene was rewritten, however, it was no different from anyone else's love scenes. And all of the charm of Spock's Vulcan attitudes was lost. Only Leonard Nimoy's skillful handling of the scene kept it from being totally out of context.*

---

* Dorothy Fontana, who wrote the script had protested the revision mightily. In a memo to the producer, she said,

"Gentlemen:

"These are not the outcries of a wounded writer, but of an ex-story editor with four years of service stripes for STAR TREK. The points I mention here appear in the yellow cover copy (first approved draft) of my script and I feel need correction.

"Sc. 93—seduction scene—Spock and Commander. Vulcans and Romulans have been firmly established as cool, unemotional creatures. True, Spock is half human—but only under the most extreme circumstances will he behave in any manner other than Vulcan. We have established Vulcans do not puzzle, kiss, hug or display any other form of *human* affection. The Vulcan outward sign of affection is expressed in a certain touching of hands as demonstrated in "Journey to Babel." If Spock behaves in such outlandishly embarrassing human manner as is indicated in this scene, he violates the character we have established for him, and the culture he comes from. And the Commander had

Other characters had chances to fall in love during the third season, Chekov, Scotty and McCoy, for instance—and each time they did, they stepped out of character to play puerile love scenes. In "The Lights of Zetar," for example, Scotty falls in love. Fine, okay—Scotty is a normal healthy Scotsman, he should have an interest in women.

But remember, Mr. Scott, as postulated in the original STAR TREK concept, loves his machines first. ("If Scotty can't fix it, it can't be fixed.") To him, relaxation is a stack of technical journals. And shore leave is an unpleasant duty, he doesn't want to go.

Yet, in "The Lights of Zetar" Mr. Scott is shown

---

jolly well better be suspicious if Spock starts slobbering all over her. Their seduction scene should be cool, suggesting an alien sexuality—but *not* human passion.

". . . Please consider making these changes, especially in regard to the seduction scene between Spock and the Commander. Frankly, our fans—especially the vocal ones who write a lot of letters to networks—are very hip to what is and what isn't 'Vulcan.' They write whole treatises and fanzines (for a large circle of fan subscribers) based on Vulcan psychology, physiology, emotions, mores, and what Spock eats for breakfast. And they will tune us out if the 'business' in this seduction scene goes unchanged.

"Respectfully,"

—D.C. Fontana

The changes weren't made, and when she found out about it, she went to the set and apologized to Leonard Nimoy. "Leonard, I didn't write the scene."

And she was right about the fans, too. Within a few weeks after "The *Enterprise* Incident" was telecast, articles started appearing in fanzines. One of them began, "Curse you, Dorothy Fontana . . . Vulcans are cool, logical, unemotional, etc. . ." And focused on that love scene as the prime example of what was wrong with the script.

Even though she was not responsible for that scene, still it was her name on the screen, so she had to take the blame for someone else's mistake.

falling head over heels in love with a woman who seems to have nothing more going for her than a short skirt and a good bust measurement. Scotty is portrayed as a pre-pubescent, terminal acne case casting lovesick, moony glances at the mother-object. It's out of character.

Sure, Scotty has the right to fall in love—but couldn't he do so as Mr. Scott?

Just as Mr. Spock should have been allowed to play a love scene as Mr. Spock, so should Scotty have been allowed to fall in love as Scotty. What an opportunity to expand on his character! What kind of a woman would Scotty love? Certainly not a librarian!

In "For the World Is Hollow and I Have Touched the Sky" McCoy gets his chance to fall in love. In it, he has an incurable disease and falls in love with the high priestess of a doomed planetoid. (He gets to fall in love and almost die in the same episode—a plethora of devices to create artificial excitement.) That he does not want to go back to a Starfleet base to die and falls in love with one of the green priestesses of the cosmic computer seems ridiculous. In this episode, he's so out of character, he really isn't Dr. McCoy at all. He's someone else with the same name.

The STAR TREK concept was carefully delineated in The STAR TREK *Writers' Guide.* But the process of erosion wore away that concept bit by bit until the point where the writers were no longer using the guide as a referral—and with that, there was no more STAR TREK concept at all.

There are too many different examples of STAR TREK's erosion to list here. Primarily, most of them were symptoms of a much larger disease, a kind of internal decaying.

During the last season, the erosion of the STAR TREK

concept was at its worst—this was because it became commonly known that the show would not be renewed for a fourth year. As a result, a kind of apathy set in among most of the cast and crew. The effort became almost a half-hearted one. And this showed in the production values.

Not that anyone was doing an inferior job, all of the work continued to be competent. But the urge to surpass one's best was gone; the high level of morale that Gene Roddenberry had inspired was no longer there, because Gene Roddenberry was no longer there. It showed not only in the scripts, but also in the acting, the directing, the background details, and the overall "feel" of the show.

And this state of affairs existed primarily because the show would not be renewed. STAR TREK during its first two years, was a family—now that family was breaking up. The cast and crew knew that there was no longer any reason to try to excel—the show was going to be cancelled no matter what they did. At that point, and one cannot fault any of them for this, their primary interest became one of finishing out the season as painlessly as possible and finding other work. STAR TREK was no longer going to be the important focus of their lives, and their attention began to turn elsewhere.

But in one respect, the ones who suffered most were the fans. They had fought to save the show with their letters and now it was dying on the vine. They didn't know what was happening or why. It was like watching a good friend die. A healthy and virile sportsman who had conquered universes had suddenly come down with leukemia, had become pale and weak, had begun to shake with palsy, had become incoherent, had lost his will to live, had begun to shrivel and waste away before the horrified eyes of those who loved him best.

By the time STAR TREK did die, it was almost a blessing . . .

There is one last aspect of STAR TREK's unfulfilled potential to consider. It is the most telling criticism of all.

It's partly an error of format, partly a piece of formula. It's a little bit of hardening of the arteries and a little bit of erosion. It's the "American Way" syndrome. It is the most deadly of all mistakes that STAR TREK ever made—not STAR TREK per se, but her writers, the men and women who were responsible for seeing that the show lived up to its potential.

I said earlier that STAR TREK is not *pure* science fiction, and never was intended to be. It was designed as a set of contemporary morality fables against a science fiction background. The stories are about twentieth century man's attitudes in a future universe. The stories are about us.

And I said that this was probably the most flexible format that had ever been designed for a television series; the format was broad enough for an almost unlimited potential.

It is my contention that it was this aspect of STAR TREK's format that made it such a special show. If our heroes represented the American attitudes, then as such, they could be thrust into a variety of situations which would test those attitudes.

And once in a while, those attitudes would be wrong. Once in a while they would come up against a culture that might be just a little more compassionate, or a little more aware, or a little more *alive*.

—And when that happened, the crew of the *Enterprise* would be students, not masters.

Once in a while, the American attitudes might be tested and found wanting.

It is precisely this potential that was STAR TREK's greatest strength. Imagine a story where the hero does everything that he believes to be correct—and the audience identifies with him totally in his actions because they believe them to be correct too. Imagine that he is ultimately *wrong* in some of his decisions—when (and if) he learns better, then so will the audience.

The self-examination of the human condition is what drama is all about—but if you are going to test yourself, then you must be prepared to be found wanting in any respect. Self-awareness includes one's faults, otherwise it becomes narcissistic onanism.

But STAR TREK rarely went that far. Too many of the stories were facile, and required not much more than a mind that was easily gulled by flashy technical effects. All that valuable background work, the props, the sets, the costumes, is a waste of time unless the story justifies it.

In 1966, when STAR TREK first came on the air, Lyndon Baines Johnson was President; it was a time when the Viet Nam "adventure" was at the core of the American dilemma—were we supposed to be the world's policeman or not?

As far as STAR TREK was concerned, we were—because STAR TREK was the galaxy's policeman. By implication, that ratified and justified the American presence in everybody else's culture.

The mistake was that the *Enterprise* was a cosmic meddler. Her attitudes were those of twentieth century America—and so her mission was (seemingly) to spread truth, justice, *and the American Way* to the far corners of the universe.

STAR TREK missed the opportunity to question this attitude. While Kirk was occasionally in error, never was there a script in which the *Enterprise*'s mission or goals were questioned. Never did they run into a situation that might have been better off without their intervention. (In "Errand of Mercy" they ran into the Organian culture, which didn't *need* their intervention, but that's not the same thing.)

There were too many stories where Kirk upset a local planet's status quo—in effect, saying, "Your culture isn't as good as mine, therefore I have the right to effect whatever changes I feel necessary. I want to make you into a carbon copy of me because I'm so good . . ."

On the surface, most of these intervention stories were intended to make very dramatic points. They had been designed as situations specifically for the making of these points.

In "A Taste of Armageddon" two planets are shown involved in a computer controlled war—this war has provided social stability for centuries through the controlled waste of material and human life. Captain Kirk restores the horror of war by destroying the war computer.

The point of this story was that death had been made "clean." Invisible. Somehow, it isn't really there. The analogy with Vietnam is strong—oh, those damnable body counts. These people were obediently and cheerfully doing their duty and trotting into the disintegrators when they were told to—never questioning why, or whether their war could be turned into a useful peace. Kirk changed the situation so that death was no longer so clean—if people were going to die, they were also going to have to see the blood and broken bodies. The point here was to force the two combatants to recognize the horror of their waste-based society—like ours.

The situation had been set up specifically to make the above point—and in order to make it, Kirk had to intervene.

In "Return of the Archons" Kirk destroys another culture-controlling computer. (How IBM must hate that man!) This one has stabilized its culture by a more direct control of its people's lives. The life-style is totalitarian, except for occasional "festivals" when the computer releases the populace from its control for short periods of time. Here too, we are told that this culture has endured for hundreds of years.

The situation was set up to say that totalitarianism—of any kind—is wrong. In order to escape, Kirk had to destroy the Landru computer, thus making the point that human beings were meant to be their own masters.

In "This Side of Paradise" a colony has found peace and contentment—and stagnation—living in symbiosis with a kind of spore. In fact, it is only the presence of the spores which allows humans to survive on this planet; the spores nullify a certain type of radiation, and also keep the colonists in excellent health. The point to be questioned was whether humans could exist in total stagnation with no creativity, no growth, no exercise of mind or talent of any kind.

Kirk's answer was to nullify the effect of the spores and remove the colonists—but he had to do so in order to escape personally. His decision was between his mission and the symbiosis.

In "Who Mourns for Adonais" Kirk decides that it is time for the human race to give up its old myths, and an ancient Greek God is destroyed. Although Kirk indicates some remorse at the end, his answer is still the same.

In "The Apple" (one of the worst offenders) Kirk destroys a garden of Eden. Vaal, the Godzilla-head rock god, controls the weather, and hence, the ecology of the planet. He provides a pastoral situation for his servants. This story, like most of STAR TREK's moral statements is oddly anti-machine. Vaal must be destroyed—no attempt is made to tame him.

In "Mirror, Mirror" an alternate *Enterprise,* one dedicated to violence, is portrayed. Kirk convinces the alternate world Spock to rebel—implying that he will eventually bring peace and justice and the "American Way" to this alternate galaxy.

In "Bread and Circuses" a modernized Roman Empire is encountered. We are shown that they have their local equivalent of Christians too. Hence, the implication is that this culture will eventually evolve into one more suitable to Starfleet's tastes.

In "The Gamesters of Triskelion" Kirk must win his freedom from an arena situation—in the process, he convinces the gamesters that gaming with human and other beings is immoral.

In "A Piece of the Action" Kirk encounters a 1920-mobster civilization. This one was a comedy, so Kirk succeeds simply by out-mobstering everybody else. He simply takes over totally and says, "Dis is de way we're going to do it from now on." But it is in character with everything he's done before.

In "Patterns of Force," a neo-Nazi culture is defeated—even though it had raised an agricultural populace into an industrial one in just one generation. Kirk feels that although the goals are laudable, the methods are wrong.

In "The Cloud Minders" another form of oppression is encountered—a cultural and social delineation produced by the fact that the elite live in sky cities floating above the harsh surface of their planet. Naturally, in just 48 minutes of story, Kirk corrects all of this.*

* "The Cloud Minders" was based on a story that I submitted called "Castles in the Sky.' It was intended as a parable between the haves and the have-nots, the haves being the elite who are removed from the realities of everyday life—they live in their floating sky cities. The have-nots were called "Mannies" (for Manual Laborers) and were forced to live on the surface of the planet where the air was denser, pressure was higher, and noxious gases made the conditions generally unlivable. The Mannies were torn between two leaders, one a militant, and one a Martin Luther King figure. (Mind you, this was in 1968, shortly after King was assassinated, and just before the assassination of Robert F. Kennedy.)

In my original version, Kirk, Spock, McCoy and Uhura were captured by the Mannies when their shuttlecraft was shot down by a missile. (The *Enterprise* desperately needed dilithium crystals. This planet was one of the Federation's biggest suppliers, and Kirk's concern was to restore the flow of crystals. He didn't care who worked the mines, just that the supply was not interrupted. The shuttlecraft was necessary because I felt that the crystals might be too dense for the transporter.) In the process of the story, Kirk realizes that unless living conditions for the Mannies are improved, the situation can never be stabilized.

Because Uhura has been injured in the shuttlecraft crash,

—It wasn't just cultures that Kirk had to contend with. It was attitudes in general:

In "The Way to Eden" the *Enterprise* picks up a shipload of cosmic hippies. Naturally, the hippies' attitudes are found to be without value. Apparently, peace and happiness are alien to the commander of the *Enterprise* by now. The kids have to be reeducated that there's no such thing as a free lunch. You pays for what you gets.

In "By Any Other Name" agents of the Kelvan empire grab the *Enterprise* for an intergalactic sojourn. Kirk grabs it right back by teaching them how to be human.

In "Plato's Stepchildren" another group of cosmic gamesters is encountered and defeated. It is not good

---

McCoy starts treating her in a Mannie hospital. But he is so appalled at the condition of the other patients there, especially the children suffering from high-pressure disease, that he begins treating them as well. Meanwhile, Kirk and Spock have convinced their captors to let them go up to the sky city and try to negotiate a settlement to the local crisis.

The story focused primarily on the lack of communication between the skymen and the Mannies. Kirk's resolution of the problem was to force the two sides into negotiation. He opened the channels of communication with a phaser in his hand. "You —sit there! You—sit there! Now, talk!" And that's all he does. He doesn't solve the problem himself, he merely provides the tools whereby the combatants can seek their own solutions, a far more moral procedure.

In the end, as the *Enterprise* breaks orbit, Kirk remarks on this, as if inaugurating the problem-solving procedure is the same as solving the problem. He pats himself on the back and says, "We've got them talking. It's just a matter of time until they find the right direction." And McCoy who is standing right next to him, looks at him and says, "Yes, but how many children will die in the meantime?"

This answer was not a facile one; the viewer was meant to be left as uneasy as Kirk.

—But in the telecast version, the whole problem was caused by Zenite gas in the mines, and "if we can just get them troglytes to all wear gas masks, then they'll be happy little darkies and they'll pick all the cotton we need . . ."

Somehow, I think it lost something in the translation.

manners to force things on people—Kirk forces them
to appreciate this attitude.

Individually, any one of the above episodes was designed to make a specific point. Slavery is wrong. Ex-
ploitation is wrong. Racism is wrong. And so on.

Cumulatively, the effect is quite different.

Cumulatively, the effect is that each situation has
been constructed for Kirk to make that point. And
cumulatively, the effect is of a set of straw men—or
straw cultures, actually—for Kirk to knock down.

While each of the individual stories may have been
valid, in the context of the series as a whole there is an
implication of Starfleet's attitudes that reflects seriously
on the attitudes of American television, as well as the
American culture.

The subtext of the series, the subvocal message, is
that if a local culture is tested and found wanting in the
eyes of a starship Captain, he may make such changes
as he feels necessary.

Granted, Kirk never touched a culture that didn't
need it in the context of the given story. But, in point
of fact, each of those stories and cultures had been set
up to make a specific point. Looking past the individual points, to the implied power of the Captain, he was
functioning not so much as Starfleet's ambassador—but
as Starfleet's *judge.*

Every culture he encountered was weighed and tested. Rarely was Captain Kirk tested.

If STAR TREK was to be about contemporary man
against a science fiction background, then it is not just
that background we are exploring—it is the nature of
contemporary man as well.

Every time Kirk knocked down a straw man culture,
he was reinforcing the message that "In the name of
my morality, this is the proper action."

The worst offender was an episode entitled "The *Enterprise* Incident." In this episode, Kirk (seemingly)
goes crazy and orders the *Enterprise* into Romulan

space. The *Enterprise* is captured, Kirk is killed (we think), Spock seduces a Romulan captain, Kirk puts on a Klingon disguise and—aha! Now we find out that it has all been an espionage plot—sneaks aboard the Romulan ship to steal their Cloak of Invisibility device. Never mind the holes in the story big enough to drive a starship through—the episode came about as a result of the Pueblo Incident. Remember the American spy ship that the North Koreans captured? Well, the way STAR TREK told it, we won.

In fact, the way STAR TREK told it, we were *justified* in spying because our side was right and theirs wasn't.

(Oh, Organia—where are you when we really need you?)

The story was as dishonest as anything ever presented on American television, and representative of STAR TREK's worst failures. Instead of testing Kirk—and by implication, contemporary man—it said that the ends justify the means; because our ends are just, then no matter what means we choose, our means will be just too. It ignored the fact that the means *shape* the ends; if a culture uses espionage and trickery and force, then no matter what is written in its laws and Constitution, it is not an honorable culture. As presented in "The *Enterprise* Incident" Starfleet was no better than the "evil" Romulans.

STAR TREK could have told a far better story if they had really retold the Pueblo Incident. And in point of fact, this is exactly what Dorothy Fontana had intended. But when she presented the idea, NBC flinched. "Too dangerous. It has to be something else."

Had the show retold the Pueblo Incident, Kirk's decision would have been a much more crucial one. He can save his honor and refuse to sign the confession that he was spying—or he can save his ship and the 431 human beings (and one Vulcan) whose lives he is responsible for. And suppose he really *had* been on a spying mission—!

The kind of human being he was presented as, Kirk would sacrifice his honor rather than one single life. Had he been forced to do so, he would have then returned to base and confronted the Starfleet authority that had ordered him on such a mission. Supposedly a shamed and defeated Captain, he would confront the Admiral who had ordered him into such a situation and he would say, "We had no right to be there, that was Romulan territory! I didn't embarrass us—you did by ordering me to undertake such a mission."

And the Admiral might reply, "You're right, Kirk—but we needed that information that you gathered in order to maintain the balance of power. I didn't like having to give you those orders, but they were necessary. And if it's necessary to repeat them in the future, I'll give those orders again. And you'll follow them too."

And Kirk might look at him and reply, "I don't know . . . I don't know . . ."

And we would leave it at that.

There is no satisfactory resolution to such a situation—only a gained awareness of the reasons for its occurrence. STAR TREK had the opportunity to comment on one of the more shameful American adventures—as it had the opportunity to comment on all of them—and muffed it thoroughly.

STAR TREK had the greatest potential of any television series ever created—but its potential was rarely fulfilled because the decisions that Kirk was called upon to make were facile ones. A facile decision doesn't test Kirk. And it doesn't test the contemporary man who is the unwritten hero of every STAR TREK episode.

Not all of it was network restrictions—if you push at the lines hard enough and long enough, you can move them. It took two years, but Archie Bunker got on the air, didn't he? It takes a conscious effort and a *continual* effort—and a refusal to let the censor tell you how to tell your story.

But there is a frightening amount of self-censorship and cowardice in American television. The restrictions may be a little more relaxed in 1973 than they were in 1966, but the same basic rules are in effect: stories about the profit motive are *verboten,* big business is never the villain, our heroes don't have genitals and always subscribe to the puritan work ethic; the "American Way" is best. We can be relevant, but we must never be dangerous. Don't slice too close to the bone.

The result—

The writers of a television series—the bad ones—set up a series of straw men for their "heroes" to knock down; phony attitudes and cultures which can be knocked down to show how strong *our* attitude and culture is, week after interminable week. We don't have to learn anything because we are already at our best. See—? Our heroes are never defeated.

But—*is* our way the best?

We'll never know—at least not until we really do get out into the stars and have to test ourselves against some real decisions.

The real question is whether or not we'll be ready for that test.

If we send Captain Kirk, then he had better be a proper representative and something more than just a modern-dress Buck Rogers, for if we choose the latter, then the answer is already determined before the question is ever asked.

This last section has been about the unfulfilled potential of STAR TREK. I've spent nearly a fourth of the book discussing and analyzing those aspects of the series that (I felt) failed to live up to the high ideals of the original concept.

I've had to do a lot of generalizing, and there are always exceptions to every generalization. There were good moments in the worst of episodes, and bad moments in the best. A generalization is valuable only when it can be used to show the direction of a trend. I have tried to use as accurate examples as possible as indicators of each point I have discussed.

Perhaps STAR TREK *was* little more than Buck Rogers updated—if you think of it in terms of battles with Klingons and Romulans and tree-men and lizard-men, then maybe that's true.

But I believe STAR TREK to be one of the finest television formats ever conceived. It proved this with episodes like "City on the Edge of Forever" and "Errand of Mercy" and "Shore Leave" and "Charlie X."

So, if I have been ruthless with the show in this discussion, it is out of love, not distaste. If STAR TREK is truly as strong a format as I believe, then it will withstand any test we can put against it. And if it *cannot* withstand some of our tests, then we are better off knowing about it now.

As a STAR TREK fan, and as a STAR TREK writer, I wanted only one thing from the show—that it should be as great as it promised it could be. And as it sometimes was.

THE RETURN OF STAR TREK...?

In 1972, an interesting rumor began circulating—that STAR TREK might return!

The rumor was not unfounded. NBC *was* interested in bringing the show back, and had begun talks with Gene Roddenberry and Paramount Studios (which now owns the show) about just such a possibility.

—What happened?!! NBC was the network that had cancelled STAR TREK—and now just three years later was doing an abrupt turnaround. What had caused it?

Let's start at the beginning. STAR TREK was saved for its third season by a massive letter campaign that brought in more than one million letters. But in addition to that, Gene Roddenberry had made a personal effort to save the show.

"I went to NBC," recalls Roddenberry, "and I said, 'I love this show. I think it could run for as long as 'Gunsmoke' if you'll give it another season, and so, NBC, I am prepared to make this offer: if you'll put STAR TREK on for a third year, I will come back, I will come out of the Executive Producer spot. I will go back and personally line-produce the third year the same way I did the first year. I guarantee it to you that if I have to work 14 hours a day, we'll have the same kind of scripts we had, the same kind of attention, and all I ask in return is that if I do that, you'll give me a good time slot. Don't kill the show with a bad time slot, because you've moved us twice now into increasingly worse spots.'

"NBC said to me, 'Yes, okay, we accept your offer. You can have either 7:30, Monday, or 8:00, Tuesday.'

And I said fine. 7:30, Monday was fine and I was prepared to do it. A few weeks before the schedules came out, I received a call from NBC, from one of the executives, and I was having breakfast at home and remember clearly and the first words of the executive was, 'Gene, baby . . .' and I almost knew I was in trouble right then. He says, 'We've really done something for you. The Research Department has been working very hard about the ideal spot for your show and we're going to do even better for you. We're going to put you at 10:00 Friday night.'

"I said, 'You're mad. What are you talking about, you're doing something for me?' He said, 'Please, our research people have really a lot of reasons for this.'

Well, I learned later in the day that their real reason for it was that *Laugh-In* had insisted on the spot they were going to give us* and it was obvious to me that 10:00 Friday was death so I said to the network in subsequent meetings, 'I will not go back and put that kind of effort, risk of life and health and everything. to a show that cannot make it no matter what I do.' Oh, and at the same time NBC had also, instead of giving us a full year's commitment, only picked us up for 13 shows, a half a year. The only clout I had to fight the network with was would I or would I not produce. Obviously, I had no other weapon. I could not get them to change the time.

"I retreated so far, finally, in an effort to save STAR TREK as to say, 'All right, if you'll give me a firm commitment for a full season, 22 episodes, I'll even produce it then. I'll take a chance that even in this bad time slot that if I can have a commitment for the full year that somehow we'll pull it off.' The network re-

---

* "Laugh-In" was scheduled for 8:00 Monday and refused to be moved to 8:30. As they had a bigger rating than STAR TREK—they were the smash hit of 1968 and '69—they had more clout. STAR TREK was outvoted.

fused to budge even there.* I said, 'If you won't, I will not produce it.' They refused to budge and I was left in a situation of having used the only threat I had. I was stuck with either backing off entirely and producing it anyway, which meant that in future dealings with NBC (which I have right now), they would never believe my word again. Or I could keep my word. So I was really forced to break off from the show, and I could see it was going to die and I spent that year trying to develop new projects for the following season.

"Later, I also found out that there would be no fourth season, no matter what. I was told that they didn't understand the show and they didn't like it and that was generally it. I suppose if we'd gotten smash ratings they couldn't have done anything about it, but there's no chance of getting smash ratings in that time slot. That was a great sorrow to me, but I have my own career to think about. If the show was going to be dead anyway, I was better off keeping my executive producer position which left me time to develop things for the following year. Since STAR TREK was gone, I had to have something else, and I spent the time writing a couple of features."

About the third season, in general, Gene Roddenberry was brief: "I think a show needs its creator with it, or if it doesn't have that it has to have someone who has continuity with the show, who you had developed to take over that position, and unfortunately, always intending to stay close to STAR TREK, I had developed no one to take it over except Gene Coon who, unfortu-

---

* The network always suspected that Gene Roddenberry had engineered the mail campaign. NBC never quite understood what it had in STAR TREK and probably would have cancelled it in 1968, had it not been for the mail campaign. Thus embarrassed, they had to keep it on the air—but they were not committed to keeping it alive. Hence, the bad time slot. It has always seemed to many of the fans that NBC was definitely trying to kill the show. It was too expensive for them and it wasn't a big enough hit. Demographics have since proven the Nielson ratings wrong on STAR TREK.

nately had gotten sick and then had a commitment over at Universal. So I brought in people who were well recommended. They saw the show their way and when you let someone produce, you've got to let them produce. If I was going to produce it for them, I'd be right back where I was, doing it my way.

"I think the experience taught NBC something. I think it taught them that it's not so much the concept in the long run—it's the people who are doing it. And I think that TV in general is beginning to learn that."

So STAR TREK went off the air. Its last episode was "Turnabout Intruder." The *Enterprise*'s five year mission had been aborted two years before completion.

Almost immediately, the show went into syndication, nationally and worldwide. Over 146 markets.

And became an even bigger hit. STAR TREK is the show that refused to die.

Until finally, there was a STAR TREK convention in January of 1972.

That first STAR TREK convention attracted more than 3300 plus people. There were also spies from two networks present. Both CBS (which has purchased two new series-projects from Gene Roddenberry) and NBC were curious as to the extent of the STAR TREK Phenomenon and had representatives in attendance to gauge the response.

Network executives seem to understand only one thing: numbers. Big ones. *Especially* big ones. The bigger the better.

That convention intrigued them. The show had been out of production for three years, but the intensity of the fans' response was greater than that for many of the shows currently on the air. There were more fans than ever—all the old ones, and the whole new generation that had discovered STAR TREK since it had gone into syndication.

NBC went back and took another look at their demographics; these are a kind of ratings—only they tell you not how many are watching a program, but *who* they are: how many housewives and husbands, how many students and senior citizens, how many children, dogs, cats, and parakeets. They also question whether the TV is just *on* or if people are *watching*.

CBS was interested too, but NBC had first dibsies. Within a few months the network was talking about the possibility of a STAR TREK movie—which would also be the pilot for a new STAR TREK series. The movie might be a two hour made-for-TV movie, or it might be released theatrically.

The key to it was *would Gene Roddenberry produce it?*

Sure, he would—but only on *his* terms. He's proven his point. Or rather, STAR TREK and STAR TREK's fans have proven it for him. Gene had said to the network in 1968, "You don't know what you have in this show. Give it a chance." And now that they're showing some signs of realizing that he was right, he's going to stick by his guns. If STAR TREK is to return, Gene Roddenberry is going to see that it comes back properly, and with the quality that it had in its first season. Or *better*.

Would Gene Roddenberry change the format or any of the characters?

"I would like to keep it pretty much as is," he says. "I can think of no basic changes in the concept that I would make. Obviously, there are, looking back over our mistakes on set, items we had that worked and didn't work. We would make improvements there. The cast I would like to keep pretty much as it was depending on availability.* I thought it was a good cast, well orchestrated, good actors.

"NBC told me, 'If we do it, let's have an updated version of the starship,' and I said, 'Look, fellows, I

---

* Most of the cast have indicated that they would be glad to return, if they were not tied down by other commitments or exclusive contracts. Leonard Nimoy has said he would return only if Gene Roddenberry were actively producing. And that's loyalty.

don't really know how to update a ship that operates on matter/anti-matter and has a transporter system and all that.' They kept saying, 'Couldn't it be more modern looking?'

"Mort Werner (of NBC) and I once had a talk about the ideal way to do the show and we both agreed that the really right way to do STAR TREK would have been to do six or seven segments a year and do them in 90 minute lengths and do them with time and money to do them right and have them play like the first Monday of every month or something like that.

"I think NBC would not object to the idea. I think the success of the long form on television might make it a little easier to convince them. Of course, the disadvantage of that is you do lose the habit pattern of tuning in that same night every week. You probably would lose some audience, not having this weekly pattern. But I think you would gain some back by the better quality.

"And I think the show will come back. The pressure is going to continue in a growing amount and I think it's got to come back in some form . . . The most exciting thing to me about bringing the show back is the fact that television has changed a lot since the early days of STAR TREK. It's opened up, you can talk about subjects now that were absolutely forbidden when we did STAR TREK. Everyone has heard the story many times of how we had to recut a film because we showed a navel. And the next year 'Laugh-In' came on and there were navels all over the place. We've had *All in the Family* which talked about menopause, impotency, unions, things we had to disguise, so I think our story opportunities would open broadly and we could do some very exciting stories that we had to toss out before.

"We might want to do a story of a strange religion. I personally think there's something patently ridiculous in many organized religions. We could invent one on another planet that could say this without ever directly criticizing what evils there are in organized religion here . . . Sex, of course, has got to lead to story ideas. I'd like to do a planet where—well, I'm a union man, I like unions, but I also think unions can be very bad if they get out of control, and I'd like to do a planet that has gone completely unionized, to the extent that all creativity and excellence in work has been destroyed. I'd like to do a planet story that shows maybe the pros and cons of socialism. All these things could be done now. We can talk about them. Still, they have to be people-stories with adventure, but they could be laid against these backgrounds.

"I think science fiction does one thing—I'm sure it's been written about, although I've never happened to read it—in that, through science fiction you can comment on our society more strongly, with greater force than you can by doing it on a contemporary level. Science fiction as an axe for the dramatist is a very focused mirror that you could really use to lay something out. For instance, if you wanted to talk about the problems of male and female, all of the incongruities of sex and getting together on this planet, it's been done almost every way already in a contemporary-Earth level. But if you invent a story where there are three sexes on another planet and it takes three to tango on that planet, and all three have to be involved for reproduction and pleasure, the very wildness of that allows you to comment forcefully on our problems. On this planet it could be practically a felony to do it with only two, which makes it a very strong statement about our contemporary values. So, I'm very hopeful about STAR TREK returning."

—And so are the fans.

There is a Detroit-based operation called S.T.A.R.—Star Trek Association for Revival. Since 1971, they have been trying to generate a new letter campaign to force the show back on the air. NBC and

Paramount receive approximately 50 letters a week as a direct result of this campaign.

A typical notice in their newsletter reads something like this:

Write Paramount. Tell them that you want STAR TREK to return. Get your friends to write Paramount. See how many other Trek fans you can reach. Let's bury the studio in a still greater avalanche of letters.

And while you are at it, write NBC too. And your local television station that is broadcasting STAR TREK. Also try to write the sponsors of the show, telling them where you have seen their advertisements and especially if you have bought their product. Write to:

Frank Yablans
Paramount Pictures
5451 Marathon St.
Los Angeles, Calif.
90038

Mort Werner
NBC-TV
30 Rockefeller Plaza
New York, N.Y.
10029

Herb Schlosser
NBC-TV
3000 Alameda Ave.
Burbank, Calif. 91505

Do not write STAR TREK on the envelope. This is automatically forwarded to Gene Roddenberry.

Do not send in petitions. One letter is worth 100 signatures.

Do not send in form letters of any kind including carbon or ditto.

Do not write 'cute' letters. This is a business letter. Anonymous letters also present a very bad image as to the caliber of the STAR TREK fan.

Do type or write a neat intelligent letter with a firm voicing of opinion.

Do use letter-headed stationery *if* it is representative of you personally. It is ideal for pointing out that the writer of the letter is a responsible individual. WRITE NOW!

It is also recommended that you keep carbons of the letters for your own files and that you also keep records of how many answers (if any) that you receive from Paramount or NBC and what their contents are.

With this kind of effort—and with the continued growth of STAR TREK conventions around the United States, it seems likely that Gene Roddenberry's prediction *could* come true. STAR TREK could return in one form or another. Paramount needs only to be convinced that there is still an audience large enough to justify the expense. The growing size and number of the conventions and the continual momentum of the letter campaign are bound to have an effect.

Both Gene Roddenberry and NBC want to do the show again. All that remains is for the right deal to be made with Paramount.

Time will tell. It is even possible that a decision may have been made by the time this book sees print.

In the meantime ...

Gene Roddenberry has a few other projects that he's working on.

For instance:

Working out of the Burbank Studios for Warner Brothers TV, Gene will produce for the CBS network, a supernatural series called "Spectre." He believes that most supernatural series eventually fail because they say there really are no ghosts, spirits or demons.

The main character of "Spectre" is a man who was the world's greatest criminologist, and who is now interested in the occult. "It's something I've wanted to do

for a long time," says Gene. "It's a continuing character, supernatural show, in which—in the tradition of
the great horror classics—we say these things are real.
I've always been offended by ghost stories which in the
end turn out to be someone trying to drive the heiress
mad so they can get her money. That's sort of a copout. I say if you're going to do ghost stories, let ghosts
spirits, demons and all these things be real because
that's what the classics, Frankenstein and Dracula and
all of those, did. It'll be in that tradition. I think the
audience wants to be frightened, not cheated, at the end.
We haven't had a supernatural series yet where reality
was the base."

Another project in the works is "Questor." This one
is being produced at Universal for the NBC network.
(Leonard Nimoy has read the script and is reported to
be *very* interested . . .) Gene says, "We're doing it as a
two-hour television movie pilot and the lead in that is
an android robot who you cannot distinguish from a
real person unless you pull back a skin flap and see
what's underneath. The theme of the show is very
much—you know the Latin expression?—*cogito ergo
sum:* I think, therefore I am. This is a fairly classical
theme because you think he is alive—has he a soul?
It's an action-adventure format, the lead is this robot
android who increasingly becomes more human as we
get to know him, and a young mechanical engineer who
travels with him, who assembled him. We discover in
the script though where the parts came from, where
these fantastic relays and units, like the nuclear fuel
stomach, came from—and it's not Earth. But some of
the programming tapes have been lost and the android
has to find out what he doesn't know. We discover that
we have always had somewhere on Earth one of these
beings who were sent to us by another race from far
away to guide us . . ."

A third project is "The Tribunes," which will be a
90-minute pilot for NBC. It will be a police show un-

like any on the air. It's about an experimental police division of 40–50 men and women, equipped with the latest scientific and technological developments to aid them.

This project is being developed with Sam Peeples, another well-known writer-producer in Hollywood, and it is based on both Roddenberry's and Peeples' background in police work. Gene was once a Los Angeles police officer and Peeples a police commissioner upstate. The show was the result of an almost casual conversation between the two, a mutual reminiscence of experiences, resulting in a discussion of, "How *should* it be done?" Followed by, "Aha! Wouldn't this be a great TV series?" So, they went over to the local executive's office and on the strength of that conversation, sold the concept.

Gene says, "Isn't it silly that a cop is out there on a beat really basically equipped no better than a policeman in 1912 was equipped, with a gun and a badge? About the only addition the average squad car has is a shotgun and a radio, and usually the radio doesn't work much better than a taxicab radio. Law enforcement is an extraordinarily important thing in our society, because law enforcement can often determine the nature of a society more than a constitution. You can have a constitution, but if your police act like Gestapo and have Gestapo powers, you're going to have a fascist civilization. We believe that there's more to police work than just repression.

"Police should be for the people, they should have options beyond just a gun, to kill or not to kill and things like that. It's really in a way a kind of science fiction format: if there was some way to get our best people, the best training (especially psychology and psychiatry) and the services of our vast technology into our police work, what would we have then?

"Our hope is that some of these ideas will filter down into actual police work. We hope that our ideas might be able to lead the way. We have some police administrators around the country who are very anxious for us to do the series."

One of the interesting aspects of "The Tribunes" is that these special officers will no longer carry guns, but weapons which are non-lethal, such as a high intensity light which temporarily blinds a suspect or sprays of non-lethal chemicals. The officers would also be magistrates; they can take testimony, settle cases on the spot, issue subpoenas, and so on.

The fourth new series of Gene's is the one which will be first on the air. It's titled *Genesis II* and the pilot episode (filmed at Warner Brothers) is scheduled for telecasting early in 1973 on the CBS network. It will be a made-for-TV movie first, and if it is successful, then it will be a series premiering in the fall of 1973. (Warner Brothers has already told Gene to film an extra 15 minutes, so that *Genesis II* can be released theatrically in the foreign markets.)

Genesis II takes place on the Earth, 108 years from now, a century after the great conflict. The premise is that just as with Rome and Babylon, all civilizations die. And that includes this one too. But each civilization is succeeded by a better one. Therefore, *Genesis II* is a story of optimism despite its background of great conflict. It revolves around an organization called Pax, a group of people seeking to preserve the treasures of the past and trying to pull a drastically changed Earth together.

The hero is Dylan Hunt, a scientist with the National Aeronautics and Space Administration who has been trapped in suspended animation for 108 years. When he awakens from his long sleep, he finds that the nations of the Earth have fragmented into many tiny city-states, each with its own separate and distinct culture, each almost like another planet, so varied are their civilizations.

One is a Matriarchy, a culture where the women are

in charge and the men are little better than pets. On the east coast of what was once the United States, he finds a black empire where white men are held as slaves. In Arizona, Hunt encounters a totalitarian Western culture, and in England a small monarchy. There are also mutant plants and animals—and a new race of men called Tyranians. These Tyranians are stronger than human beings, more intelligent, and cruel and vicious as well; their goal is to take over the Earth and enslave all human beings.*

Hunt becomes a member of Pax, a super-scientific organization with its headquarters deep in Carlbad Caverns, and ultimately is assigned to be the head of *Team 21*, a highly-specialized crew of troubleshooters that specialize in coping with cultural problems all over the Earth. They stop feuds before they turn into wars, bring vaccines to plague spots, spread knowledge and so on.

The means of transportation for this team is an underground shuttle system with trains that travel hundreds of miles an hour. (An early conception of it looked amazingly like the BART system in San Francisco-Oakland.)

In a sense, *Genesis II* is STAR TREK without the *Enterprise*. It is (Gene Roddenberry's phrase) "the hundred worlds concept." Each civilization visited would be separate from all the others, even if they were only a couple hundred miles apart. The underground shuttle system is the equivalent of the transporter room, getting the characters into and out of the stories. It promises to have almost as vast a scope and storytelling potential as STAR TREK did.

---

* They can be recognized by the fact that they have two navels. Because Gene Roddenberry had to cut all the navels out of STAR TREK, this is his way of making up for it. He's putting them all back in. (The sci-fi justification is that Tyranians have double circulatory systems, hence babies would need two umbilici.)

Oh, yes. One more thing. What if STAR TREK *doesn't* come back . . .?

"Well," says Gene. "I have a lot of notes on a new concept, a planet-travel show. Not for this season, but for the next one. I'm going to start putting it together . . ."

You see, the fans are right. STAR TREK lives!

ACKNOWLEDGMENTS

There are so many people who helped make this book possible that to list them all would be another chapter in itself.

Of course, first on the list are the cast and crew of the show; all of them fine people who took time out to talk with me—particularly Leonard Nimoy, William Shatner, De Forest Kelley, James Doohan, Nichelle Nichols, Walter Koenig, George Takei and Majel Barrett. Thanks also to William Campbell and John Dwyer.

There were others who helped in other ways. It was Gene L. Coon's direction that provided much of the insight for this work. Others are Tony Sauber in the legal department at Paramount, Stan Burns and his incredible camera, and Bjo Trimble—who not only provided the material for two chapters, but most of the film clips that were used in the photo sections. In addition, Bjo Trimble's STAR TREK CONCORDANCE was an invaluable research aid. Many of the details about specific episodes were drawn directly from this work.*

Invaluable help also came from three of the staunchest Trekkies in Los Angeles: Cheryl Etchison, Ruth Rigel, and Rita Ratcliffe—who provided extra film clips, important information at odd hours of the night, transcription of interview tapes—and a lot of good will.

There were two people without whom this book could not have been written as thoroughly as it was:

---

* THE STAR TREK CONCORDANCE is available for $5.00. It is an 84-page encyclopedia of everything you want to know about STAR TREK, plus illustrations. Write to *Star Trek Concordance*, PO Box 74866, Los Angeles, Calif. 90004. Tell them where you read about it.

Betty Ballantine and Dorothy Fontana—both of whom supplied moral support, editorial guidance, and much needed "second opinions."

And finally, the one person without whom this book could not have been written at all—the Great Bird of the Galaxy, Gene Roddenberry himself. He made it all happen in the first place. Thank you again, Gene.

About the Author

DAVID GERROLD was born in Los Angeles in 1944. He majored in Cinema at the University of Southern California and minored in Art and Journalism. He graduated with a B.A. in Theatre Arts from California State at Northridge in 1967. Even before he graduated though, he was a working writer.

Gerrold had been submitting outlines and story premises to various television series, beginning in 1966. In early '67, the TV series, *Star Trek*, took an interest in one of his outlines and asked to see more. In the summer of 1967, he made his first professional sale; the story and script became *Star Trek*'s highly acclaimed episode, "The Trouble With Tribbles." It was nominated for the International Hugo Award for the best dramatic presentation in science fiction in 1967 and placed a close second in the balloting. Other sales to *Star Trek* included some rewrite work and an original story which became "The Cloud Minders" episode.

In 1969, David Gerrold turned his attention to the prose form, and in a short time had sold stories to *Galaxy* magazine and a serial to *If*, another science fiction magazine. He has been anthologized several times, most notably in Harlan Ellison's *Again, Dangerous Visions*.

David Gerrold has edited three anthologies of his own: *Protostars, Generation,* and *Generation Two*. He has written one collection of short stories, *With a Finger in My I* and several novels including *The Flying Sorcerers* (in collaboration with Larry Niven), *Space Skimmer, Yesterday's Children, When Harlie Was One, The Man Who Folded Himself,* and *Battle for the Planet of the Apes*. David Gerrold has also written two non-fiction books, both about *Star Trek: The Trouble With Tribbles* and *The World of Star Trek*.